reet

Cram101 Textbook Outlines to accompany:

Health Fitness Instructor's Handbook

Howley, Franks, 4th Edition

An Academic Internet Publishers (AIPI) publication (c) 2007.

You have a discounted membership at www.Cram101.com with this book.

Get all of the practice tests for the chapters of this textbook, and access in-depth reference material for writing essays and papers. Here is an example from a Cram101 Biology text:

When you need problem solving help with math, stats, and other disciplines, www.Cram101.com will walk through the formulas and solutions step by step.

With Cram101.com online, you also have access to extensive reference material.

You will nail those essays and papers. Here is an example from a Cram101 Biology text:

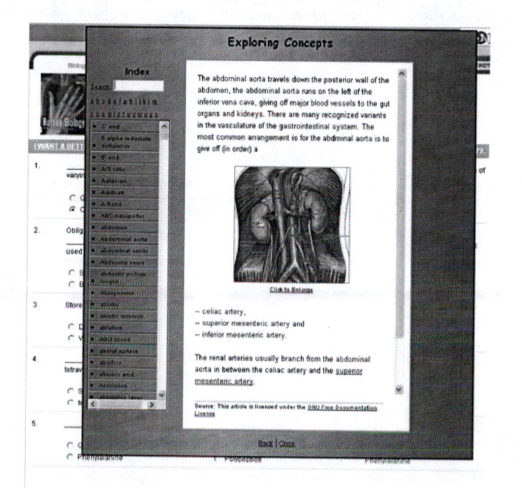

Visit **www.Cram101.com**, click Sign Up at the top of the screen, and enter DK73DW3458 in the promo code box on the registration screen. Access to www.Cram101.com is normally $9.95, but because you have purchased this book, your access fee is only $4.95. Sign up and stop highlighting textbooks forever.

Learning System

Cram101 Textbook Outlines is a learning system. The notes in this book are the highlights of your textbook, you will never have to highlight a book again.

How to use this book. Take this book to class, it is your notebook for the lecture. The notes and highlights on the left hand side of the pages follow the outline and order of the textbook. All you have to do is follow along while your intructor presents the lecture. Circle the items emphasized in class and add other important information on the right side. With Cram101 Textbook Outlines you'll spend less time writing and more time listening. Learning becomes more efficient.

Cram101.com Online

Increase your studying efficiency by using Cram101.com's practice tests and online reference material. It is the perfect complement to Cram101 Textbook Outlines. Use self-teaching matching tests or simulate in-class testing with comprehensive multiple choice tests, or simply use Cram's true and false tests for quick review. Cram101.com even allows you to enter your in-class notes for an integrated studying format combining the textbook notes with your class notes.

Visit **www.Cram101.com**, click Sign Up at the top of the screen, and enter **DK73DW3458** in the promo code box on the registration screen. Access to www.Cram101.com is normally $9.95, but because you have purchased this book, your access fee is only $4.95. Sign up and stop highlighting textbooks forever.

Health Fitness Instructor's Handbook
Howley, Franks, 4th

CONTENTS

Health	Health is a term that refers to a combination of the absence of illness, the ability to cope with everyday activities, physical fitness, and high quality of life.
Population	Population refers to all members of a well-defined group of organisms, events, or things.
Quality of life	Quality of life refers to the perception of individuals or groups that their needs are being satisfied and that they are not being denied opportunities to achieve happiness and fulfillment.
Coronary	Referring to the heart or the blood vessels of the heart is referred to as coronary.
Coronary heart disease	Coronary heart disease is the end result of the accumulation of atheromatous plaques within the walls of the arteries that supply the myocardium (the muscle of the heart).
Risk factor	A risk factor is a variable associated with an increased risk of disease or infection but risk factors are not necessarily causal.
Rehabilitation	Rehabilitation is the restoration of lost capabilities, or the treatment aimed at producing it. Also refers to treatment for dependency on psychoactive substances such as alcohol, prescription drugs, and illicit drugs such as cocaine, heroin or amphetamines.
Hypertension	Hypertension is a medical condition where the blood pressure in the arteries is chronically elevated. Persistent hypertension is one of the risk factors for strokes, heart attacks, heart failure and arterial aneurysm, and is a leading cause of chronic renal failure.
Cholesterol	Cholesterol is a steroid, a lipid, and an alcohol, found in the cell membranes of all body tissues, and transported in the blood plasma of all animals. It is an important component of the membranes of cells, providing stability; it makes the membrane's fluidity stable over a bigger temperature interval.
Consensus	General agreement is a consensus.
Blood	Blood is a circulating tissue composed of fluid plasma and cells. The main function of blood is to supply nutrients (oxygen, glucose) and constitutional elements to tissues and to remove waste products.
Blood pressure	Blood pressure is the pressure exerted by the blood on the walls of the blood vessels.
Outcome	Outcome is the impact of care provided to a patient. They can be positive, such as the ability to walk freely as a result of rehabilitation, or negative, such as the occurrence of bedsores as a result of lack of mobility of a patient.
Health outcome	Any medically or epidemiologically defined characteristic of a patient or population that results from health promotion or care provided or required, as measured at one point in time is a health outcome.
Mortality	The incidence of death in a population is mortality.
Lifestyle	The culturally, socially, economically, and environmentally conditioned complex of actions characteristic of an individual, group, or community as a pattern of habituated behavior over time that is health related but not necessarily health directed is a lifestyle.
Mental health	Mental health refers to the 'thinking' part of psychosocial health; includes your values, attitudes, and beliefs.
Wellness	A dimension of health beyond the absence of disease or infirmity, including social, emotional, and spiritual aspects of health is called wellness.
Heredity	Heredity refers to the transmission of genetic information from parent to offspring.
Lead	Lead is a chemical element in the periodic table that has the symbol Pb and atomic number 82. A soft, heavy, toxic and malleable poor metal, lead is bluish white when freshly cut but tarnishes to dull gray when exposed to air. Lead is used in building construction, lead-acid batteries, bullets and shot, and is part of solder, pewter, and fusible alloys.
Affect	Affect is the scientific term used to describe a subject's externally displayed mood. This can be assesed by the nurse by observing facial expression, tone of voice, and body language.

Go to **Cram101.com** for the Practice Tests for this Chapter.

Value	Value is worth in general, and it is thought to be connected to reasons for certain practices, policies, actions, beliefs or emotions. Value is "that which one acts to gain and/or keep."
Insight	Insight refers to a sudden awareness of the relationships among various elements that had previously appeared to be independent of one another.
Older adult	Older adult is an adult over the age of 65.
Insight in	Gestalt psychology, a sudden perception of relationships depth based on the fact that a nearby object obscures a more distant object behind it is an insight in.
Aerobic	An aerobic organism is an organism that has an oxygen based metabolism. Aerobes, in a process known as cellular respiration, use oxygen to oxidize substrates (for example sugars and fats) in order to obtain energy.
Chronic disease	Disease of long duration often not detected in its early stages and from which the patient will not recover is referred to as a chronic disease.
Resistance	Resistance refers to a nonspecific ability to ward off infection or disease regardless of whether the body has been previously exposed to it. A force that opposes the flow of a fluid such as air or blood. Compare with immunity.
Variable	A characteristic or aspect in which people, objects, events, or conditions vary is called variable.
Alcohol	Alcohol is a general term, applied to any organic compound in which a hydroxyl group (-OH) is bound to a carbon atom, which in turn is bound to other hydrogen and/or carbon atoms. The general formula for a simple acyclic alcohol is $C_nH_{2n+1}OH$.
Abstinence	Abstinence has diverse forms. In its oldest sense it is sexual, as in the practice of continence, chastity, and celibacy.
Diabetes	Diabetes is a medical disorder characterized by varying or persistent elevated blood sugar levels, especially after eating. All types of diabetes share similar symptoms and complications at advanced stages: dehydration and ketoacidosis, cardiovascular disease, chronic renal failure, retinal damage which can lead to blindness, nerve damage which can lead to erectile dysfunction, gangrene with risk of amputation of toes, feet, and even legs.
Obesity	The state of being more than 20 percent above the average weight for a person of one's height is called obesity.
Cancer	Cancer is a class of diseases or disorders characterized by uncontrolled division of cells and the ability of these cells to invade other tissues, either by direct growth into adjacent tissue through invasion or by implantation into distant sites by metastasis.
Osteoporosis	Osteoporosis is a disease of bone in which bone mineral density (BMD) is reduced, bone microarchitecture is disrupted, the amount and variety of non-collagenous proteins in bone is changed, and a concomitantly fracture risk is increased.
Angina	Angina pectoris is chest pain due to ischemia (a lack of blood and hence oxygen supply) to the heart muscle, generally due to obstruction or spasm of the coronary arteries (the heart's blood vessels). Coronary artery disease, the main cause of angina, is due to atherosclerosis of the cardiac arteries.
Artery	Vessel that takes blood away from the heart to the tissues and organs of the body is called an artery.
Stress	Stress refers to a condition that is a response to factors that change the human systems normal state.
Muscle	Muscle is a contractile form of tissue. It is one of the four major tissue types, the other three being epithelium, connective tissue and nervous tissue. Muscle contraction is used to move parts of the body, as well as to move substances within the body.
Oxygen	Oxygen is a chemical element in the periodic table. It has the symbol O and atomic number 8. Oxygen is the second most common element on Earth, composing around 46% of the mass of Earth's crust and 28% of

the mass of Earth as a whole, and is the third most common element in the universe.

Pain	Pain is an unpleasant sensation which may be associated with actual or potential tissue damage and which may have physical and emotional components.
Coronary arteries	Arteries that directly supply the heart with blood are referred to as coronary arteries.
Coronary artery	An artery that supplies blood to the wall of the heart is called a coronary artery.
Myocardium	Myocardium is the muscular tissue of the heart. The myocardium is composed of specialized cardiac muscle cells with an ability not possessed by muscle tissue elsewhere in the body.
Stroke	A stroke or cerebrovascular accident (CVA) occurs when the blood supply to a part of the brain is suddenly interrupted.
Cardiovascular disease	Cardiovascular disease refers to afflictions in the mechanisms, including the heart, blood vessels, and their controllers, that are responsible for transporting blood to the body's tissues and organs. Psychological factors may play important roles in such diseases and their treatments.
Brain	The part of the central nervous system involved in regulating and controlling body activity and interpreting information from the senses transmitted through the nervous system is referred to as the brain.
Blood vessel	A blood vessel is a part of the circulatory system and function to transport blood throughout the body. The most important types, arteries and veins, are so termed because they carry blood away from or towards the heart, respectively.
Hemorrhage	Loss of blood from the circulatory system is referred to as a hemorrhage.
Consciousness	Consciousness refers to the ability to perceive, communicate, remember, understand, appreciate, and initiate voluntary movements; a functioning sensorium.
Paralysis	Paralysis is the complete loss of muscle function for one or more muscle groups. Paralysis may be localized, or generalized, or it may follow a certain pattern.
Glucose	Glucose, a simple monosaccharide sugar, is one of the most important carbohydrates and is used as a source of energy in animals and plants. Glucose is one of the main products of photosynthesis and starts respiration.
Serum	Serum is the same as blood plasma except that clotting factors (such as fibrin) have been removed. Blood plasma contains fibrinogen.
Intolerance	Intolerance refers to a type of interaction in which two or more drugs produce extremely uncomfortable symptoms.
Tolerance	Drug tolerance occurs when a subject's reaction to a drug decreases so that larger doses are required to achieve the same effect.
Chronic obstructive pulmonary disease	Chronic obstructive pulmonary disease is an umbrella term for a group of respiratory tract diseases that are characterized by airflow obstruction or limitation. It is usually caused by tobacco smoking.
Housework	Unpaid work carried on in and around the home such as cooking, cleaning and shopping, is referred to as a housework.
Acute	In medicine, an acute disease is a disease with either or both of: a rapid onset; and a short course (as opposed to a chronic course).
Cardiovascular system	The circulatory system or cardiovascular system is the organ system which circulates blood around the body of most animals.

Lipoprotein	A lipoprotein is a biochemical assembly that contains both proteins and lipids and may be structural or catalytic in function. They may be enzymes, proton pumps, ion pumps, or some combination of these functions.
Syndrome	Syndrome is the association of several clinically recognizable features, signs, symptoms, phenomena or characteristics which often occur together, so that the presence of one feature alerts the physician to the presence of the others
Stenosis	A stenosis is an abnormal narrowing in a blood vessel or other tubular organ or structure. It is also sometimes called a "stricture" (as in urethral stricture).
Advocate	An advocate is one who speaks on behalf of another, especially in a legal context. Implicit in the concept is the notion that the represented lacks the knowledge, skill, ability, or standing to speak for themselves.
Medicine	Medicine is the branch of health science and the sector of public life concerned with maintaining or restoring human health through the study, diagnosis and treatment of disease and injury.
Longevity	A long duration of life is referred to as longevity.
Elderly	Old age consists of ages nearing the average life span of human beings, and thus the end of the human life cycle. Euphemisms for older people include advanced adult, elderly, and senior or senior citizen.
Independence	The condition in which one variable has no effect on another is referred to as independence.
Centers for Disease Control and Prevention	The Centers for Disease Control and Prevention in Atlanta, Georgia, is recognized as the lead United States agency for protecting the public health and safety of people by providing credible information to enhance health decisions, and promoting health through strong partnerships with state health departments and other organizations.
Health promotion	Any planned combination of educational, political, regulatory, and organizational supports for actions and conditions of living conducive to the health of individuals, groups, or communities is called health promotion.

Health	Health is a term that refers to a combination of the absence of illness, the ability to cope with everyday activities, physical fitness, and high quality of life.
Extension	Movement increasing the angle between parts at a joint is referred to as extension.
Immunization	Use of a vaccine to protect the body against specific disease-causing agents is called immunization.
Solution	Solution refers to homogenous mixture formed when a solute is dissolved in a solvent.
Cardiovascular disease	Cardiovascular disease refers to afflictions in the mechanisms, including the heart, blood vessels, and their controllers, that are responsible for transporting blood to the body's tissues and organs. Psychological factors may play important roles in such diseases and their treatments.
Quality of life	Quality of life refers to the perception of individuals or groups that their needs are being satisfied and that they are not being denied opportunities to achieve happiness and fulfillment.
Osteoporosis	Osteoporosis is a disease of bone in which bone mineral density (BMD) is reduced, bone microarchitecture is disrupted, the amount and variety of non-collagenous proteins in bone is changed, and a concomitantly fracture risk is increased.
Lead	Lead is a chemical element in the periodic table that has the symbol Pb and atomic number 82. A soft, heavy, toxic and malleable poor metal, lead is bluish white when freshly cut but tarnishes to dull gray when exposed to air. Lead is used in building construction, lead-acid batteries, bullets and shot, and is part of solder, pewter, and fusible alloys.
Obesity	The state of being more than 20 percent above the average weight for a person of one's height is called obesity.
Aerobic	An aerobic organism is an organism that has an oxygen based metabolism. Aerobes, in a process known as cellular respiration, use oxygen to oxidize substrates (for example sugars and fats) in order to obtain energy.
Conditioning	Processes by which behaviors can be learned or modified through interaction with the environment are conditioning.
Elderly	Old age consists of ages nearing the average life span of human beings, and thus the end of the human life cycle. Euphemisms for older people include advanced adult, elderly, and senior or senior citizen.
Lifestyle	The culturally, socially, economically, and environmentally conditioned complex of actions characteristic of an individual, group, or community as a pattern of habituated behavior over time that is health related but not necessarily health directed is a lifestyle.
Course	Pattern of development and change of a disorder over time is a course.
Sleep deprivation	Sleep deprivation is an overall lack of the necessary amount of sleep. A person can be deprived of sleep by their own body and mind, insomnia, or actively deprived by another individual.
Base	The common definition of a base is a chemical compound that absorbs hydronium ions when dissolved in water (a proton acceptor). An alkali is a special example of a base, where in an aqueous environment, hydroxide ions are donated.
Oxygen	Oxygen is a chemical element in the periodic table. It has the symbol O and atomic number 8. Oxygen is the second most common element on Earth, composing around 46% of the mass of Earth's crust and 28% of the mass of Earth as a whole, and is the third most common element in the universe.

Go to **Cram101.com** for the Practice Tests for this Chapter.

Heart rate	Heart rate is a term used to describe the frequency of the cardiac cycle. It is considered one of the four vital signs. Usually it is calculated as the number of contractions of the heart in one minute and expressed as "beats per minute".
Alcohol	Alcohol is a general term, applied to any organic compound in which a hydroxyl group (-OH) is bound to a carbon atom, which in turn is bound to other hydrogen and/or carbon atoms. The general formula for a simple acyclic alcohol is $C_nH_{2n+1}OH$.
Stress	Stress refers to a condition that is a response to factors that change the human systems normal state.
Resistance	Resistance refers to a nonspecific ability to ward off infection or disease regardless of whether the body has been previously exposed to it. A force that opposes the flow of a fluid such as air or blood. Compare with immunity.
Stressor	A factor capable of stimulating a stress response is a stressor.
Drug abuse	Drug abuse has a wide range of definitions, all of them relating either to the misuse or overuse of a psychoactive drug or performance enhancing drug for a non-therapeutic or non-medical effect, or referring to any use of illegal drug in the absence of a required, yet practically impossible to get, license from a government authority.
Carbohydrate	Carbohydrate is a chemical compound that contains oxygen, hydrogen, and carbon atoms. They consist of monosaccharide sugars of varying chain lengths and that have the general chemical formula $C_n(H_2O)_n$ or are derivatives of such.
Protein	A protein is a complex, high-molecular-weight organic compound that consists of amino acids joined by peptide bonds. They are essential to the structure and function of all living cells and viruses. Many are enzymes or subunits of enzymes.
Blood	Blood is a circulating tissue composed of fluid plasma and cells. The main function of blood is to supply nutrients (oxygen, glucose) and constitutional elements to tissues and to remove waste products.
Salt	Salt is a term used for ionic compounds composed of positively charged cations and negatively charged anions, so that the product is neutral and without a net charge.
Vaccine	A harmless variant or derivative of a pathogen used to stimulate a host organism's immune system to mount a long-term defense against the pathogen is referred to as vaccine.
Risk factor	A risk factor is a variable associated with an increased risk of disease or infection but risk factors are not necessarily causal.
Evaluation	The fifth step of the nursing process where nursing care and the patient's goal achievement are measured is the evaluation.
Public health	Public health is concerned with threats to the overall health of a community based on population health analysis.
Health promotion	Any planned combination of educational, political, regulatory, and organizational supports for actions and conditions of living conducive to the health of individuals, groups, or communities is called health promotion.

Go to **Cram101.com** for the Practice Tests for this Chapter.

Health	Health is a term that refers to a combination of the absence of illness, the ability to cope with everyday activities, physical fitness, and high quality of life.
Population	Population refers to all members of a well-defined group of organisms, events, or things.
Lifestyle	The culturally, socially, economically, and environmentally conditioned complex of actions characteristic of an individual, group, or community as a pattern of habituated behavior over time that is health related but not necessarily health directed is a lifestyle.
Risk factor	A risk factor is a variable associated with an increased risk of disease or infection but risk factors are not necessarily causal.
Blood	Blood is a circulating tissue composed of fluid plasma and cells. The main function of blood is to supply nutrients (oxygen, glucose) and constitutional elements to tissues and to remove waste products.
Electrocardi-gram	An electrocardiogram is a graphic produced by an electrocardiograph, which records the electrical voltage in the heart in the form of a continuous strip graph. It is the prime tool in cardiac electrophysiology, and has a prime function in screening and diagnosis of cardiovascular diseases..
Blood pressure	Blood pressure is the pressure exerted by the blood on the walls of the blood vessels.
Heart rate	Heart rate is a term used to describe the frequency of the cardiac cycle. It is considered one of the four vital signs. Usually it is calculated as the number of contractions of the heart in one minute and expressed as "beats per minute".
Glucose	Glucose, a simple monosaccharide sugar, is one of the most important carbohydrates and is used as a source of energy in animals and plants. Glucose is one of the main products of photosynthesis and starts respiration.
Triglycerides	Triglycerides refer to fats and oils composed of fatty acids and glycerol; are the body's most concentrated source of energy fuel; also known as neutral fats.
Triglyceride	Triglyceride is a glyceride in which the glycerol is esterified with three fatty acids. They are the main constituent of vegetable oil and animal fats and play an important role in metabolism as energy sources. They contain a bit more than twice as much energy as carbohydrates and proteins.
Lipoprotein	A lipoprotein is a biochemical assembly that contains both proteins and lipids and may be structural or catalytic in function. They may be enzymes, proton pumps, ion pumps, or some combination of these functions.
Cholesterol	Cholesterol is a steroid, a lipid, and an alcohol, found in the cell membranes of all body tissues, and transported in the blood plasma of all animals. It is an important component of the membranes of cells, providing stability; it makes the membrane's fluidity stable over a bigger temperature interval.
Heart attack	A heart attack, is a serious, sudden heart condition usually characterized by varying degrees of chest pain or discomfort, weakness, sweating, nausea, vomiting, and arrhythmias, sometimes causing loss of consciousness. It occurs when the blood supply to a part of the heart is interrupted, causing death and scarring of the local heart tissue.
Palpitation	A palpitation is an awareness of the beating of the heart, whether it is too slow, too fast, irregular, or at its normal frequency; brought on by overexertion, adrenaline, alcohol, disease or drugs, or as a symptom of panic disorder.
Coronary	Referring to the heart or the blood vessels of the heart is referred to as coronary.
Planning	In agreement with the patient, the nurse addresses each of the problems identified in the planning phase. For each problem a measurable goal is set. For example, for the patient

discussed above, the goal would be for the patient's skin to remain intact. The result is a nursing care plan. This is the third step.

Fever	Fever (also known as pyrexia, or a febrile response, and archaically known as ague) is a medical symptom that describes an increase in internal body temperature to levels that are above normal (37°C, 98.6°F).
Agent	Agent refers to an epidemiological term referring to the organism or object that transmits a disease from the environment to the host.
Physiology	The study of the function of cells, tissues, and organs is referred to as physiology.
Baseline	Measure of a particular behavior or process taken before the introduction of the independent variable or treatment is called the baseline.
Oxygen	Oxygen is a chemical element in the periodic table. It has the symbol O and atomic number 8. Oxygen is the second most common element on Earth, composing around 46% of the mass of Earth's crust and 28% of the mass of Earth as a whole, and is the third most common element in the universe.
Medicine	Medicine is the branch of health science and the sector of public life concerned with maintaining or restoring human health through the study, diagnosis and treatment of disease and injury.
Variable	A characteristic or aspect in which people, objects, events, or conditions vary is called variable.
Value	Value is worth in general, and it is thought to be connected to reasons for certain practices, policies, actions, beliefs or emotions. Value is "that which one acts to gain and/or keep."
Diastolic blood pressure	The pressure present in a large artery when the heart is at the resting phase of the cardiac cycle is called diastolic blood pressure.
Stress	Stress refers to a condition that is a response to factors that change the human systems normal state.
Base	The common definition of a base is a chemical compound that absorbs hydronium ions when dissolved in water (a proton acceptor). An alkali is a special example of a base, where in an aqueous environment, hydroxide ions are donated.
Diabetes	Diabetes is a medical disorder characterized by varying or persistent elevated blood sugar levels, especially after eating. All types of diabetes share similar symptoms and complications at advanced stages: dehydration and ketoacidosis, cardiovascular disease, chronic renal failure, retinal damage which can lead to blindness, nerve damage which can lead to erectile dysfunction, gangrene with risk of amputation of toes, feet, and even legs.
Serum	Serum is the same as blood plasma except that clotting factors (such as fibrin) have been removed. Blood plasma contains fibrinogen.
Lipid	Lipid is one class of aliphatic hydrocarbon-containing organic compounds essential for the structure and function of living cells. They are characterized by being water-insoluble but soluble in nonpolar organic solvents.
Vital capacity	Vital capacity is the total amount of air that a person can expire after a complete inspiration.
Evaluation	The fifth step of the nursing process where nursing care and the patient's goal achievement are measured is the evaluation.
Affect	Affect is the scientific term used to describe a subject's externally displayed mood. This

can be assesed by the nurse by observing facial expression, tone of voice, and body language.

Aerobic
An aerobic organism is an organism that has an oxygen based metabolism. Aerobes, in a process known as cellular respiration, use oxygen to oxidize substrates (for example sugars and fats) in order to obtain energy.

Lead
Lead is a chemical element in the periodic table that has the symbol Pb and atomic number 82. A soft, heavy, toxic and malleable poor metal, lead is bluish white when freshly cut but tarnishes to dull gray when exposed to air. Lead is used in building construction, lead-acid batteries, bullets and shot, and is part of solder, pewter, and fusible alloys.

Atropine
Atropine is a tropane alkaloid extracted from the deadly nightshade and other plants of the family Solanaceae. It is a secondary metabolite of these plants and serves as a drug with a wide variety of effects.

Alcohol
Alcohol is a general term, applied to any organic compound in which a hydroxyl group (-OH) is bound to a carbon atom, which in turn is bound to other hydrogen and/or carbon atoms. The general formula for a simple acyclic alcohol is $C_nH_{2n+1}OH$.

Bronchodilator
A bronchodilator is a medication intended to improve bronchial airflow. Treatment of bronchial asthma is the most common application of these drugs.

Dehydration
Dehydration is the removal of water from an object. Medically, dehydration is a serious and potentially life-threatening condition in which the body contains an insufficient volume of water for normal functioning.

Carrier
Person in apparent health whose chromosomes contain a pathologic mutant gene that may be transmitted to his or her children is a carrier.

Stroke
A stroke or cerebrovascular accident (CVA) occurs when the blood supply to a part of the brain is suddenly interrupted.

Primary prevention
Primary prevention is any effort to avoid the development of a disease or condition.

Cardiovascular disease
Cardiovascular disease refers to afflictions in the mechanisms, including the heart, blood vessels, and their controllers, that are responsible for transporting blood to the body's tissues and organs. Psychological factors may play important roles in such diseases and their treatments.

Joint
A joint (articulation) is the location at which two bones make contact (articulate). They are constructed to both allow movement and provide mechanical support.

Oxygen	Oxygen is a chemical element in the periodic table. It has the symbol O and atomic number 8. Oxygen is the second most common element on Earth, composing around 46% of the mass of Earth's crust and 28% of the mass of Earth as a whole, and is the third most common element in the universe.
Skin	Skin is an organ of the integumentary system composed of a layer of tissues that protect underlying muscles and organs.
Carbohydrate	Carbohydrate is a chemical compound that contains oxygen, hydrogen, and carbon atoms. They consist of monosaccharide sugars of varying chain lengths and that have the general chemical formula $C_n(H_2O)_n$ or are derivatives of such.
Constant	A behavior or characteristic that does not vary from one observation to another is referred to as a constant.
Protein	A protein is a complex, high-molecular-weight organic compound that consists of amino acids joined by peptide bonds. They are essential to the structure and function of all living cells and viruses. Many are enzymes or subunits of enzymes.
Calorie	Calorie refers to a unit used to measure heat energy and the energy contents of foods.
Value	Value is worth in general, and it is thought to be connected to reasons for certain practices, policies, actions, beliefs or emotions. Value is "that which one acts to gain and/or keep."
Urea	Urea is an organic compound of carbon, nitrogen, oxygen and hydrogen, CON_2H_4 or $(NH_2)_2CO$. Urea is essentially a waste product: it has no physiological function. It is dissolved in blood and excreted by the kidney.
Carbon	Carbon is a chemical element in the periodic table that has the symbol C and atomic number 6. An abundant nonmetallic, tetravalent element, carbon has several allotropic forms.
Ratio	In number and more generally in algebra, a ratio is the linear relationship between two quantities.
Carbon dioxide	Carbon dioxide is an atmospheric gas comprized of one carbon and two oxygen atoms. A very widely known chemical compound, it is frequently called by its formula CO_2. In its solid state, it is commonly known as dry ice.
Gas exchange	In humans and other mammals, respiratory gas exchange or ventilation is carried out by mechanisms of the lungs. The actual gas exchange occurs in the alveoli.
Spirometer	A spirometer is an apparatus for measuring the volume of air inspired and expired by the lungs. It is a precision differential pressure transducer for the measurements of respiration flow rates.
Insight	Insight refers to a sudden awareness of the relationships among various elements that had previously appeared to be independent of one another.
Muscle	Muscle is a contractile form of tissue. It is one of the four major tissue types, the other three being epithelium, connective tissue and nervous tissue. Muscle contraction is used to move parts of the body, as well as to move substances within the body.
Adenosine	Adenosine is a nucleoside comprized of adenine attached to a ribose (ribofuranose) moiety via a β-N_9-glycosidic bond. Adenosine plays an important role in biochemical processes, such as energy transfer - as adenosine triphosphate (ATP) and adenosine diphosphate (ADP) - as well as in signal transduction as cyclic adenosine monophosphate, cAMP.
Leveling	The communication of a clear, simple, and honest message is a leveling.
Aerobic	An aerobic organism is an organism that has an oxygen based metabolism. Aerobes, in a process

Go to **Cram101.com** for the Practice Tests for this Chapter.

	known as cellular respiration, use oxygen to oxidize substrates (for example sugars and fats) in order to obtain energy.
Adenosine triphosphate	Organic molecule that stores energy and releases energy for use in cellular processes is adenosine triphosphate.
Metabolism	Metabolism is the biochemical modification of chemical compounds in living organisms and cells. This includes the biosynthesis of complex organic molecules (anabolism) and their breakdown (catabolism).
Substrate	A substrate is a molecule which is acted upon by an enzyme. Each enzyme recognizes only the specific substrate of the reaction it catalyzes. A surface in or on which an organism lives.
Metabolic rate	Energy expended by the body per unit time is called metabolic rate.
Population	Population refers to all members of a well-defined group of organisms, events, or things.
Course	Pattern of development and change of a disorder over time is a course.
Rehabilitation	Rehabilitation is the restoration of lost capabilities, or the treatment aimed at producing it. Also refers to treatment for dependency on psychoactive substances such as alcohol, prescription drugs, and illicit drugs such as cocaine, heroin or amphetamines.
Trauma	Trauma refers to a severe physical injury or wound to the body caused by an external force, or a psychological shock having a lasting effect on mental life.
Joint	A joint (articulation) is the location at which two bones make contact (articulate). They are constructed to both allow movement and provide mechanical support.
Hip	In anatomy, the hip is the bony projection of the femur, known as the greater trochanter, and the overlying muscle and fat.
Resistance	Resistance refers to a nonspecific ability to ward off infection or disease regardless of whether the body has been previously exposed to it. A force that opposes the flow of a fluid such as air or blood. Compare with immunity.
Elderly	Old age consists of ages nearing the average life span of human beings, and thus the end of the human life cycle. Euphemisms for older people include advanced adult, elderly, and senior or senior citizen.
Variable	A characteristic or aspect in which people, objects, events, or conditions vary is called variable.
Muscle contraction	A muscle contraction occurs when a muscle cell (called a muscle fiber) shortens. There are three general types: skeletal, heart, and smooth.
Stroke	A stroke or cerebrovascular accident (CVA) occurs when the blood supply to a part of the brain is suddenly interrupted.
Physiology	The study of the function of cells, tissues, and organs is referred to as physiology.
Medicine	Medicine is the branch of health science and the sector of public life concerned with maintaining or restoring human health through the study, diagnosis and treatment of disease and injury.
Assessment	In clinical practice, the process by which a mental health professional gathers and compiles information about a client for the purpose of describing the person's problems or disorder and developing a plan of treatment is an assessment.
Myocardial infarction	Acute myocardial infarction, commonly known as a heart attack, is a serious, sudden heart condition usually characterized by varying degrees of chest pain or discomfort, weakness, sweating, nausea, vomiting, and arrhythmias, sometimes causing loss of consciousness.

Go to **Cram101.com** for the Practice Tests for this Chapter.

Infarction	The sudden death of tissue from a lack of blood perfusion is referred to as an infarction.
Cardiology	Cardiology is the branch of medicine dealing with disorders of the heart and blood vessels. The field is commonly divided in the branches of congenital heart defects, coronary artery disease, heart failure, valvular heart disease and electrophysiology.
Health	Health is a term that refers to a combination of the absence of illness, the ability to cope with everyday activities, physical fitness, and high quality of life.
Compatibility	The capability of living together in harmony is referred to as compatibility.

Variable	A characteristic or aspect in which people, objects, events, or conditions vary is called variable.
Sphygmomanometer	A sphygmomanometer or blood pressure meter is an inflatable cuff used to measure blood pressure.
Rehabilitation	Rehabilitation is the restoration of lost capabilities, or the treatment aimed at producing it. Also refers to treatment for dependency on psychoactive substances such as alcohol, prescription drugs, and illicit drugs such as cocaine, heroin or amphetamines.
Health	Health is a term that refers to a combination of the absence of illness, the ability to cope with everyday activities, physical fitness, and high quality of life.
Aerobic	An aerobic organism is an organism that has an oxygen based metabolism. Aerobes, in a process known as cellular respiration, use oxygen to oxidize substrates (for example sugars and fats) in order to obtain energy.
Muscle	Muscle is a contractile form of tissue. It is one of the four major tissue types, the other three being epithelium, connective tissue and nervous tissue. Muscle contraction is used to move parts of the body, as well as to move substances within the body.
Oxygen	Oxygen is a chemical element in the periodic table. It has the symbol O and atomic number 8. Oxygen is the second most common element on Earth, composing around 46% of the mass of Earth's crust and 28% of the mass of Earth as a whole, and is the third most common element in the universe.
Blood	Blood is a circulating tissue composed of fluid plasma and cells. The main function of blood is to supply nutrients (oxygen, glucose) and constitutional elements to tissues and to remove waste products.
Lungs	Lungs are the essential organs of respiration in air-breathing vertebrates. Their principal function is to transport oxygen from the atmosphere into the bloodstream, and to excrete carbon dioxide from the bloodstream into the atmosphere.
Blood vessel	A blood vessel is a part of the circulatory system and function to transport blood throughout the body. The most important types, arteries and veins, are so termed because they carry blood away from or towards the heart, respectively.
Ventilation	Ventilation refers to a mechanism that provides contact between an animal's respiratory surface and the air or water to which it is exposed. It is also called breathing.
Conditioning	Processes by which behaviors can be learned or modified through interaction with the environment are conditioning.
Obesity	The state of being more than 20 percent above the average weight for a person of one's height is called obesity.
Quality of life	Quality of life refers to the perception of individuals or groups that their needs are being satisfied and that they are not being denied opportunities to achieve happiness and fulfillment.
Risk factor	A risk factor is a variable associated with an increased risk of disease or infection but risk factors are not necessarily causal.
Informed consent	The term used by psychologists to indicate that a person has agreed to participate in research after receiving information about the purposes of the study and the nature of the treatments is informed consent. Even with informed consent, subjects may withdraw from any experiment at any time.
Psychological test	Psychological test refers to a standardized measure of a sample of a person's behavior.

Go to **Cram101.com** for the Practice Tests for this Chapter.

Informed consent form	An informed consent form explains a study to a potential subject before he or she agrees to participate.
Evaluation	The fifth step of the nursing process where nursing care and the patient's goal achievement are measured is the evaluation.
Value	Value is worth in general, and it is thought to be connected to reasons for certain practices, policies, actions, beliefs or emotions. Value is "that which one acts to gain and/or keep."
Infection	The invasion and multiplication of microorganisms in body tissues is called an infection.
Coronary	Referring to the heart or the blood vessels of the heart is referred to as coronary.
Aneurysm	An aneurysm is a localized dilation or ballooning of a blood vessel by more than 50% of the diameter of the vessel. Aneurysms most commonly occur in the arteries at the base of the brain and in the aorta (the main artery coming out of the heart) - this is an aortic aneurysm.
Diabetes	Diabetes is a medical disorder characterized by varying or persistent elevated blood sugar levels, especially after eating. All types of diabetes share similar symptoms and complications at advanced stages: dehydration and ketoacidosis, cardiovascular disease, chronic renal failure, retinal damage which can lead to blindness, nerve damage which can lead to erectile dysfunction, gangrene with risk of amputation of toes, feet, and even legs.
Ischemia	Narrowing of arteries caused by plaque buildup within the arteries is called ischemia.
Stenosis	A stenosis is an abnormal narrowing in a blood vessel or other tubular organ or structure. It is also sometimes called a "stricture" (as in urethral stricture).
Embolus	Embolus refers to any abnormal traveling object in the bloodstream, such as agglutinated bacteria or blood cells, a blood clot, or an air bubble.
Angina	Angina pectoris is chest pain due to ischemia (a lack of blood and hence oxygen supply) to the heart muscle, generally due to obstruction or spasm of the coronary arteries (the heart's blood vessels). Coronary artery disease, the main cause of angina, is due to atherosclerosis of the cardiac arteries.
Acute	In medicine, an acute disease is a disease with either or both of: a rapid onset; and a short course (as opposed to a chronic course).
Cardiac arrhythmia	Cardiac arrhythmia is a group of conditions in which the muscle contraction of the heart is irregular or is faster or slower than normal.
Infectious disease	In medicine, infectious disease or communicable disease is disease caused by a biological agent such as by a virus, bacterium or parasite. This is contrasted to physical causes, such as burns or chemical ones such as through intoxication.
Unstable angina	Worsening angina attacks, sudden-onset angina at rest, and angina lasting more than 15 minutes are symptoms of unstable angina or acute coronary syndrome. As these may herald myocardial infarction (a heart attack), they require urgent medical attention and are generally treated quite similarly
Aortic stenosis	Aortic stenosis is a heart condition caused by the incomplete opening of the aortic valve.
Hypomagnesemia	Hypomagnesemia is an electrolyte disturbance in which there is an abnormally low level of magnesium in the blood.
Myocardial infarction	Acute myocardial infarction, commonly known as a heart attack, is a serious, sudden heart condition usually characterized by varying degrees of chest pain or discomfort, weakness, sweating, nausea, vomiting, and arrhythmias, sometimes causing loss of consciousness.

Go to **Cram101.com** for the Practice Tests for this Chapter.

Hypertension	Hypertension is a medical condition where the blood pressure in the arteries is chronically elevated. Persistent hypertension is one of the risk factors for strokes, heart attacks, heart failure and arterial aneurysm, and is a leading cause of chronic renal failure.
Pericarditis	Pericarditis is inflalt can cause fluid to build up in the sac (pericardial effusion). Excessive amounts of fluid may lead to cardiac tamponade by physically blocking the heart from beating properly or compression of the great vessels of the heart.mmation of the pericardium.
Hypokalemia	Hypokalemia is a potentially fatal condition in which the body fails to retain sufficient potassium to maintain health.
Electrolyte	An electrolyte is a substance that dissociates into free ions when dissolved (or molten), to produce an electrically conductive medium. Because they generally consist of ions in solution, they are also known as ionic solutions.
Arrhythmias	Arrhythmias refers to abnormal heart rhythms which may be too slow, too early, too rapid, or irregular.
Arrhythmia	Cardiac arrhythmia is a group of conditions in which muscle contraction of the heart is irregular for any reason.
Infarction	The sudden death of tissue from a lack of blood perfusion is referred to as an infarction.
Hepatitis	Hepatitis is a gastroenterological disease, featuring inflammation of the liver. The clinical signs and prognosis, as well as the therapy, depend on the cause.
Cardiology	Cardiology is the branch of medicine dealing with disorders of the heart and blood vessels. The field is commonly divided in the branches of congenital heart defects, coronary artery disease, heart failure, valvular heart disease and electrophysiology.
Asymptomatic	A disease is asymptomatic when it is at a stage where the patient does not experience symptoms. By their nature, asymptomatic diseases are not usually discovered until the patient undergoes medical tests (X-rays or other investigations). Some diseases remain asymptomatic for a remarkably long time, including some forms of cancer.
Correlation	A statistical technique for determining the degree of association between two or more variables is referred to as correlation.
Outcome	Outcome is the impact of care provided to a patient. They can be positive, such as the ability to walk freely as a result of rehabilitation, or negative, such as the occurrence of bedsores as a result of lack of mobility of a patient.
Affect	Affect is the scientific term used to describe a subject's externally displayed mood. This can be assesed by the nurse by observing facial expression, tone of voice, and body language.
Resistance	Resistance refers to a nonspecific ability to ward off infection or disease regardless of whether the body has been previously exposed to it. A force that opposes the flow of a fluid such as air or blood. Compare with immunity.
Constant	A behavior or characteristic that does not vary from one observation to another is referred to as a constant.
Cardiovascular system	The circulatory system or cardiovascular system is the organ system which circulates blood around the body of most animals.
Protocol	Protocol is a document with the aim of guiding decisions and criteria in specific areas of healthcare, as defined by an authoritative examination of current evidence. It details the activities to be executed in specific situations.
Heart rate	Heart rate is a term used to describe the frequency of the cardiac cycle. It is considered

Go to **Cram101.com** for the Practice Tests for this Chapter.

one of the four vital signs. Usually it is calculated as the number of contractions of the heart in one minute and expressed as "beats per minute".

Artery	Vessel that takes blood away from the heart to the tissues and organs of the body is called an artery.
Palpation	Palpation is a method of examination in which the examiner feels the size or shape or firmness or location of something.
Carotid artery	In human anatomy, the carotid artery refers to a number of major arteries in the head and neck.
Radial artery	The radial artery is the main blood vessel, with oxygenated blood, of the lateral aspect of the forearm. It arises from the brachial artery and terminates in the deep palmar arch.
Bladder	A hollow muscular storage organ for storing urine is a bladder.
Pain	Pain is an unpleasant sensation which may be associated with actual or potential tissue damage and which may have physical and emotional components.
Eye	An eye is an organ that detects light. Different kinds of light-sensitive organs are found in a variety of creatures. The simplest eyes do nothing but detect whether the surroundings are light or dark, while more complex eyes can distinguish shapes and colors.
Stress	Stress refers to a condition that is a response to factors that change the human systems normal state.
Blood pressure	Blood pressure is the pressure exerted by the blood on the walls of the blood vessels.
Diastolic pressure	Diastolic pressure refers to arterial blood pressure during the diastolic phase of the cardiac cycle.
Systolic pressure	The force of blood against the walls of the arteries when the heart contracts to pump blood to the rest of the body is systolic pressure.
Cyanosis	Bluish skin coloration due to decreased blood oxygen concentration is called cyanosis.
Ataxia	Ataxia is unsteady and clumsy motion of the limbs or trunk due to a failure of the gross coordination of muscle movements. Ataxia often occurs when parts of the nervous system that control movement are damaged.
Pallor	Pallor is an abnormal loss of skin or mucous membrane color. It can develop suddenly or gradually, depending of the cause.
Skin	Skin is an organ of the integumentary system composed of a layer of tissues that protect underlying muscles and organs.
Medicine	Medicine is the branch of health science and the sector of public life concerned with maintaining or restoring human health through the study, diagnosis and treatment of disease and injury.
Insight	Insight refers to a sudden awareness of the relationships among various elements that had previously appeared to be independent of one another.
Baseline	Measure of a particular behavior or process taken before the introduction of the independent variable or treatment is called the baseline.
Stroke	A stroke or cerebrovascular accident (CVA) occurs when the blood supply to a part of the brain is suddenly interrupted.
Steady state	Steady state is a system in which a particular variable is not changing but energy must be continuously added to maintain this variable constant.

Go to **Cram101.com** for the Practice Tests for this Chapter.

Pulse	The rhythmic stretching of the arteries caused by the pressure of blood forced through the arteries by contractions of the ventricles during systole is a pulse.
Adjustment	Adjustment is an attempt to cope with a given situation.
Elevation	Elevation refers to upward movement of a part of the body.
Displacement	An unconscious defense mechanism in which the individual directs aggressive or sexual feelings away from the primary object to someone or something safe is referred to as displacement. Displacement in linguistics is simply the ability to talk about things not present.
Mercury	Mercury is a chemical element in the periodic table that has the symbol Hg and atomic number 80. A heavy, silvery, transition metal, mercury is one of five elements that are liquid at or near standard room temperature (the others are the metals caesium, francium, and gallium, and the nonmetal bromine).
Meniscus	The meniscus is either of two parts of the human knee. The knee contains a lateral meniscus and a medial meniscus, and both are cartilaginous tissues that provide structural integrity to the knee when it undergoes tension and torsion.
Alcohol	Alcohol is a general term, applied to any organic compound in which a hydroxyl group (-OH) is bound to a carbon atom, which in turn is bound to other hydrogen and/or carbon atoms. The general formula for a simple acyclic alcohol is $C_nH_{2n+1}OH$.
Gauge	The diameter of the needle is indicated by the needle gauge.
Physiology	The study of the function of cells, tissues, and organs is referred to as physiology.
Assessment	In clinical practice, the process by which a mental health professional gathers and compiles information about a client for the purpose of describing the person's problems or disorder and developing a plan of treatment is an assessment.
Mortality	The incidence of death in a population is mortality.
Methodology	Techniques of measurement used to collect and manipulate empirical data refer to a methodology.
Ergonomics	Ergonomics refers to the branch of psychology concerned with the interaction of people and technology; also called engineering psychology or human factors.
Coronary heart disease	Coronary heart disease is the end result of the accumulation of atheromatous plaques within the walls of the arteries that supply the myocardium (the muscle of the heart).

Go to **Cram101.com** for the Practice Tests for this Chapter.
And, **NEVER** highlight a book again!

Hydrostatic weighing	Hydrostatic weighing refers to method used to determine the difference between a person's scale weight and weight underwater. A leaner person of a given weight will weigh more under water than a fatter person of the same weight.
Displacement	An unconscious defense mechanism in which the individual directs aggressive or sexual feelings away from the primary object to someone or something safe is referred to as displacement. Displacement in linguistics is simply the ability to talk about things not present.
Assess	Assess is to systematically and continuously collect, validate, and communicate patient data.
Assessment	In clinical practice, the process by which a mental health professional gathers and compiles information about a client for the purpose of describing the person's problems or disorder and developing a plan of treatment is an assessment.
Health	Health is a term that refers to a combination of the absence of illness, the ability to cope with everyday activities, physical fitness, and high quality of life.
Tissue	A collection of interconnected cells that perform a similar function within an organism is called tissue.
Value	Value is worth in general, and it is thought to be connected to reasons for certain practices, policies, actions, beliefs or emotions. Value is "that which one acts to gain and/or keep."
Obesity	The state of being more than 20 percent above the average weight for a person of one's height is called obesity.
Coronary	Referring to the heart or the blood vessels of the heart is referred to as coronary.
Diabetes	Diabetes is a medical disorder characterized by varying or persistent elevated blood sugar levels, especially after eating. All types of diabetes share similar symptoms and complications at advanced stages: dehydration and ketoacidosis, cardiovascular disease, chronic renal failure, retinal damage which can lead to blindness, nerve damage which can lead to erectile dysfunction, gangrene with risk of amputation of toes, feet, and even legs.
Artery	Vessel that takes blood away from the heart to the tissues and organs of the body is called an artery.
Cancer	Cancer is a class of diseases or disorders characterized by uncontrolled division of cells and the ability of these cells to invade other tissues, either by direct growth into adjacent tissue through invasion or by implantation into distant sites by metastasis.
Stroke	A stroke or cerebrovascular accident (CVA) occurs when the blood supply to a part of the brain is suddenly interrupted.
Lipid	Lipid is one class of aliphatic hydrocarbon-containing organic compounds essential for the structure and function of living cells. They are characterized by being water-insoluble but soluble in nonpolar organic solvents.
Joint	A joint (articulation) is the location at which two bones make contact (articulate). They are constructed to both allow movement and provide mechanical support.
Blood	Blood is a circulating tissue composed of fluid plasma and cells. The main function of blood is to supply nutrients (oxygen, glucose) and constitutional elements to tissues and to remove waste products.
Body mass index	Body mass index refers to a number derived from an individual's weight and height used to estimate body fat. The formula is- weight /height' .
Coronary artery	An artery that supplies blood to the wall of the heart is called a coronary artery.

Go to **Cram101.com** for the Practice Tests for this Chapter.

Osteoarthritis	Osteoarthritis is a condition in which low-grade inflammation results in pain in the joints, caused by wearing of the cartilage that covers and acts as a cushion inside joints.
Coronary artery disease	Coronary artery disease (CAD) is the end result of the accumulation of atheromatous plaques within the walls of the arteries that supply the myocardium (the muscle of the heart).
Hypertension	Hypertension is a medical condition where the blood pressure in the arteries is chronically elevated. Persistent hypertension is one of the risk factors for strokes, heart attacks, heart failure and arterial aneurysm, and is a leading cause of chronic renal failure.
Adipose tissue	Adipose tissue is an anatomical term for loose connective tissue composed of adipocytes. Its main role is to store energy in the form of fat, although it also cushions and insulates the body. It has an important endocrine function in producing recently-discovered hormones such as leptin, resistin and TNFalpha.
Affect	Affect is the scientific term used to describe a subject's externally displayed mood. This can be assesed by the nurse by observing facial expression, tone of voice, and body language.
Distribution	Distribution in pharmacology is a branch of pharmacokinetics describing reversible transfer of drug from one location to another within the body.
Hip	In anatomy, the hip is the bony projection of the femur, known as the greater trochanter, and the overlying muscle and fat.
Cardiovascular disease	Cardiovascular disease refers to afflictions in the mechanisms, including the heart, blood vessels, and their controllers, that are responsible for transporting blood to the body's tissues and organs. Psychological factors may play important roles in such diseases and their treatments.
Ratio	In number and more generally in algebra, a ratio is the linear relationship between two quantities.
Outcome	Outcome is the impact of care provided to a patient. They can be positive, such as the ability to walk freely as a result of rehabilitation, or negative, such as the occurrence of bedsores as a result of lack of mobility of a patient.
Infertility	The inability to conceive after one year of regular, unprotected intercourse is infertility.
Depression	In everyday language depression refers to any downturn in mood, which may be relatively transitory and perhaps due to something trivial. This is differentiated from Clinical depression which is marked by symptoms that last two weeks or more and are so severe that they interfere with daily living.
Lead	Lead is a chemical element in the periodic table that has the symbol Pb and atomic number 82. A soft, heavy, toxic and malleable poor metal, lead is bluish white when freshly cut but tarnishes to dull gray when exposed to air. Lead is used in building construction, lead-acid batteries, bullets and shot, and is part of solder, pewter, and fusible alloys.
Criterion	Criterion refers to a standard of comparison. For performance appraisal, it is the definition of good performance.
Methodology	Techniques of measurement used to collect and manipulate empirical data refer to a methodology.
Oxygen	Oxygen is a chemical element in the periodic table. It has the symbol O and atomic number 8. Oxygen is the second most common element on Earth, composing around 46% of the mass of Earth's crust and 28% of the mass of Earth as a whole, and is the third most common element in the universe.
Conversion	Conversion syndrome describes a condition in which physical symptoms arise for which there is no clear explanation.

Hydration	Hydration can create a hydrate from which water can be reextracted. When hydration occurs in a chemical reaction it is called a hydration reaction, in which water is permanently and chemically combined with a reactant in a way that it can no longer be reextracted.
Hydrostatic weighing techniques	Methods of determining body fat by measuring the amount of water displaced when a person is completely submerged are referred to as hydrostatic weighing techniques.
Trial	In classical conditioning, any presentation of a stimulus or pair of stimuli is called a trial.
Residual volume	Residual volume is the amount of air left in the lungs after a maximal exhalation. This averages about 1.5 L..
Hydrogen	Hydrogen is a chemical element in the periodic table that has the symbol H and atomic number 1. At standard temperature and pressure it is a colorless, odorless, nonmetallic, univalent, tasteless, highly flammable diatomic gas.
Isotope	An isotope is a form of an element whose nuclei have the same atomic number - the number of protons in the nucleus - but different mass numbers because they contain different numbers of neutrons.
Total body water	Total body water is the total amount of water in the body expressed as a percentage of body weight.
Urine	Concentrated filtrate produced by the kidneys and excreted via the bladder is called urine.
Protein	A protein is a complex, high-molecular-weight organic compound that consists of amino acids joined by peptide bonds. They are essential to the structure and function of all living cells and viruses. Many are enzymes or subunits of enzymes.
Population	Population refers to all members of a well-defined group of organisms, events, or things.
Concept	A mental category used to class together objects, relations, events, abstractions, or qualities that have common properties is called concept.
Diaphragm	The diaphragm is a shelf of muscle extending across the bottom of the ribcage. It is critically important in respiration: in order to draw air into the lungs, the diaphragm contracts, thus enlarging the thoracic cavity and reducing intra-thoracic pressure.
Resistance	Resistance refers to a nonspecific ability to ward off infection or disease regardless of whether the body has been previously exposed to it. A force that opposes the flow of a fluid such as air or blood. Compare with immunity.
Alcohol	Alcohol is a general term, applied to any organic compound in which a hydroxyl group (-OH) is bound to a carbon atom, which in turn is bound to other hydrogen and/or carbon atoms. The general formula for a simple acyclic alcohol is $C_nH_{2n+1}OH$.
Skin	Skin is an organ of the integumentary system composed of a layer of tissues that protect underlying muscles and organs.
Diuretic	A diuretic is any drug that elevates the rate of bodily urine excretion.
Menstrual cycle	The menstrual cycle is the set of recurring physiological changes in a female's body that are under the control of the reproductive hormone system and necessary for reproduction. Besides humans, only other great apes exhibit menstrual cycles, in contrast to the estrus cycle of most mammalian species.
Muscle	Muscle is a contractile form of tissue. It is one of the four major tissue types, the other three being epithelium, connective tissue and nervous tissue. Muscle contraction is used to move parts of the body, as well as to move substances within the body.

Go to **Cram101.com** for the Practice Tests for this Chapter.

Radiation	The emission of electromagnetic waves by all objects warmer than absolute zero is referred to as radiation.
Clinical assessment	A clinical assessment is a systematic evaluation and measurement of psychological, biological, and social factors in a person presenting with a possible psychological disorder.
Clinician	A health professional authorized to provide services to people suffering from one or more pathologies is a clinician.
Computed tomography	Computed tomography is an imaging method employing tomography where digital processing is used to generate a three-dimensional image of the internals of an object from a large series of two-dimensional X-ray images taken around a single axis of rotation.
Magnetic resonance imaging	Magnetic resonance imaging refers to imaging technology that uses magnetism and radio waves to induce hydrogen nuclei in water molecules to emit faint radio signals. A computer creates images of the body from the radio signals.
Visceral	Visceral refers to the internal organs of an animal.
Umbilicus	The umbilicus is essentially a scar caused at birth by the removal of the umbilical cord from a newborn baby. The scar can appear as a depression or as a protrusion.
Acromion	The acromion process, or simply the acromion, is an anatomical feature on the scapula. It is a continuation of the scapular spine, and hooks over anteriorly. The acromion articulates with the clavicle to form the acromioclavicular joint.
Olecranon	The olecranon is a large, thick, curved eminence, situated at the upper and back part of the ulna. It is bent forward at the summit so as to present a prominent lip which is received into the olecranon fossa of the humerus in extension of the forearm.
Scapula	In anatomy, the scapula, or shoulder blade, is the bone that connects the humerus (arm bone) with the clavicle (collar bone).
Inferior angle	The inferior angle, thick and rough, is formed by the union of the vertebral and axillary borders; its dorsal surface affords attachment to the Teres major and frequently to a few fibers of the Latissimus dorsi.
Iliac	In human anatomy, iliac artery refers to several anatomical structures located in the pelvis.
Patella	The patella is a thick, triangular bone which articulates with the femur and covers and protects the front of the knee joint. The patella increases the leverage that the tendon can exert on the femur by increasing the angle at which it acts.
Regression	Return to a form of behavior characteristic of an earlier stage of development is a regression.
Abdomen	The abdomen is a part of the body. In humans, and in many other vertebrates, it is the region between the thorax and the pelvis. In fully developed insects, the abdomen is the third (or posterior) segment, after the head and thorax.
Anthropometric	Anthropometric is the actual measurements of the body and body parts.
Constant	A behavior or characteristic that does not vary from one observation to another is referred to as a constant.
Correlation	A statistical technique for determining the degree of association between two or more variables is referred to as correlation.
Medicine	Medicine is the branch of health science and the sector of public life concerned with maintaining or restoring human health through the study, diagnosis and treatment of disease and injury.

Go to **Cram101.com** for the Practice Tests for this Chapter.

Tuberculosis	Tuberculosis is an infection caused by the bacterium Mycobacterium tuberculosis, which most commonly affects the lungs but can also affect the central nervous system, lymphatic system, circulatory system, genitourinary system, bones and joints.
Plethysmograph	A plethysmograph is an instrument for measuring changes in volume within an organ or whole body (usually resulting from fluctuations in the amount of blood or air it contains).
Evaluation	The fifth step of the nursing process where nursing care and the patient's goal achievement are measured is the evaluation.
Epidemic	An epidemic is a disease that appears as new cases in a given human population, during a given period, at a rate that substantially exceeds what is "expected", based on recent experience.
Physiology	The study of the function of cells, tissues, and organs is referred to as physiology.

Go to **Cram101.com** for the Practice Tests for this Chapter.

Calorie	Calorie refers to a unit used to measure heat energy and the energy contents of foods.
Minerals	Minerals refer to inorganic chemical compounds found in nature; salts.
Vitamin	An organic compound other than a carbohydrate, lipid, or protein that is needed for normal metabolism but that the body cannot synthesize in adequate amounts is called a vitamin.
Assessment	In clinical practice, the process by which a mental health professional gathers and compiles information about a client for the purpose of describing the person's problems or disorder and developing a plan of treatment is an assessment.
Lipid	Lipid is one class of aliphatic hydrocarbon-containing organic compounds essential for the structure and function of living cells. They are characterized by being water-insoluble but soluble in nonpolar organic solvents.
Blood	Blood is a circulating tissue composed of fluid plasma and cells. The main function of blood is to supply nutrients (oxygen, glucose) and constitutional elements to tissues and to remove waste products.
Cardiovascular disease	Cardiovascular disease refers to afflictions in the mechanisms, including the heart, blood vessels, and their controllers, that are responsible for transporting blood to the body's tissues and organs. Psychological factors may play important roles in such diseases and their treatments.
Hydration	Hydration can create a hydrate from which water can be reextracted. When hydration occurs in a chemical reaction it is called a hydration reaction, in which water is permanently and chemically combined with a reactant in a way that it can no longer be reextracted.
Protein	A protein is a complex, high-molecular-weight organic compound that consists of amino acids joined by peptide bonds. They are essential to the structure and function of all living cells and viruses. Many are enzymes or subunits of enzymes.
Glycogen	Glycogen refers to a complex, extensively branched polysaccharide of many glucose monomers; serves as an energy-storage molecule in liver and muscle cells.
Health	Health is a term that refers to a combination of the absence of illness, the ability to cope with everyday activities, physical fitness, and high quality of life.
Distribution	Distribution in pharmacology is a branch of pharmacokinetics describing reversible transfer of drug from one location to another within the body.
Outcome	Outcome is the impact of care provided to a patient. They can be positive, such as the ability to walk freely as a result of rehabilitation, or negative, such as the occurrence of bedsores as a result of lack of mobility of a patient.
Lead	Lead is a chemical element in the periodic table that has the symbol Pb and atomic number 82. A soft, heavy, toxic and malleable poor metal, lead is bluish white when freshly cut but tarnishes to dull gray when exposed to air. Lead is used in building construction, lead-acid batteries, bullets and shot, and is part of solder, pewter, and fusible alloys.
Susceptibility	The degree of resistance of a host to a pathogen is susceptibility.
Malnutrition	Malnutrition is a general term for the medical condition in a person or animal caused by an unbalanced diet—either too little or too much food, or a diet missing one or more important nutrients.
Essential nutrient	An essential nutrient is a nutrient required for normal body functioning that can not be synthesized by the body. Categories of essential nutrient include vitamins, dietary minerals, essential fatty acids and essential amino acids.
Tissue	A collection of interconnected cells that perform a similar function within an organism is

Go to **Cram101.com** for the Practice Tests for this Chapter.

called tissue.

Carbohydrate	Carbohydrate is a chemical compound that contains oxygen, hydrogen, and carbon atoms. They consist of monosaccharide sugars of varying chain lengths and that have the general chemical formula $C_n(H_2O)_n$ or are derivatives of such.
Hydrogen	Hydrogen is a chemical element in the periodic table that has the symbol H and atomic number 1. At standard temperature and pressure it is a colorless, odorless, nonmetallic, univalent, tasteless, highly flammable diatomic gas.
Carbon	Carbon is a chemical element in the periodic table that has the symbol C and atomic number 6. An abundant nonmetallic, tetravalent element, carbon has several allotropic forms.
Oxygen	Oxygen is a chemical element in the periodic table. It has the symbol O and atomic number 8. Oxygen is the second most common element on Earth, composing around 46% of the mass of Earth's crust and 28% of the mass of Earth as a whole, and is the third most common element in the universe.
Sugar	A sugar is the simplest molecule that can be identified as a carbohydrate. These include monosaccharides and disaccharides, trisaccharides and the oligosaccharides. The term "glyco-" indicates the presence of a sugar in an otherwise non-carbohydrate substance.
Monosaccharide	A monosaccharide is simplest form of a carbohydrate. They consist of one sugar and are usually colorless, water-soluble, crystalline solids. Some monosaccharides have a sweet taste. They are the building blocks of disaccharides like sucrose and polysaccharides.
Polysaccharide	A carbohydrate composed of many joined monosaccharides is called a polysaccharide.
Disaccharide	A disaccharide is a sugar (a carbohydrate) composed of two monosaccharides. The two monosaccharides are bonded via a condensation reaction.
Glucose	Glucose, a simple monosaccharide sugar, is one of the most important carbohydrates and is used as a source of energy in animals and plants. Glucose is one of the main products of photosynthesis and starts respiration.
Starch	Biochemically, starch is a combination of two polymeric carbohydrates (polysaccharides) called amylose and amylopectin.
Muscle	Muscle is a contractile form of tissue. It is one of the four major tissue types, the other three being epithelium, connective tissue and nervous tissue. Muscle contraction is used to move parts of the body, as well as to move substances within the body.
Liver	The liver is an organ in vertebrates, including humans. It plays a major role in metabolism and has a number of functions in the body including drug detoxification, glycogen storage, and plasma protein synthesis. It also produces bile, which is important for digestion.
Skeletal muscle	Skeletal muscle is a type of striated muscle, attached to the skeleton. They are used to facilitate movement, by applying force to bones and joints; via contraction. They generally contract voluntarily (via nerve stimulation), although they can contract involuntarily.
Saturated fat	Saturated fat is fat that consists of triglycerides containing only fatty acids that have no double bonds between the carbon atoms of the fatty acid chain (hence, they are fully saturated with hydrogen atoms).
Fiber	Fibers used by man come from a wide variety of sources: Natural fiber include those made out of plants, animal and mineral sources. Natural fibers can be classified according to their origin.
Dietary fiber	Dietary fiber is the indigestible portion of plant foods that move food through the digestive system and absorb water.

Go to **Cram101.com** for the Practice Tests for this Chapter.

Digestive system	The organ system that ingests food, breaks it down into smaller chemical units, and absorbs the nutrient molecules is referred to as the digestive system.
Cancer	Cancer is a class of diseases or disorders characterized by uncontrolled division of cells and the ability of these cells to invade other tissues, either by direct growth into adjacent tissue through invasion or by implantation into distant sites by metastasis.
Constipation	Constipation is a condition of the digestive system where a person (or other animal) experiences hard feces that are difficult to eliminate; it may be extremely painful, and in severe cases (fecal impaction) lead to symptoms of bowel obstruction.
Hemorrhoids	Hemorrhoids are varicosities or swelling and inflammation of veins in the rectum and anus.
Hemorrhoid	A pronounced swelling in a large vein, particularly veins found in the anal region is referred to as hemorrhoid.
Pancreas	The pancreas is a retroperitoneal organ that serves two functions: exocrine - it produces pancreatic juice containing digestive enzymes, and endocrine - it produces several important hormones, namely insulin.
Insulin	Insulin is a polypeptide hormone that regulates carbohydrate metabolism. Apart from being the primary effector in carbohydrate homeostasis, it also has a substantial effect on small vessel muscle tone, controls storage and release of fat (triglycerides) and cellular uptake of both amino acids and some electrolytes.
Affect	Affect is the scientific term used to describe a subject's externally displayed mood. This can be assesed by the nurse by observing facial expression, tone of voice, and body language.
Kidney	The kidney is a bean-shaped excretory organ in vertebrates. Part of the urinary system, the kidneys filter wastes (especially urea) from the blood and excrete them, along with water, as urine.
Diabetes	Diabetes is a medical disorder characterized by varying or persistent elevated blood sugar levels, especially after eating. All types of diabetes share similar symptoms and complications at advanced stages: dehydration and ketoacidosis, cardiovascular disease, chronic renal failure, retinal damage which can lead to blindness, nerve damage which can lead to erectile dysfunction, gangrene with risk of amputation of toes, feet, and even legs.
Comorbidity	Comorbidity refers to the presence of more than one mental disorder occurring in an individual at the same time.
Metabolism	Metabolism is the biochemical modification of chemical compounds in living organisms and cells. This includes the biosynthesis of complex organic molecules (anabolism) and their breakdown (catabolism).
Organ	Organ refers to a structure consisting of several tissues adapted as a group to perform specific functions.
Triglycerides	Triglycerides refer to fats and oils composed of fatty acids and glycerol; are the body's most concentrated source of energy fuel; also known as neutral fats.
Triglyceride	Triglyceride is a glyceride in which the glycerol is esterified with three fatty acids. They are the main constituent of vegetable oil and animal fats and play an important role in metabolism as energy sources. They contain a bit more than twice as much energy as carbohydrates and proteins.
Aerobic	An aerobic organism is an organism that has an oxygen based metabolism. Aerobes, in a process known as cellular respiration, use oxygen to oxidize substrates (for example sugars and fats) in order to obtain energy.
Phospholipid	Phospholipid is a class of lipids formed from four components: fatty acids, a negatively-

charged phosphate group, an alcohol and a backbone. Phospholipids with a glycerol backbone are known as glycerophospholipids or phosphoglycerides.

Phosphate group	The functional group $-OPO_3H_2$; the transfer of energy from one compound to another is often accomplished by the transfer of a phosphate group.
Phosphate	A phosphate is a polyatomic ion or radical consisting of one phosphorus atom and four oxygen. In the ionic form, it carries a -3 formal charge, and is denoted $PO_4{}^{3-}$.
Hormone	A hormone is a chemical messenger from one cell to another. All multicellular organisms produce hormones. The best known hormones are those produced by endocrine glands of vertebrate animals, but hormones are produced by nearly every organ system and tissue type in a human or animal body. Hormone molecules are secreted directly into the bloodstream, they move by circulation or diffusion to their target cells, which may be nearby cells in the same tissue or cells of a distant organ of the body.
Sterol	A sterol, or steroid alcohols are a subgroup of steroids with a hydroxyl group in the 3-position of the A-ring. They are amphipathic lipids synthetized from Acetyl coenzyme A.
Atom	An atom is the smallest possible particle of a chemical element that retains its chemical properties.
Cholesterol	Cholesterol is a steroid, a lipid, and an alcohol, found in the cell membranes of all body tissues, and transported in the blood plasma of all animals. It is an important component of the membranes of cells, providing stability; it makes the membrane's fluidity stable over a bigger temperature interval.
Egg	An egg is the zygote, resulting from fertilization of the ovum. It nourishes and protects the embryo.
Lipoprotein	A lipoprotein is a biochemical assembly that contains both proteins and lipids and may be structural or catalytic in function. They may be enzymes, proton pumps, ion pumps, or some combination of these functions.
Double bond	Double bond refers to a type of covalent bond in which two atoms share two pairs of electrons; symbolized by a pair of lines between the bonded atoms. An example is in ethylene (between the carbon atoms). It usually consists of one sigma bond and one pi bond.
Unsaturated fat	An unsaturated fat is a fat or fatty acid in which there is one or more double bonds between carbon atoms of the fatty acid chain. Such fat molecules are monounsaturated if each contains one double bond, and polyunsaturated if each contain more than one.
Acid	An acid is a water-soluble, sour-tasting chemical compound that when dissolved in water, gives a solution with a pH of less than 7.
Monounsaturated fats	In nutrition, monounsaturated fats are dietary fats with one double-bonded carbon in the molecule, with all of the others single-bonded carbons.
Fatty acid	A fatty acid is a carboxylic acid (or organic acid), often with a long aliphatic tail (long chains), either saturated or unsaturated.
Carboxyl	A carboxyl is the univalent radical -COOH; present in and characteristic of organic acids.
Carboxyl group	In an organic molecule, a functional group consisting of an oxygen atom doublebonded to a carbon atom that is also bonded to a hydroxyl group is referred to as a carboxyl group.
Amino group	An amino group is an ammonia-like functional group composed of a nitrogen and two hydrogen atoms covalently linked. $-NH_2$
Amino acid	An amino acid is any molecule that contains both amino and carboxylic acid functional groups. They are the basic structural building units of proteins. They form short polymer chains

Go to **Cram101.com** for the Practice Tests for this Chapter.

called peptides or polypeptides which in turn form structures called proteins.

Essential amino acid
An essential amino acid for an organism is an amino acid that cannot be synthesized by the organism from other available resources, and therefore must be supplied as part of its diet.

Blood clotting
A complex process by which platelets, the protein fibrin, and red blood cells block an irregular surface in or on the body, such as a damaged blood vessel, sealing the wound is referred to as blood clotting.

Beriberi
Beriberi is a nervous system ailment caused by a deficiency of vitamin B1 (thiamine), the symptoms of which may include weight loss, emotional disturbances, impaired sensory perception (Wernicke's encephalopathy), weakness and pain in the limbs, and periods of irregular heartbeat.

Thiamin
Thiamin, also known as vitamin B1, is a colorless compound with chemical formula $C_{12}H_{17}N_4OS$. It is soluble in water and insoluble in alcohol. Thiamin decomposes if heated.

Scurvy
Scurvy refers to the deficiency disease that results after a few weeks to months of consuming a diet that lacks vitamin C; pinpoint sites of bleeding on the skin are an early sign.

DNA
Deoxyribonucleic acid (DNA) is a nucleic acid —usually in the form of a double helix— that contains the genetic instructions specifying the biological development of all cellular forms of life, and most viruses.

Free radicals
Free radicals are atomic or molecular species with unpaired electrons on an otherwise open shell configuration.

Enzyme
An enzyme is a protein that catalyzes, or speeds up, a chemical reaction. They are essential to sustain life because most chemical reactions in biological cells would occur too slowly, or would lead to different products, without them.

Older adult
Older adult is an adult over the age of 65.

Adequate intakes
Adequate intakes refers to best estimates of nutritional needs.

Adequate intake
Adequate intake are recommendations for nutrient intake when not enough information is available to establish an RDA.

Calcium
Calcium is the chemical element in the periodic table that has the symbol Ca and atomic number 20. Calcium is a soft grey alkaline earth metal that is used as a reducing agent in the extraction of thorium, zirconium and uranium. Calcium is also the fifth most abundant element in the Earth's crust.

Sodium
Sodium is the chemical element in the periodic table that has the symbol Na (Natrium in Latin) and atomic number 11. Sodium is a soft, waxy, silvery reactive metal belonging to the alkali metals that is abundant in natural compounds (especially halite). It is highly reactive.

Sulfur
Sulfur is the chemical element in the periodic table that has the symbol S and atomic number 16. It is an abundant, tasteless, odorless, multivalent non-metal. Sulfur, in its native form, is a yellow crystaline solid. In nature, it can be found as the pure element or as sulfide and sulfate minerals.

Macromineral
An inorganic substance that is necessary for metabolism and is one of a group that accounts for 75% of the mineral elements within the body is called a macromineral.

Phosphorus
Phosphorus is the chemical element in the periodic table that has the symbol P and atomic number 15.

Potassium
Potassium is a chemical element in the periodic table. It has the symbol K (L. kalium) and

atomic number 19. Potassium is a soft silvery-white metallic alkali metal that occurs naturally bound to other elements in seawater and many minerals.

Magnesium	Magnesium is the chemical element in the periodic table that has the symbol Mg and atomic number 12 and an atomic mass of 24.31.
Osteoporosis	Osteoporosis is a disease of bone in which bone mineral density (BMD) is reduced, bone microarchitecture is disrupted, the amount and variety of non-collagenous proteins in bone is changed, and a concomitantly fracture risk is increased.
Iron	Iron is essential to all organisms, except for a few bacteria. It is mostly stably incorporated in the inside of metalloproteins, because in exposed or in free form it causes production of free radicals that are generally toxic to cells.
Red blood cells	Red blood cells are the most common type of blood cell and are the vertebrate body's principal means of delivering oxygen from the lungs or gills to body tissues via the blood.
Red blood cell	The red blood cell is the most common type of blood cell and is the vertebrate body's principal means of delivering oxygen from the lungs or gills to body tissues via the blood.
Hemoglobin	Hemoglobin is the iron-containing oxygen-transport metalloprotein in the red cells of the blood in mammals and other animals. Hemoglobin transports oxygen from the lungs to the rest of the body, such as to the muscles, where it releases the oxygen load.
Anemia	Anemia is a deficiency of red blood cells and/or hemoglobin. This results in a reduced ability of blood to transfer oxygen to the tissues, and this causes hypoxia; since all human cells depend on oxygen for survival, varying degrees of anemia can have a wide range of clinical consequences.
Hypertension	Hypertension is a medical condition where the blood pressure in the arteries is chronically elevated. Persistent hypertension is one of the risk factors for strokes, heart attacks, heart failure and arterial aneurysm, and is a leading cause of chronic renal failure.
Salt	Salt is a term used for ionic compounds composed of positively charged cations and negatively charged anions, so that the product is neutral and without a net charge.
Diuretic	A diuretic is any drug that elevates the rate of bodily urine excretion.
Consensus	General agreement is a consensus.
Diabetes mellitus	Diabetes mellitus is a medical disorder characterized by varying or persistent hyperglycemia (elevated blood sugar levels), especially after eating. All types of diabetes mellitus share similar symptoms and complications at advanced stages.
Assess	Assess is to systematically and continuously collect, validate, and communicate patient data.
Anger	Anger is an emotional response often based on a sensation or perception of threat to one's needs.
Alcoholic	An alcoholic is dependent on alcohol as characterized by craving, loss of control, physical dependence and withdrawal symptoms, and tolerance.
Value	Value is worth in general, and it is thought to be connected to reasons for certain practices, policies, actions, beliefs or emotions. Value is "that which one acts to gain and/or keep."
Standard deviation	In probability and statistics, the standard deviation is the most commonly used measure of statistical dispersion. Simply put, it measures how spread out the values in a data set are.
Specificity	A medical diagnostic test for a certain disease, specificity is the proportion of true negatives of all the negative samples tested.

Daily values	A set of standard nutrient-intake values developed by FDA and used as a reference for expressing nutrient content on nutrition labels are called daily values.
Daily value	Daily value refers to dietary reference values useful for planning a healthy diet. The daily values are taken from the Reference Daily Intakes and the Daily Reference Values.
Risk factor	A risk factor is a variable associated with an increased risk of disease or infection but risk factors are not necessarily causal.
Hydrophobic	Hydrophobic refers to being electrically neutral and nonpolar, and thus prefering other neutral and nonpolar solvents or molecular environments. Hydrophobic is often used interchangeably with "oily" or "lipophilic."
Macromolecule	A macromolecule is a molecule with a large molecular mass, but generally the use of the term is restricted to polymers and molecules which structurally include polymers.
Artery	Vessel that takes blood away from the heart to the tissues and organs of the body is called an artery.
Lifestyle changes	Lifestyle changes are changes to the way a person lives which are often called for when treating chronic disease.
Lifestyle	The culturally, socially, economically, and environmentally conditioned complex of actions characteristic of an individual, group, or community as a pattern of habituated behavior over time that is health related but not necessarily health directed is a lifestyle.
Trans fat	Trans fat is an unsaturated fatty acid whose molecules contain trans double bonds between carbon atoms, which makes the molecules less kinked compared with those of 'cis fat'.
Aerobic exercise	Exercise in which oxygen is used to produce ATP is aerobic exercise.
Joint	A joint (articulation) is the location at which two bones make contact (articulate). They are constructed to both allow movement and provide mechanical support.
Dehydration	Dehydration is the removal of water from an object. Medically, dehydration is a serious and potentially life-threatening condition in which the body contains an insufficient volume of water for normal functioning.
Stroke	A stroke or cerebrovascular accident (CVA) occurs when the blood supply to a part of the brain is suddenly interrupted.
Cramp	A cramp is an unpleasant sensation caused by contraction, usually of a muscle. It can be caused by cold or overexertion.
Absorption	Absorption is a physical or chemical phenomenon or a process in which atoms, molecules, or ions enter some bulk phase - gas, liquid or solid material. In nutrition, amino acids are broken down through digestion, which begins in the stomach.
Resistance	Resistance refers to a nonspecific ability to ward off infection or disease regardless of whether the body has been previously exposed to it. A force that opposes the flow of a fluid such as air or blood. Compare with immunity.
Normal distribution	A normal distribution is a symmetrical distribution of scores that is assumed to reflect chance fluctuations; approximately 68% of cases lie within a single standard deviation of the mean.
Macronutrients	Macrominerals are macronutrients that are chemical elements. They include calcium, magnesium, sodium, potassium, phosphorus and chlorine. They are dietary minerals needed by the human body in high quantities (generally more than 100 mg/day) as opposed to microminerals (trace elements) which are only required in very small amounts.
Macronutrient	A chemical substance that an organism must obtain in relatively large amounts is referred to

58

	as macronutrient.
Agent	Agent refers to an epidemiological term referring to the organism or object that transmits a disease from the environment to the host.
Steroid	A steroid is a lipid characterized by a carbon skeleton with four fused rings. Different steroids vary in the functional groups attached to these rings. Hundreds of distinct steroids have been identified in plants and animals. Their most important role in most living systems is as hormones.
Anabolic steroid	An anabolic steroid is a class of natural and synthetic steroid hormones that promote cell growth and division, resulting in growth of muscle tissue and sometimes bone size and strength. They act in different ways on the body to promote muscle growth, and each has androgenic and anabolic properties.
Menstrual cycle	The menstrual cycle is the set of recurring physiological changes in a female's body that are under the control of the reproductive hormone system and necessary for reproduction. Besides humans, only other great apes exhibit menstrual cycles, in contrast to the estrus cycle of most mammalian species.
Iron deficiency	Iron deficiency (or "sideropenia") is the most common known form of nutritional deficiency.
Creatine phosphate	Compound unique to muscles that contains a high-energy phosphate bond is creatine phosphate or phosphocreatine.
Carbohydrate loading	Carbohydrate loading refers to a week-long program of diet and exercise that results in an increase in muscle glycogen stores.
Solution	Solution refers to homogenous mixture formed when a solute is dissolved in a solvent.
Sucrose	A disaccharide composed of glucose and fructose is called sucrose.
Anorexia	Anorexia nervosa is an eating disorder characterized by voluntary starvation and exercise stress.
Bulimia	Bulimia refers to a disorder in which a person binges on incredibly large quantities of food, then purges by vomiting or by using laxatives. Bulimia is often less about food, and more to do with deep psychological issues and profound feelings of lack of control.
Stress	Stress refers to a condition that is a response to factors that change the human systems normal state.
Amenorrhea	Amenorrhea is the absence of a menstrual period in a woman of reproductive age. Physiologic states of amenorrhea are seen during pregnancy and lactation (breastfeeding).
Medicine	Medicine is the branch of health science and the sector of public life concerned with maintaining or restoring human health through the study, diagnosis and treatment of disease and injury.
Insight	Insight refers to a sudden awareness of the relationships among various elements that had previously appeared to be independent of one another.
Acceptable macronutrient distribution range	Acceptable macronutrient distribution range refers to range of intake for a specific macronutrient that is associated with a reduced risk of chronic diseases while providing for recommended intakes of essential nutrients.
Case study	A carefully drawn biography that may be obtained through interviews, questionnaires, and psychological tests is called a case study.
Plasma	Fluid portion of circulating blood is called plasma.

Chromium	Chromium is a chemical element in the periodic table that has the symbol Cr and atomic number 24. Chromium (0) is unstable in oxygen, immediately producing a thin oxide layer that is impermeable to oxygen and protects the metal below.
Vanadium	Vanadium is a chemical element in the periodic table that has the symbol V and atomic number 23. A rare, soft and ductile element, vanadium is found combined in certain minerals and is used mainly to produce certain alloys. It is one of the 26 elements commonly found in living things.
Silicon	Silicon is the chemical element in the periodic table that has the symbol Si and atomic number 14. It is the second most abundant element in the Earth's crust, making up 25.7% of it by weight.
Arsenic	Arsenic is a chemical element in the periodic table that has the symbol As and atomic number 33. This is a notoriously poisonous metalloid that has many allotropic forms; yellow, black and grey are a few that are regularly seen. Arsenic and its compounds are used as pesticides, herbicides, insecticides and various alloys.
Copper	Copper is a chemical element in the periodic table that has the symbol Cu (L.: Cuprum) and atomic number 29. It is a ductile metal with excellent electrical conductivity, and finds extensive use as a building material, as an electrical conductor, and as a component of various alloys.
Iodine	Iodine is a chemical element in the periodic table that has the symbol I and atomic number 53. It is required as a trace element for most living organisms. Chemically, iodine is the least reactive of the halogens, and the most electropositive halogen. Iodine is primarily used in medicine, photography and in dyes.
Nickel	Nickel is a metallic chemical element in the periodic table that has the symbol Ni and atomic number 28. Notable characteristicsNickel is a silvery white metal that takes on a high polish. It belongs to the iron group, and is hard, malleable, and ductile. It occurs combined with sulfur in millerite, with arsenic in the mineral niccolite, and with arsenic and sulfur in nickel glance.
Boron	Boron is a chemical element in the periodic table that has the symbol B and atomic number 5. A trivalent metalloid element, boron occurs abundantly in the ore borax.
Zinc	Zinc is a chemical element in the periodic table that has the symbol Zn and atomic number 30.
Molybdenum	Molybdenum is a chemical element in the periodic table. Its symbol is Mo and its atomic number 42. Molybdenum is a transition metal. The pure metal is silvery white in color and very hard, and has one of the highest melting points of all pure elements.
Manganese	Manganese is a chemical element in the periodic table that has the symbol Mn and atomic number 25.
Obesity	The state of being more than 20 percent above the average weight for a person of one's height is called obesity.
Diagnosis	In medicine, diagnosis is the process of identifying a medical condition or disease by its signs, symptoms, and from the results of various diagnostic procedures.
Chronic disease	Disease of long duration often not detected in its early stages and from which the patient will not recover is referred to as a chronic disease.
Concept	A mental category used to class together objects, relations, events, abstractions, or qualities that have common properties is called concept.

Health	Health is a term that refers to a combination of the absence of illness, the ability to cope with everyday activities, physical fitness, and high quality of life.
Older adult	Older adult is an adult over the age of 65.
Assess	Assess is to systematically and continuously collect, validate, and communicate patient data.
Coronary	Referring to the heart or the blood vessels of the heart is referred to as coronary.
Blood	Blood is a circulating tissue composed of fluid plasma and cells. The main function of blood is to supply nutrients (oxygen, glucose) and constitutional elements to tissues and to remove waste products.
Blood pressure	Blood pressure is the pressure exerted by the blood on the walls of the blood vessels.
Coronary heart disease	Coronary heart disease is the end result of the accumulation of atheromatous plaques within the walls of the arteries that supply the myocardium (the muscle of the heart).
Hypertension	Hypertension is a medical condition where the blood pressure in the arteries is chronically elevated. Persistent hypertension is one of the risk factors for strokes, heart attacks, heart failure and arterial aneurysm, and is a leading cause of chronic renal failure.
Assessment	In clinical practice, the process by which a mental health professional gathers and compiles information about a client for the purpose of describing the person's problems or disorder and developing a plan of treatment is an assessment.
Baseline	Measure of a particular behavior or process taken before the introduction of the independent variable or treatment is called the baseline.
Evaluation	The fifth step of the nursing process where nursing care and the patient's goal achievement are measured is the evaluation.
Protocol	Protocol is a document with the aim of guiding decisions and criteria in specific areas of healthcare, as defined by an authoritative examination of current evidence. It details the activities to be executed in specific situations.
Adaptation	A biological adaptation is an anatomical structure, physiological process or behavioral trait of an organism that has evolved over a period of time by the process of natural selection such that it increases the expected long-term reproductive success of the organism.
Population	Population refers to all members of a well-defined group of organisms, events, or things.
Resistance	Resistance refers to a nonspecific ability to ward off infection or disease regardless of whether the body has been previously exposed to it. A force that opposes the flow of a fluid such as air or blood. Compare with immunity.
Muscle	Muscle is a contractile form of tissue. It is one of the four major tissue types, the other three being epithelium, connective tissue and nervous tissue. Muscle contraction is used to move parts of the body, as well as to move substances within the body.
Constant	A behavior or characteristic that does not vary from one observation to another is referred to as a constant.
Range of motion	Range of motion is a measurement of movement through a particular joint or muscle range.
Activation	As reflected by facial expressions, the degree of arousal a person is experiencing is referred to as activation.
Gold	Gold is a chemical element in the periodic table that has the symbol Au and atomic number 79. A soft, shiny, yellow, dense, malleable, ductile (trivalent and univalent) transition metal, gold does not react with most chemicals but is attacked by chlorine, fluorine and aqua regia.
Ratio	In number and more generally in algebra, a ratio is the linear relationship between two

	quantities.
Ethnicity	While ethnicity and race are related concepts, the concept of ethnicity is rooted in the idea of social groups, marked especially by shared nationality, tribal affiliation, religious faith, shared language, or cultural and traditional origins and backgrounds, whereas race is rooted in the idea of biological classification of Homo sapiens to subspecies according to chosen genotypic and/or phenotypic traits.
Course	Pattern of development and change of a disorder over time is a course.
Deltoid	The deltoid muscle is the muscle forming the rounded contour of the human shoulder.
Flexor	A muscle or tendon which bends a limb, part of a limb, or part of the body is a flexor.
Stress	Stress refers to a condition that is a response to factors that change the human systems normal state.
Hip	In anatomy, the hip is the bony projection of the femur, known as the greater trochanter, and the overlying muscle and fat.
Extension	Movement increasing the angle between parts at a joint is referred to as extension.
Elevation	Elevation refers to upward movement of a part of the body.
Individual test	A psychological test administered to only one person at a time is referred to as individual test.
Test battery	A group of tests and interviews given to the same individual is a test battery.
Insight	Insight refers to a sudden awareness of the relationships among various elements that had previously appeared to be independent of one another.
Validity	The extent to which a test measures what it is intended to measure is called validity.
Correlation	A statistical technique for determining the degree of association between two or more variables is referred to as correlation.
Criterion	Criterion refers to a standard of comparison. For performance appraisal, it is the definition of good performance.
Construct	Generalized concept, such as anxiety or gravity, which is constructed in a theoretical manner is referred to as construct.
Angina	Angina pectoris is chest pain due to ischemia (a lack of blood and hence oxygen supply) to the heart muscle, generally due to obstruction or spasm of the coronary arteries (the heart's blood vessels). Coronary artery disease, the main cause of angina, is due to atherosclerosis of the cardiac arteries.
Rehabilitation	Rehabilitation is the restoration of lost capabilities, or the treatment aimed at producing it. Also refers to treatment for dependency on psychoactive substances such as alcohol, prescription drugs, and illicit drugs such as cocaine, heroin or amphetamines.
Congestive heart failure	Congestive heart failure is the inability of the heart to pump a sufficient amount of blood throughout the body, or requiring elevated filling pressures in order to pump effectively.
Arrhythmias	Arrhythmias refers to abnormal heart rhythms which may be too slow, too early, too rapid, or irregular.
Arrhythmia	Cardiac arrhythmia is a group of conditions in which muscle contraction of the heart is irregular for any reason.
Unstable angina	Worsening angina attacks, sudden-onset angina at rest, and angina lasting more than 15 minutes are symptoms of unstable angina or acute coronary syndrome. As these may herald

	myocardial infarction (a heart attack), they require urgent medical attention and are generally treated quite similarly
Angina pectoris	Angina pectoris is chest pain due to ischemia (a lack of blood and hence oxygen supply) to the heart muscle, generally due to obstruction or spasm of the coronary arteries (the heart's blood vessels).
Diabetes	Diabetes is a medical disorder characterized by varying or persistent elevated blood sugar levels, especially after eating. All types of diabetes share similar symptoms and complications at advanced stages: dehydration and ketoacidosis, cardiovascular disease, chronic renal failure, retinal damage which can lead to blindness, nerve damage which can lead to erectile dysfunction, gangrene with risk of amputation of toes, feet, and even legs.
Thyroid	The thyroid is one of the larger endocrine glands in the body. It is located in the neck and produces hormones, principally thyroxine and triiodothyronine, that regulate the rate of metabolism and affect the growth and rate of function of many other systems in the body.
Value	Value is worth in general, and it is thought to be connected to reasons for certain practices, policies, actions, beliefs or emotions. Value is "that which one acts to gain and/or keep."
Cardiovascular disease	Cardiovascular disease refers to afflictions in the mechanisms, including the heart, blood vessels, and their controllers, that are responsible for transporting blood to the body's tissues and organs. Psychological factors may play important roles in such diseases and their treatments.
Outcome	Outcome is the impact of care provided to a patient. They can be positive, such as the ability to walk freely as a result of rehabilitation, or negative, such as the occurrence of bedsores as a result of lack of mobility of a patient.
Complement	Complement is a group of proteins of the complement system, found in blood serum which act in concert with antibodies to achieve the destruction of non-self particles such as foreign blood cells or bacteria.
Diagnosis	In medicine, diagnosis is the process of identifying a medical condition or disease by its signs, symptoms, and from the results of various diagnostic procedures.
Medicine	Medicine is the branch of health science and the sector of public life concerned with maintaining or restoring human health through the study, diagnosis and treatment of disease and injury.
Base	The common definition of a base is a chemical compound that absorbs hydronium ions when dissolved in water (a proton acceptor). An alkali is a special example of a base, where in an aqueous environment, hydroxide ions are donated.
Artery	Vessel that takes blood away from the heart to the tissues and organs of the body is called an artery.
Coronary artery	An artery that supplies blood to the wall of the heart is called a coronary artery.
Coronary artery disease	Coronary artery disease (CAD) is the end result of the accumulation of atheromatous plaques within the walls of the arteries that supply the myocardium (the muscle of the heart).
Cardiology	Cardiology is the branch of medicine dealing with disorders of the heart and blood vessels. The field is commonly divided in the branches of congenital heart defects, coronary artery disease, heart failure, valvular heart disease and electrophysiology.
Mortality	The incidence of death in a population is mortality.
Gerontology	The interdisciplinary study of aging and of the special problems of the elderly is referred to as gerontology.

Go to **Cram101.com** for the Practice Tests for this Chapter.

Pain	Pain is an unpleasant sensation which may be associated with actual or potential tissue damage and which may have physical and emotional components.
Physical therapy	Physical therapy is a health profession concerned with the assessment, diagnosis, and treatment of disease and disability through physical means. It is based upon principles of medical science, and is generally held to be within the sphere of conventional medicine.
Methodology	Techniques of measurement used to collect and manipulate empirical data refer to a methodology.
Trial	In classical conditioning, any presentation of a stimulus or pair of stimuli is called a trial.
Statistics	Statistics is a type of data analysis which practice includes the planning, summarizing, and interpreting of observations of a system possibly followed by predicting or forecasting of future events based on a mathematical model of the system being observed.
Statistic	A statistic is an observable random variable of a sample.
Secondary prevention	Psychological counseling, psychotropic medications, and other rehabilitation treatment programs designed to prevent repeat offenses are called secondary prevention.

Extension	Movement increasing the angle between parts at a joint is referred to as extension.
Flexion	In anatomy, Flexion is movement whereby bones or other parts of the body, including the trunk, are brought closer together by decreasing the joint angle. The opposite term is extention, or straightening.
Sacrum	The sacrum is a large, triangular bone at the base of the vertebral column and at the upper and back part of the pelvic cavity, where it is inserted like a wedge between the two hip bones. Its upper part or base articulates with the last lumbar vertebra, its apex with the coccyx.
Lumbar	In anatomy, lumbar is an adjective that means of or pertaining to the abdominal segment of the torso, between the diaphragm and the sacrum (pelvis). The five vertebra in the lumbar region are the largest and strongest in the spinal column.
Joint	A joint (articulation) is the location at which two bones make contact (articulate). They are constructed to both allow movement and provide mechanical support.
Hip	In anatomy, the hip is the bony projection of the femur, known as the greater trochanter, and the overlying muscle and fat.
Sagittal	A sagittal plane is an X-Z plane, perpendicular to the ground and to the coronal plane, which separates left from right. The midsagittal plane is the specific sagittal plane that is exactly in the middle of the body.
Anatomy	Anatomy is the branch of biology that deals with the structure and organization of living things. It can be divided into animal anatomy (zootomy) and plant anatomy (phytonomy).
Sagittal plane	Sagittal plane refers to any plane that extends from ventral to dorsal and cephalic to caudal and divides the body into right and left portions. Compare with midsagittal plane.
Hyperextension	Hyperextension is the movement of a body part beyond the normal range of motion, such as the position of the head when looking upwards into the sky.
Range of motion	Range of motion is a measurement of movement through a particular joint or muscle range.
Affect	Affect is the scientific term used to describe a subject's externally displayed mood. This can be assesed by the nurse by observing facial expression, tone of voice, and body language.
Genotype	Genotype refers to the combination of genes present within a zygote or within the cells of an individual.
Variable	A characteristic or aspect in which people, objects, events, or conditions vary is called variable.
Demographic variable	A varying characteristic that is a vital or social statistic of an individual, sample group, or population, for example, age, sex, socioeconomic status, racial origin, education is called a demographic variable.
Activities of daily living	Activities of daily living is a way to describe the functional status of a person.
Arthritis	Arthritis is a group of conditions that affect the health of the bone joints in the body. Arthritis can be caused from strains and injuries caused by repetitive motion, sports, overexertion, and falls. Unlike the autoimmune diseases, it largely affects older people and results from the degeneration of joint cartilage.
Osteoporosis	Osteoporosis is a disease of bone in which bone mineral density (BMD) is reduced, bone microarchitecture is disrupted, the amount and variety of non-collagenous proteins in bone is changed, and a concomitantly fracture risk is increased.
Articular	The articular is a bone in the lower jaw of most tetrapods, including reptiles, birds, and

amphibians, but has become a middle ear bone (the malleus) in mammals. It is the site of articulation between the lower jaw and the skull, and is connected to two other lower jaw bones, the suprangular and the angular.

Cartilage	Cartilage is a type of dense connective tissue. Cartilage is composed of cells called chondrocytes which are dispersed in a firm gel-like ground substance, called the matrix. Cartilage is avascular (contains no blood vessels) and nutrients are diffused through the matrix.
Ligament	A ligament is a short band of tough fibrous connective tissue composed mainly of long, stringy collagen fibres. They connect bones to other bones to form a joint. (They do not connect muscles to bones.)
Tissue	A collection of interconnected cells that perform a similar function within an organism is called tissue.
Tendon	A tendon or sinew is a tough band of fibrous connective tissue that connects muscle to bone. They are similar to ligaments except that ligaments join one bone to another.
Stress	Stress refers to a condition that is a response to factors that change the human systems normal state.
Connective tissue	Connective tissue is any type of biological tissue with an extensive extracellular matrix and often serves to support, bind together, and protect organs.
Blood	Blood is a circulating tissue composed of fluid plasma and cells. The main function of blood is to supply nutrients (oxygen, glucose) and constitutional elements to tissues and to remove waste products.
Hyaline cartilage	Hyaline cartilage is the most abundant type of cartilage. Hyaline cartilage is a translucent matrix or ground substance found lining bones in joints. It is also present inside bones, serving as a center of ossification or bone growth
Fibrocartilage	Fibrocartilage, as its name implies, is a type of cartilage arranged in a fibrous matrix that is similar to fibrous connective tissues. It is found in areas that require tensile strength, such as intervertebral disks.
Rheumatoid arthritis	Rheumatoid arthritis is a chronic, inflammatory autoimmune disorder that causes the immune system to attack the joints. It is a disabling and painful inflammatory condition, which can lead to substantial loss of mobility due to pain and joint destruction.
Osteoarthritis	Osteoarthritis is a condition in which low-grade inflammation results in pain in the joints, caused by wearing of the cartilage that covers and acts as a cushion inside joints.
Autoimmune disease	Disease that results when the immune system mistakenly attacks the body's own tissues is referred to as autoimmune disease.
Autoimmune	Autoimmune refers to immune reactions against normal body cells; self against self.
Population	Population refers to all members of a well-defined group of organisms, events, or things.
Diffusion	Random movement of molecules from a region of higher concentration toward one of lower concentration is referred to as diffusion.
Bone mineral density	A bone mineral density test is used to measure bone density and determine fracture risk for osteoporosis.
Menopause	Menopause is the physiological cessation of menstrual cycles associated with advancing age in species that experience such cycles. Menopause is sometimes referred to as change of life or climacteric.
Cancellous	Cancellous bone is a spongy type of bone with a very high surface area, found at the ends of

long bones. The spongy bone contains red bone marrow which leads to the production of red blood cells.

Vertebrae	Vertebrae are the individual bones that make up the vertebral column (aka spine) - a flexuous and flexible column.
Heredity	Heredity refers to the transmission of genetic information from parent to offspring.
Synovial joint	Synovial joint refers to freely moving joint in which two bones are separated by a cavity.
Pain	Pain is an unpleasant sensation which may be associated with actual or potential tissue damage and which may have physical and emotional components.
Rotation	Movement turning a body part on its longitudinal axis is rotation.
Pelvis	The pelvis is the bony structure located at the base of the spine (properly known as the caudal end). The pelvis incorporates the socket portion of the hip joint for each leg (in bipeds) or hind leg (in quadrupeds). It forms the lower limb (or hind-limb) girdle of the skeleton.
Scoliosis	Scoliosis is a condition that involves a lateral curvature of the spine; that is, the spine is bent sideways. Scoliosis is incurable, but its natural course can be affected with treatments such as surgery or bracing.
Muscle	Muscle is a contractile form of tissue. It is one of the four major tissue types, the other three being epithelium, connective tissue and nervous tissue. Muscle contraction is used to move parts of the body, as well as to move substances within the body.
Rectus abdominis	The Rectus abdominis is a long flat muscle, which extends along the whole length of the front of the abdomen, and is separated from its fellow of the opposite side by the linea alba.
Femur	The femur or thigh bone is the longest, most voluminous and strongest bone of the human body. It forms part of the hip and part of the knee.
Transverse plane	A plane running from right to left, dividing the body into superior and inferior parts is a transverse plane.
Transverse	A transverse (also known as axial or horizontal) plane is an X-Y plane, parallel to the ground, which (in humans) separates the superior from the inferior, or put another way, the head from the feet.
Lordosis	Lordosis is a term used for an anterior curvature of the vertebral column. Two segments of the vertebral column, namely cervical and lumbar, are normally lordotic, that is, they are set in a curve that has its convexity in front and concavity behind, in the context of human anatomy.
Symmetry	Symmetry is the balanced distribution of duplicate body parts or shapes from one side of the body to the other.
Value	Value is worth in general, and it is thought to be connected to reasons for certain practices, policies, actions, beliefs or emotions. Value is "that which one acts to gain and/or keep."
Host	Host is an organism that harbors a parasite, mutual partner, or commensal partner; or a cell infected by a virus.
Protocol	Protocol is a document with the aim of guiding decisions and criteria in specific areas of healthcare, as defined by an authoritative examination of current evidence. It details the activities to be executed in specific situations.
Flexor	A muscle or tendon which bends a limb, part of a limb, or part of the body is a flexor.

Go to **Cram101.com** for the Practice Tests for this Chapter.

Iliac	In human anatomy, iliac artery refers to several anatomical structures located in the pelvis.
Elevation	Elevation refers to upward movement of a part of the body.
Syndrome	Syndrome is the association of several clinically recognizable features, signs, symptoms, phenomena or characteristics which often occur together, so that the presence of one feature alerts the physician to the presence of the others
Patella	The patella is a thick, triangular bone which articulates with the femur and covers and protects the front of the knee joint. The patella increases the leverage that the tendon can exert on the femur by increasing the angle at which it acts.
Medial	In anatomical terms of location toward or near the midline is called medial.
Abductor	An abductor is any muscle that when activated, normally moves a limb or body part away from the body.
Assessment	In clinical practice, the process by which a mental health professional gathers and compiles information about a client for the purpose of describing the person's problems or disorder and developing a plan of treatment is an assessment.
Greater trochanter	The Greater Trochanter (great trochanter) of the femur is a large, irregular, quadrilateral eminence, situated at the junction of the neck with the upper part of the body.
Nerve	A nerve is an enclosed, cable-like bundle of nerve fibers or axons, which includes the glia that ensheath the axons in myelin.
Medicine	Medicine is the branch of health science and the sector of public life concerned with maintaining or restoring human health through the study, diagnosis and treatment of disease and injury.
Validity	The extent to which a test measures what it is intended to measure is called validity.
In vivo	In vivo is used to indicate the presence of a whole/living organism, in distinction to a partial or dead organism, or a computer model. Animal testing and clinical trials are forms of in vivo research.
Young adult	An young adult is someone between the ages of 20 and 40 years old.
Conditioning	Processes by which behaviors can be learned or modified through interaction with the environment are conditioning.
Diagnosis	In medicine, diagnosis is the process of identifying a medical condition or disease by its signs, symptoms, and from the results of various diagnostic procedures.
Anthropometric	Anthropometric is the actual measurements of the body and body parts.
Rehabilitation	Rehabilitation is the restoration of lost capabilities, or the treatment aimed at producing it. Also refers to treatment for dependency on psychoactive substances such as alcohol, prescription drugs, and illicit drugs such as cocaine, heroin or amphetamines.
Physical therapy	Physical therapy is a health profession concerned with the assessment, diagnosis, and treatment of disease and disability through physical means. It is based upon principles of medical science, and is generally held to be within the sphere of conventional medicine.
Skeletal muscle	Skeletal muscle is a type of striated muscle, attached to the skeleton. They are used to facilitate movement, by applying force to bones and joints; via contraction. They generally contract voluntarily (via nerve stimulation), although they can contract involuntarily.
Cardiac muscle	Cardiac muscle is a type of striated muscle found within the heart. Its function is to "pump" blood through the circulatory system. Unlike skeletal muscle, which contracts in response to nerve stimulation, and like smooth muscle, cardiac muscle is myogenic, meaning that it

Go to **Cram101.com** for the Practice Tests for this Chapter.

	stimulates its own contraction without a requisite electrical impulse.
Organ	Organ refers to a structure consisting of several tissues adapted as a group to perform specific functions.
Reversibility	Reversibility according to Piaget, is recognition that processes can be undone, that things can be made as they were.
Specificity	A medical diagnostic test for a certain disease, specificity is the proportion of true negatives of all the negative samples tested.
Fiber	Fibers used by man come from a wide variety of sources: Natural fiber include those made out of plants, animal and mineral sources. Natural fibers can be classified according to their origin.
Muscle fiber	Cell with myofibrils containing actin and myosin filaments arranged within sarcomeres is a muscle fiber.
Adaptation	A biological adaptation is an anatomical structure, physiological process or behavioral trait of an organism that has evolved over a period of time by the process of natural selection such that it increases the expected long-term reproductive success of the organism.
Capillary	A capillary is the smallest of a body's blood vessels, measuring 5-10 micro meters. They connect arteries and veins, and most closely interact with tissues. Their walls are composed of a single layer of cells, the endothelium. This layer is so thin that molecules such as oxygen, water and lipids can pass through them by diffusion and enter the tissues.
Mitochondria	Cytoplasmic organelles responsible for ATP generation for cellular activities are referred to as mitochondria.
Capillaries	Capillaries refer to the smallest of the blood vessels and the sites of exchange between the blood and tissue cells.
Protein	A protein is a complex, high-molecular-weight organic compound that consists of amino acids joined by peptide bonds. They are essential to the structure and function of all living cells and viruses. Many are enzymes or subunits of enzymes.
Actin	A protein in a muscle fiber that, together with myosin, is responsible for contraction and relaxation is actin.
Hypertrophy	Hypertrophy is the increase of the size of an organ. It should be distinguished from hyperplasia which occurs due to cell division; hypertrophy occurs due to an increase in cell size rather than division. It is most commonly seen in muscle that has been actively stimulated, the most well-known method being exercise.

Go to **Cram101.com** for the Practice Tests for this Chapter.

Health	Health is a term that refers to a combination of the absence of illness, the ability to cope with everyday activities, physical fitness, and high quality of life.
Public health	Public health is concerned with threats to the overall health of a community based on population health analysis.
Concept	A mental category used to class together objects, relations, events, abstractions, or qualities that have common properties is called concept.
Specificity	A medical diagnostic test for a certain disease, specificity is the proportion of true negatives of all the negative samples tested.
Population	Population refers to all members of a well-defined group of organisms, events, or things.
Coronary	Referring to the heart or the blood vessels of the heart is referred to as coronary.
Outcome	Outcome is the impact of care provided to a patient. They can be positive, such as the ability to walk freely as a result of rehabilitation, or negative, such as the occurrence of bedsores as a result of lack of mobility of a patient.
Coronary heart disease	Coronary heart disease is the end result of the accumulation of atheromatous plaques within the walls of the arteries that supply the myocardium (the muscle of the heart).
Variability	Statistically, variability refers to how much the scores in a distribution spread out, away from the mean.
Calorie	Calorie refers to a unit used to measure heat energy and the energy contents of foods.
Serum	Serum is the same as blood plasma except that clotting factors (such as fibrin) have been removed. Blood plasma contains fibrinogen.
Cholesterol	Cholesterol is a steroid, a lipid, and an alcohol, found in the cell membranes of all body tissues, and transported in the blood plasma of all animals. It is an important component of the membranes of cells, providing stability; it makes the membrane's fluidity stable over a bigger temperature interval.
Value	Value is worth in general, and it is thought to be connected to reasons for certain practices, policies, actions, beliefs or emotions. Value is "that which one acts to gain and/or keep."
Insight	Insight refers to a sudden awareness of the relationships among various elements that had previously appeared to be independent of one another.
Health outcome	Any medically or epidemiologically defined characteristic of a patient or population that results from health promotion or care provided or required, as measured at one point in time is a health outcome.
Variable	A characteristic or aspect in which people, objects, events, or conditions vary is called variable.
Acute	In medicine, an acute disease is a disease with either or both of: a rapid onset; and a short course (as opposed to a chronic course).
Insulin	Insulin is a polypeptide hormone that regulates carbohydrate metabolism. Apart from being the primary effector in carbohydrate homeostasis, it also has a substantial effect on small vessel muscle tone, controls storage and release of fat (triglycerides) and cellular uptake of both amino acids and some electrolytes.
Lipid	Lipid is one class of aliphatic hydrocarbon-containing organic compounds essential for the structure and function of living cells. They are characterized by being water-insoluble but soluble in nonpolar organic solvents.

Go to **Cram101.com** for the Practice Tests for this Chapter.

Oxygen	Oxygen is a chemical element in the periodic table. It has the symbol O and atomic number 8. Oxygen is the second most common element on Earth, composing around 46% of the mass of Earth's crust and 28% of the mass of Earth as a whole, and is the third most common element in the universe.
Respiratory system	The respiratory system is the biological system of any organism that engages in gas exchange.In humans and other mammals, the respiratory system consists of the airways, the lungs, and the respiratory muscles that mediate the movement of air into and out of the body.
Lifestyle	The culturally, socially, economically, and environmentally conditioned complex of actions characteristic of an individual, group, or community as a pattern of habituated behavior over time that is health related but not necessarily health directed is a lifestyle.
Reversibility	Reversibility according to Piaget, is recognition that processes can be undone, that things can be made as they were.
Risk factor	A risk factor is a variable associated with an increased risk of disease or infection but risk factors are not necessarily causal.
Muscle	Muscle is a contractile form of tissue. It is one of the four major tissue types, the other three being epithelium, connective tissue and nervous tissue. Muscle contraction is used to move parts of the body, as well as to move substances within the body.
Clinician	A health professional authorized to provide services to people suffering from one or more pathologies is a clinician.
Incidence	In epidemiological studies of a particular disorder, the rate at which new cases occur in a given place at a given time is called incidence.
Criterion	Criterion refers to a standard of comparison. For performance appraisal, it is the definition of good performance.
Hydration	Hydration can create a hydrate from which water can be reextracted. When hydration occurs in a chemical reaction it is called a hydration reaction, in which water is permanently and chemically combined with a reactant in a way that it can no longer be reextracted.
Heart rate	Heart rate is a term used to describe the frequency of the cardiac cycle. It is considered one of the four vital signs. Usually it is calculated as the number of contractions of the heart in one minute and expressed as "beats per minute".
Aerobic	An aerobic organism is an organism that has an oxygen based metabolism. Aerobes, in a process known as cellular respiration, use oxygen to oxidize substrates (for example sugars and fats) in order to obtain energy.
Adaptation	A biological adaptation is an anatomical structure, physiological process or behavioral trait of an organism that has evolved over a period of time by the process of natural selection such that it increases the expected long-term reproductive success of the organism.
Standard deviation	In probability and statistics, the standard deviation is the most commonly used measure of statistical dispersion. Simply put, it measures how spread out the values in a data set are.
Ventilation	Ventilation refers to a mechanism that provides contact between an animal's respiratory surface and the air or water to which it is exposed. It is also called breathing.
Conditioning	Processes by which behaviors can be learned or modified through interaction with the environment are conditioning.
Evaluation	The fifth step of the nursing process where nursing care and the patient's goal achievement are measured is the evaluation.
Diabetes	Diabetes is a medical disorder characterized by varying or persistent elevated blood sugar

Go to **Cram101.com** for the Practice Tests for this Chapter.

	levels, especially after eating. All types of diabetes share similar symptoms and complications at advanced stages: dehydration and ketoacidosis, cardiovascular disease, chronic renal failure, retinal damage which can lead to blindness, nerve damage which can lead to erectile dysfunction, gangrene with risk of amputation of toes, feet, and even legs.
Asthma	Asthma is a complex disease characterized by bronchial hyperresponsiveness (BHR), inflammation, mucus production and intermittent airway obstruction.
Hypertension	Hypertension is a medical condition where the blood pressure in the arteries is chronically elevated. Persistent hypertension is one of the risk factors for strokes, heart attacks, heart failure and arterial aneurysm, and is a leading cause of chronic renal failure.
Inpatient	Inpatient refers to a person who enters a healthcare setting for a stay ranging from 24 hours to many years.
Outpatient	Outpatient refers to a patient who requires treatment but does not need to be admitted into the institution for those sevices.
Pulse	The rhythmic stretching of the arteries caused by the pressure of blood forced through the arteries by contractions of the ventricles during systole is a pulse.
Carbohydrate	Carbohydrate is a chemical compound that contains oxygen, hydrogen, and carbon atoms. They consist of monosaccharide sugars of varying chain lengths and that have the general chemical formula $C_n(H_2O)_n$ or are derivatives of such.
Salt	Salt is a term used for ionic compounds composed of positively charged cations and negatively charged anions, so that the product is neutral and without a net charge.
Skin	Skin is an organ of the integumentary system composed of a layer of tissues that protect underlying muscles and organs.
Radiation	The emission of electromagnetic waves by all objects warmer than absolute zero is referred to as radiation.
Metabolic rate	Energy expended by the body per unit time is called metabolic rate.
Acclimatization	The word acclimatization is used to describe the process of an organism adjusting to changes in its environment, often involving temperature or climate. Acclimatization usually occurs in a short time, and within one organism's lifetime.
Dehydration	Dehydration is the removal of water from an object. Medically, dehydration is a serious and potentially life-threatening condition in which the body contains an insufficient volume of water for normal functioning.
Stress	Stress refers to a condition that is a response to factors that change the human systems normal state.
Hypothermia	Hypothermia is a low core body temperature, defined clinically as a temperature of less than 35 degrees celsius.
Freezing	Freezing is the process in which blood is frozen and all of the plasma and 99% of the WBCs are eliminated when thawing takes place and the nontransferable cryoprotectant is removed.
Gauge	The diameter of the needle is indicated by the needle gauge.
Cold stress	Cold stress is a body temperature of less than 97.6F (36.5C) in the newborn.
Insulation	The practice of managing our role performances so that role partners cannot observe our behavior in two or more conflicting roles is referred to as an insulation.
Subcutaneous	Subcutaneous injections are given by injecting a fluid into the subcutis. It is relatively painless and an effective way to administer particular types of medication.

Go to **Cram101.com** for the Practice Tests for this Chapter.

Core temperature	Core temperature is the operating temperature of an organism, specifically in deep structures of the body such as the liver, in comparison to temperatures of peripheral tissues.
Affect	Affect is the scientific term used to describe a subject's externally displayed mood. This can be assesed by the nurse by observing facial expression, tone of voice, and body language.
Eye	An eye is an organ that detects light. Different kinds of light-sensitive organs are found in a variety of creatures. The simplest eyes do nothing but detect whether the surroundings are light or dark, while more complex eyes can distinguish shapes and colors.
Airway resistance	Airway resistance is the opposition of the tracheobronchial tree to air flow: the mouth-to-alveoli pressure difference divided by the air flow.
Resistance	Resistance refers to a nonspecific ability to ward off infection or disease regardless of whether the body has been previously exposed to it. A force that opposes the flow of a fluid such as air or blood. Compare with immunity.
Ozone	Ozone (O_3) is an allotrope of oxygen, the molecule consisting of three oxygen atoms, a triatomic molecule, instead of the more stable diatomic O_2. Ozone is a powerful oxidizing agent. It is also unstable, decaying to ordinary oxygen through the reaction: $2O_3 \rightarrow 3O_2$.
Sulfur	Sulfur is the chemical element in the periodic table that has the symbol S and atomic number 16. It is an abundant, tasteless, odorless, multivalent non-metal. Sulfur, in its native form, is a yellow crystaline solid. In nature, it can be found as the pure element or as sulfide and sulfate minerals.
Sulfur dioxide	Sulfur dioxide refers to a major air pollutant, this toxic gas is formed as a result of burning sulfur. The major sources are burning coal that contain some sulfur and refining metal ores that contain sulfur.
Carbon	Carbon is a chemical element in the periodic table that has the symbol C and atomic number 6. An abundant nonmetallic, tetravalent element, carbon has several allotropic forms.
Sodium	Sodium is the chemical element in the periodic table that has the symbol Na (Natrium in Latin) and atomic number 11. Sodium is a soft, waxy, silvery reactive metal belonging to the alkali metals that is abundant in natural compounds (especially halite). It is highly reactive.
Hemoglobin	Hemoglobin is the iron-containing oxygen-transport metalloprotein in the red cells of the blood in mammals and other animals. Hemoglobin transports oxygen from the lungs to the rest of the body, such as to the muscles, where it releases the oxygen load.
Blood	Blood is a circulating tissue composed of fluid plasma and cells. The main function of blood is to supply nutrients (oxygen, glucose) and constitutional elements to tissues and to remove waste products.
Course	Pattern of development and change of a disorder over time is a course.
Cardiovascular system	The circulatory system or cardiovascular system is the organ system which circulates blood around the body of most animals.
Cardiac output	Cardiac output is the volume of blood being pumped by the heart in a minute. It is equal to the heart rate multiplied by the stroke volume.
Bolus	A bolus is any kind of ball-shaped organic structure of an organism or of its discharged substances..
Partial pressure	The partial pressure of a gas in a mixture or solution is what the pressure of that gas would be if all other components of the mixture or solution suddenly vanished without its temperature changing.

Tissue	A collection of interconnected cells that perform a similar function within an organism is called tissue.
Heart attack	A heart attack, is a serious, sudden heart condition usually characterized by varying degrees of chest pain or discomfort, weakness, sweating, nausea, vomiting, and arrhythmias, sometimes causing loss of consciousness. It occurs when the blood supply to a part of the heart is interrupted, causing death and scarring of the local heart tissue.
Blood pressure	Blood pressure is the pressure exerted by the blood on the walls of the blood vessels.
Medicine	Medicine is the branch of health science and the sector of public life concerned with maintaining or restoring human health through the study, diagnosis and treatment of disease and injury.
Pain	Pain is an unpleasant sensation which may be associated with actual or potential tissue damage and which may have physical and emotional components.
Mortality	The incidence of death in a population is mortality.
Artery	Vessel that takes blood away from the heart to the tissues and organs of the body is called an artery.
Coronary artery	An artery that supplies blood to the wall of the heart is called a coronary artery.
Coronary artery disease	Coronary artery disease (CAD) is the end result of the accumulation of atheromatous plaques within the walls of the arteries that supply the myocardium (the muscle of the heart).
Physiology	The study of the function of cells, tissues, and organs is referred to as physiology.
Tolerance	Drug tolerance occurs when a subject's reaction to a drug decreases so that larger doses are required to achieve the same effect.
Implementation	The methods by which the goal will be achieved is also recorded at this fourth stage. The methods of implementation must be recorded in an explicit and tangible format in a way that the patient can understand should he wish to read it. Clarity is essential as it will aid communication between those tasked with carrying out patient care.
Cardiology	Cardiology is the branch of medicine dealing with disorders of the heart and blood vessels. The field is commonly divided in the branches of congenital heart defects, coronary artery disease, heart failure, valvular heart disease and electrophysiology.
Rehabilitation	Rehabilitation is the restoration of lost capabilities, or the treatment aimed at producing it. Also refers to treatment for dependency on psychoactive substances such as alcohol, prescription drugs, and illicit drugs such as cocaine, heroin or amphetamines.
Plasma	Fluid portion of circulating blood is called plasma.
Triglyceride	Triglyceride is a glyceride in which the glycerol is esterified with three fatty acids. They are the main constituent of vegetable oil and animal fats and play an important role in metabolism as energy sources. They contain a bit more than twice as much energy as carbohydrates and proteins.
Stimulus	Stimulus in a nervous system, a factor that triggers sensory transduction.
Regression	Return to a form of behavior characteristic of an earlier stage of development is a regression.
Adjustment	Adjustment is an attempt to cope with a given situation.
Longevity	A long duration of life is referred to as longevity.
Centers for Disease Control	The Centers for Disease Control and Prevention in Atlanta, Georgia, is recognized as the lead United States agency for protecting the public health and safety of people by providing

Go to **Cram101.com** for the Practice Tests for this Chapter.

and Prevention	credible information to enhance health decisions, and promoting health through strong partnerships with state health departments and other organizations.
Channel	Channel, in communications (sometimes called communications channel), refers to the medium used to convey information from a sender (or transmitter) to a receiver.
Health promotion	Any planned combination of educational, political, regulatory, and organizational supports for actions and conditions of living conducive to the health of individuals, groups, or communities is called health promotion.

Health	Health is a term that refers to a combination of the absence of illness, the ability to cope with everyday activities, physical fitness, and high quality of life.
Obesity	The state of being more than 20 percent above the average weight for a person of one's height is called obesity.
Population	Population refers to all members of a well-defined group of organisms, events, or things.
Tissue	A collection of interconnected cells that perform a similar function within an organism is called tissue.
Adipose tissue	Adipose tissue is an anatomical term for loose connective tissue composed of adipocytes. Its main role is to store energy in the form of fat, although it also cushions and insulates the body. It has an important endocrine function in producing recently-discovered hormones such as leptin, resistin and TNFalpha.
Muscle	Muscle is a contractile form of tissue. It is one of the four major tissue types, the other three being epithelium, connective tissue and nervous tissue. Muscle contraction is used to move parts of the body, as well as to move substances within the body.
Creeping obesity	The gradual and consistent increase in body fat weight over the years, is referred to as a creeping obesity.
Etiology	The apparent causation and developmental history of an illness is an etiology.
Calorie	Calorie refers to a unit used to measure heat energy and the energy contents of foods.
Lead	Lead is a chemical element in the periodic table that has the symbol Pb and atomic number 82. A soft, heavy, toxic and malleable poor metal, lead is bluish white when freshly cut but tarnishes to dull gray when exposed to air. Lead is used in building construction, lead-acid batteries, bullets and shot, and is part of solder, pewter, and fusible alloys.
Lifestyle	The culturally, socially, economically, and environmentally conditioned complex of actions characteristic of an individual, group, or community as a pattern of habituated behavior over time that is health related but not necessarily health directed is a lifestyle.
Genes	Genes are the units of heredity in living organisms. They are encoded in the organism's genetic material (usually DNA or RNA), and control the development and behavior of the organism.
Affect	Affect is the scientific term used to describe a subject's externally displayed mood. This can be assesed by the nurse by observing facial expression, tone of voice, and body language.
Adaptation	A biological adaptation is an anatomical structure, physiological process or behavioral trait of an organism that has evolved over a period of time by the process of natural selection such that it increases the expected long-term reproductive success of the organism.
Constant	A behavior or characteristic that does not vary from one observation to another is referred to as a constant.
Hydrogen	Hydrogen is a chemical element in the periodic table that has the symbol H and atomic number 1. At standard temperature and pressure it is a colorless, odorless, nonmetallic, univalent, tasteless, highly flammable diatomic gas.
Isotope	An isotope is a form of an element whose nuclei have the same atomic number - the number of protons in the nucleus - but different mass numbers because they contain different numbers of neutrons.
Oxygen	Oxygen is a chemical element in the periodic table. It has the symbol O and atomic number 8. Oxygen is the second most common element on Earth, composing around 46% of the mass of Earth's crust and 28% of the mass of Earth as a whole, and is the third most common element

Go to **Cram101.com** for the Practice Tests for this Chapter.

	in the universe.
Carbohydrate	Carbohydrate is a chemical compound that contains oxygen, hydrogen, and carbon atoms. They consist of monosaccharide sugars of varying chain lengths and that have the general chemical formula $C_n(H_2O)_n$ or are derivatives of such.
Protein	A protein is a complex, high-molecular-weight organic compound that consists of amino acids joined by peptide bonds. They are essential to the structure and function of all living cells and viruses. Many are enzymes or subunits of enzymes.
Sugar	A sugar is the simplest molecule that can be identified as a carbohydrate. These include monosaccharides and disaccharides, trisaccharides and the oligosaccharides. The term "glyco-" indicates the presence of a sugar in an otherwise non-carbohydrate substance.
Culture	Culture, generally refers to patterns of human activity and the symbolic structures that give such activity significance.
Planning	In agreement with the patient, the nurse addresses each of the problems identified in the planning phase. For each problem a measurable goal is set. For example, for the patient discussed above, the goal would be for the patient's skin to remain intact. The result is a nursing care plan. This is the third step.
Metabolic rate	Energy expended by the body per unit time is called metabolic rate.
Assessment	In clinical practice, the process by which a mental health professional gathers and compiles information about a client for the purpose of describing the person's problems or disorder and developing a plan of treatment is an assessment.
Value	Value is worth in general, and it is thought to be connected to reasons for certain practices, policies, actions, beliefs or emotions. Value is "that which one acts to gain and/or keep."
Aerobic	An aerobic organism is an organism that has an oxygen based metabolism. Aerobes, in a process known as cellular respiration, use oxygen to oxidize substrates (for example sugars and fats) in order to obtain energy.
Resistance	Resistance refers to a nonspecific ability to ward off infection or disease regardless of whether the body has been previously exposed to it. A force that opposes the flow of a fluid such as air or blood. Compare with immunity.
Variable	A characteristic or aspect in which people, objects, events, or conditions vary is called variable.
Outcome	Outcome is the impact of care provided to a patient. They can be positive, such as the ability to walk freely as a result of rehabilitation, or negative, such as the occurrence of bedsores as a result of lack of mobility of a patient.
Behavior modification	Behavior Modification is a technique of altering an individual's reactions to stimuli through positive reinforcement and the extinction of maladaptive behavior.
Cation	An ion with more protons than electrons and consequently a net positive charge is called a cation.
Aerobic exercise	Exercise in which oxygen is used to produce ATP is aerobic exercise.
Lifestyle changes	Lifestyle changes are changes to the way a person lives which are often called for when treating chronic disease.
Human nature	Human nature refers to those traits, qualities, potentials, and behavior patterns most characteristic of the human species.
Lipid	Lipid is one class of aliphatic hydrocarbon-containing organic compounds essential for the

Go to **Cram101.com** for the Practice Tests for this Chapter.

structure and function of living cells. They are characterized by being water-insoluble but soluble in nonpolar organic solvents.

Blood	Blood is a circulating tissue composed of fluid plasma and cells. The main function of blood is to supply nutrients (oxygen, glucose) and constitutional elements to tissues and to remove waste products.
Solution	Solution refers to homogenous mixture formed when a solute is dissolved in a solvent.
Dehydration	Dehydration is the removal of water from an object. Medically, dehydration is a serious and potentially life-threatening condition in which the body contains an insufficient volume of water for normal functioning.
Essential nutrient	An essential nutrient is a nutrient required for normal body functioning that can not be synthesized by the body. Categories of essential nutrient include vitamins, dietary minerals, essential fatty acids and essential amino acids.
Eating disorders	Psychological disorders characterized by distortion of the body image and gross disturbances in eating patterns are called eating disorders.
Anorexia	Anorexia nervosa is an eating disorder characterized by voluntary starvation and exercise stress.
Bulimia	Bulimia refers to a disorder in which a person binges on incredibly large quantities of food, then purges by vomiting or by using laxatives. Bulimia is often less about food, and more to do with deep psychological issues and profound feelings of lack of control.
Binge	Binge refers to relatively brief episode of uncontrolled, excessive consumption.
Binge eating disorder	Binge eating disorder is a syndrome in which people feel their eating is out of control; eat what most would think is an unusually large amount of food; eat much more quickly than usual; eat until so full they are uncomfortable; eat large amounts of food, even when they are not really hungry; eat alone because they are embarrassed about the amount of food they eat; feel disgusted, depressed, or guilty after overeating.
Anorexia nervosa	Anorexia nervosa is an eating disorder characterized by voluntary starvation and exercise stress.
Bulimia nervosa	Bulimia nervosa is a psychological condition in which the subject engages in recurrent binge eating followed by intentionally; vomiting, misuse of laxatives or other medication, excessive exercising, and fasting, in order to compensate for the intake of the food and prevent weight gain:
Body image	A person's body image is their perception of their physical appearance. It is more than what a person thinks they will see in a mirror, it is inextricably tied to their self-esteem and acceptance by peers.
Anxiety	Anxiety is a complex combination of the feeling of fear, apprehension and worry often accompanied by physical sensations such as palpitations, chest pain and/or shortness of breath.
Diagnosis	In medicine, diagnosis is the process of identifying a medical condition or disease by its signs, symptoms, and from the results of various diagnostic procedures.
Intervention	Intervention refers to a planned attempt to break through addicts' or abusers' denial and get them into treatment. Interventions most often occur when legal, workplace, health, relationship, or financial problems have become intolerable.
Creatine phosphate	Compound unique to muscles that contains a high-energy phosphate bond is creatine phosphate or phosphocreatine.

Go to **Cram101.com** for the Practice Tests for this Chapter.

Phosphate	A phosphate is a polyatomic ion or radical consisting of one phosphorus atom and four oxygen. In the ionic form, it carries a -3 formal charge, and is denoted $PO_4{}^{3-}$.
Evaluation	The fifth step of the nursing process where nursing care and the patient's goal achievement are measured is the evaluation.
Medicine	Medicine is the branch of health science and the sector of public life concerned with maintaining or restoring human health through the study, diagnosis and treatment of disease and injury.
Mental disorder	Mental disorder refers to a disturbance in a person's emotions, drives, thought processes, or behavior that involves serious and relatively prolonged distress and/or impairment in ability to function, is not simply a normal response to some event or set of events in the person's environment.
Diagnostic and Statistical Manual of Mental Disorders	The Diagnostic and Statistical Manual of Mental Disorders, published by the American Psychiatric Association, is the handbook used most often in diagnosing mental disorders in the United States and internationally.
Distribution	Distribution in pharmacology is a branch of pharmacokinetics describing reversible transfer of drug from one location to another within the body.
Epidemic	An epidemic is a disease that appears as new cases in a given human population, during a given period, at a rate that substantially exceeds what is "expected", based on recent experience.
Consensus	General agreement is a consensus.
Comorbidity	Comorbidity refers to the presence of more than one mental disorder occurring in an individual at the same time.
Diabetes	Diabetes is a medical disorder characterized by varying or persistent elevated blood sugar levels, especially after eating. All types of diabetes share similar symptoms and complications at advanced stages: dehydration and ketoacidosis, cardiovascular disease, chronic renal failure, retinal damage which can lead to blindness, nerve damage which can lead to erectile dysfunction, gangrene with risk of amputation of toes, feet, and even legs.
Kidney	The kidney is a bean-shaped excretory organ in vertebrates. Part of the urinary system, the kidneys filter wastes (especially urea) from the blood and excrete them, along with water, as urine.
Adoption study	A study in which investigators seek to discover whether, in behavior and psychological characteristics, adopted children are more like their adoptive parents, who provided a home environment, or more like their biological parents, who contributed their genetic code is called adoption study.
Cohort	A cohort is a group of individuals defined by their date of birth.

Go to **Cram101.com** for the Practice Tests for this Chapter.

Health	Health is a term that refers to a combination of the absence of illness, the ability to cope with everyday activities, physical fitness, and high quality of life.
Variable	A characteristic or aspect in which people, objects, events, or conditions vary is called variable.
Acute	In medicine, an acute disease is a disease with either or both of: a rapid onset; and a short course (as opposed to a chronic course).
Concept	A mental category used to class together objects, relations, events, abstractions, or qualities that have common properties is called concept.
Muscle	Muscle is a contractile form of tissue. It is one of the four major tissue types, the other three being epithelium, connective tissue and nervous tissue. Muscle contraction is used to move parts of the body, as well as to move substances within the body.
Resistance	Resistance refers to a nonspecific ability to ward off infection or disease regardless of whether the body has been previously exposed to it. A force that opposes the flow of a fluid such as air or blood. Compare with immunity.
Conditioning	Processes by which behaviors can be learned or modified through interaction with the environment are conditioning.
Heredity	Heredity refers to the transmission of genetic information from parent to offspring.
Specificity	A medical diagnostic test for a certain disease, specificity is the proportion of true negatives of all the negative samples tested.
Adaptation	A biological adaptation is an anatomical structure, physiological process or behavioral trait of an organism that has evolved over a period of time by the process of natural selection such that it increases the expected long-term reproductive success of the organism.
Hydration	Hydration can create a hydrate from which water can be reextracted. When hydration occurs in a chemical reaction it is called a hydration reaction, in which water is permanently and chemically combined with a reactant in a way that it can no longer be reextracted.
Stimulus	Stimulus in a nervous system, a factor that triggers sensory transduction.
Stress	Stress refers to a condition that is a response to factors that change the human systems normal state.
Affect	Affect is the scientific term used to describe a subject's externally displayed mood. This can be assesed by the nurse by observing facial expression, tone of voice, and body language.
Evaluation	The fifth step of the nursing process where nursing care and the patient's goal achievement are measured is the evaluation.
Compliance	In medicine, a patient's (or doctor's) adherence to a recommended course of treatment is considered compliance.
Lead	Lead is a chemical element in the periodic table that has the symbol Pb and atomic number 82. A soft, heavy, toxic and malleable poor metal, lead is bluish white when freshly cut but tarnishes to dull gray when exposed to air. Lead is used in building construction, lead-acid batteries, bullets and shot, and is part of solder, pewter, and fusible alloys.
Assess	Assess is to systematically and continuously collect, validate, and communicate patient data.
Constant	A behavior or characteristic that does not vary from one observation to another is referred to as a constant.
Isometric contraction	A muscle contraction in which there is no movement and the length of the muscle does not change is an isometric contraction.

Go to **Cram101.com** for the Practice Tests for this Chapter.

Joint	A joint (articulation) is the location at which two bones make contact (articulate). They are constructed to both allow movement and provide mechanical support.
Isometric exercise	Isometric exercise is a form of physical exercise in which the muscles flex and hold a stationary position. No movement of a load takes place, and the exercises require little in the way of equipment.
Atrophy	Atrophy is the partial or complete wasting away of a part of the body. Causes of atrophy include poor nourishment, poor circulation, loss of hormonal support, loss of nerve supply to the target organ, disuse or lack of exercise, or disease intrinsic to the tissue itself.
Valsalva maneuver	A Valsalva maneuver is any attempted exhalation against a closed glottis or against a closed mouth and nose. A Valsalva maneuver performed against a closed glottis results in a drastic increase in pressure in the thoracic cavity, the airtight section of the torso that houses the lungs and heart.
Fiber	Fibers used by man come from a wide variety of sources: Natural fiber include those made out of plants, animal and mineral sources. Natural fibers can be classified according to their origin.
Muscle fiber	Cell with myofibrils containing actin and myosin filaments arranged within sarcomeres is a muscle fiber.
Proprioception	Proprioception is the sense of the position of parts of the body, relative to other parts of the body. Unlike the six exteroception senses of sight, taste, smell, touch, hearing, and balance, that advise us of the outside world, proprioception is a sense that provides feedback solely on the status of the body internally.
Insight	Insight refers to a sudden awareness of the relationships among various elements that had previously appeared to be independent of one another.
Value	Value is worth in general, and it is thought to be connected to reasons for certain practices, policies, actions, beliefs or emotions. Value is "that which one acts to gain and/or keep."
Bone mineral density	A bone mineral density test is used to measure bone density and determine fracture risk for osteoporosis.
Protocol	Protocol is a document with the aim of guiding decisions and criteria in specific areas of healthcare, as defined by an authoritative examination of current evidence. It details the activities to be executed in specific situations.
Angular	The angular is a large bone in the lower jaw of amphibians, birds and reptiles, which is connected to all other lower jaw bones: the dentary (which is the entire lower jaw in mammals), the splenial, the suprangular, and the articular.
Rehabilitation	Rehabilitation is the restoration of lost capabilities, or the treatment aimed at producing it. Also refers to treatment for dependency on psychoactive substances such as alcohol, prescription drugs, and illicit drugs such as cocaine, heroin or amphetamines.
Medicine	Medicine is the branch of health science and the sector of public life concerned with maintaining or restoring human health through the study, diagnosis and treatment of disease and injury.
Tissue	A collection of interconnected cells that perform a similar function within an organism is called tissue.
Connective tissue	Connective tissue is any type of biological tissue with an extensive extracellular matrix and often serves to support, bind together, and protect organs.
Extension	Movement increasing the angle between parts at a joint is referred to as extension.

Go to **Cram101.com** for the Practice Tests for this Chapter.

Population	Population refers to all members of a well-defined group of organisms, events, or things.
Individual differences	The stable, consistent ways that people are different from each other are called individual differences.
Skin	Skin is an organ of the integumentary system composed of a layer of tissues that protect underlying muscles and organs.
Rods	Rods, are photoreceptor cells in the retina of the eye that can function in less intense light than can the other type of photoreceptor, cone cells.
Aerobic	An aerobic organism is an organism that has an oxygen based metabolism. Aerobes, in a process known as cellular respiration, use oxygen to oxidize substrates (for example sugars and fats) in order to obtain energy.
Blood	Blood is a circulating tissue composed of fluid plasma and cells. The main function of blood is to supply nutrients (oxygen, glucose) and constitutional elements to tissues and to remove waste products.
Aerobic exercise	Exercise in which oxygen is used to produce ATP is aerobic exercise.
Range of motion	Range of motion is a measurement of movement through a particular joint or muscle range.
Flexion	In anatomy, Flexion is movement whereby bones or other parts of the body, including the trunk, are brought closer together by decreasing the joint angle. The opposite term is extention, or straightening.
Rotation	Movement turning a body part on its longitudinal axis is rotation.
Rotator Cuff	The rotator cuff is an anatomical term given to the group of muscles and their tendons that act to stabilize the shoulder. These muscles arise from the scapula and connect to the head of the humerus forming a cuff at shoulder joint.
Hypertrophy	Hypertrophy is the increase of the size of an organ. It should be distinguished from hyperplasia which occurs due to cell division; hypertrophy occurs due to an increase in cell size rather than division. It is most commonly seen in muscle that has been actively stimulated, the most well-known method being exercise.
Acid	An acid is a water-soluble, sour-tasting chemical compound that when dissolved in water, gives a solution with a pH of less than 7.
Tolerance	Drug tolerance occurs when a subject's reaction to a drug decreases so that larger doses are required to achieve the same effect.
Abduction	Abduction is movement of a limb away from the body's midline, or of a digit away from the long axis of a limb.
Adduction	Adduction is where there is a reduction in the angle between bones or parts of the body. This only applies to movement along the coronal plane.
Hip	In anatomy, the hip is the bony projection of the femur, known as the greater trochanter, and the overlying muscle and fat.
Syndrome	Syndrome is the association of several clinically recognizable features, signs, symptoms, phenomena or characteristics which often occur together, so that the presence of one feature alerts the physician to the presence of the others
Selye	Selye did much important theoretical work on the non-specific response of the organism to stress. Selye discovered and documented that stress differs from other physical responses in that stress is stressful whether the one receives good or bad news, whether the impulse is positive or negative. He called negative stress distress and positive stress eustress.

General adaptation syndrome	The predictable sequence of reactions that organisms show in response to stressors is called the general adaptation syndrome.
Anecdotal evidence	Anecdotal evidence is unreliable evidence based on personal experience that has not been empirically tested, and which is often used in an argument as if it had been scientifically or statistically proven. The person using anecdotal evidence may or may not be aware of the fact that, by doing so, they are generalizing.
Androgen	Androgen is the generic term for any natural or synthetic compound, usually a steroid hormone, that stimulates or controls the development and maintenance of masculine characteristics in vertebrates by binding to androgen receptors.
Control subjects	Control subjects are participants in an experiment who do not receive the treatment effect but for whom all other conditions are held comparable to those of experimental subjects.
Pain	Pain is an unpleasant sensation which may be associated with actual or potential tissue damage and which may have physical and emotional components.
Biopsy	Removal of small tissue sample from the body for microscopic examination is called biopsy.
Metabolic rate	Energy expended by the body per unit time is called metabolic rate.
Older adult	Older adult is an adult over the age of 65.
Skeletal muscle	Skeletal muscle is a type of striated muscle, attached to the skeleton. They are used to facilitate movement, by applying force to bones and joints; via contraction. They generally contract voluntarily (via nerve stimulation), although they can contract involuntarily.
Reversibility	Reversibility according to Piaget, is recognition that processes can be undone, that things can be made as they were.
Fetus	Fetus refers to a developing human from the ninth week of gestation until birth; has all the major structures of an adult.
First trimester	The first trimester is the period of time from the first day of the last menstrual period through 12 weeks of gestation. It is during this period that the embryo undergoes most of its early structural development. Most miscarriages occur during this period.
Trimester	In human development, one of three 3-mnonth-long periods of pregnancy is called trimester.
Blood pressure	Blood pressure is the pressure exerted by the blood on the walls of the blood vessels.
Heart rate	Heart rate is a term used to describe the frequency of the cardiac cycle. It is considered one of the four vital signs. Usually it is calculated as the number of contractions of the heart in one minute and expressed as "beats per minute".
Coronary	Referring to the heart or the blood vessels of the heart is referred to as coronary.
Sternum	Sternum or breastbone is a long, flat bone located in the center of the thorax (chest). It connects to the rib bones via cartilage, forming the rib cage with them, and thus helps to protect the lungs and heart from physical trauma.
Artery	Vessel that takes blood away from the heart to the tissues and organs of the body is called an artery.
Bypass	In medicine, a bypass generally means an alternate or additional route for blood flow, which is created in bypass surgery, e.g. coronary artery bypass surgery by moving blood vessels or implanting synthetic tubing.
Coronary artery	An artery that supplies blood to the wall of the heart is called a coronary artery.
Coronary artery	A coronary artery bypass graft (CABG) or heart bypass is a surgical procedure performed in

Go to **Cram101.com** for the Practice Tests for this Chapter.

bypass graft	patients with coronary artery disease (see atherosclerosis) for the relief of angina and possible improved heart muscle function.
Gluteus maximus	The gluteus maximus muscle is the largest of the gluteal muscles which are located in each buttock. By some definitions, the gluteus maxima are the most powerful muscles of the human body.
Deltoid	The deltoid muscle is the muscle forming the rounded contour of the human shoulder.
Pectoralis major	The Pectoralis major is a thick, fan-shaped muscle, situated at the upper front (anterior) of the chest wall. It makes up the bulk of the chest muscles in the male and lies under the breast in the female.
Rectus abdominis	The Rectus abdominis is a long flat muscle, which extends along the whole length of the front of the abdomen, and is separated from its fellow of the opposite side by the linea alba.
Arrhythmias	Arrhythmias refers to abnormal heart rhythms which may be too slow, too early, too rapid, or irregular.
Arrhythmia	Cardiac arrhythmia is a group of conditions in which muscle contraction of the heart is irregular for any reason.
Incidence	In epidemiological studies of a particular disorder, the rate at which new cases occur in a given place at a given time is called incidence.
Outpatient	Outpatient refers to a patient who requires treatment but does not need to be admitted into the institution for those sevices.
Outcome	Outcome is the impact of care provided to a patient. They can be positive, such as the ability to walk freely as a result of rehabilitation, or negative, such as the occurrence of bedsores as a result of lack of mobility of a patient.
Critical thinking	Critical thinking consists of a mental process of analyzing or evaluating information, particularly statements or propositions that people have offered as true. It forms a process of reflecting upon the meaning of statements, examining the offered evidence and reasoning, and forming judgments about the facts.
Gerontology	The interdisciplinary study of aging and of the special problems of the elderly is referred to as gerontology.
Elderly	Old age consists of ages nearing the average life span of human beings, and thus the end of the human life cycle. Euphemisms for older people include advanced adult, elderly, and senior or senior citizen.
Diastolic pressure	Diastolic pressure refers to arterial blood pressure during the diastolic phase of the cardiac cycle.
Left ventricle	The left ventricle is one of four chambers (two atria and two ventricles) in the human heart. It receives oxygenated blood from the left atrium via the mitral valve, and pumps it into the aorta via the aortic valve.
Ventricle	In the heart, a ventricle is a heart chamber which collects blood from an atrium (another heart chamber) and pumps it out of the heart.
Physiology	The study of the function of cells, tissues, and organs is referred to as physiology.
Extensor	A muscle or tendon that straightens or extends a limb is called an extensor.
Cardiology	Cardiology is the branch of medicine dealing with disorders of the heart and blood vessels. The field is commonly divided in the branches of congenital heart defects, coronary artery disease, heart failure, valvular heart disease and electrophysiology.

Go to **Cram101.com** for the Practice Tests for this Chapter.

Intervention	Intervention refers to a planned attempt to break through addicts' or abusers' denial and get them into treatment. Interventions most often occur when legal, workplace, health, relationship, or financial problems have become intolerable.
Risk factor	A risk factor is a variable associated with an increased risk of disease or infection but risk factors are not necessarily causal.
Cardiovascular disease	Cardiovascular disease refers to afflictions in the mechanisms, including the heart, blood vessels, and their controllers, that are responsible for transporting blood to the body's tissues and organs. Psychological factors may play important roles in such diseases and their treatments.

Lumbar vertebrae	The lumbar vertebrae are the largest segments of the movable part of the vertebral column, and can be distinguished by the absence of a foramen (hole) in the transverse process, and by the absence of facets on the sides of the body.
Anatomy	Anatomy is the branch of biology that deals with the structure and organization of living things. It can be divided into animal anatomy (zootomy) and plant anatomy (phytonomy).
Sacrum	The sacrum is a large, triangular bone at the base of the vertebral column and at the upper and back part of the pelvic cavity, where it is inserted like a wedge between the two hip bones. Its upper part or base articulates with the last lumbar vertebra, its apex with the coccyx.
Lumbar	In anatomy, lumbar is an adjective that means of or pertaining to the abdominal segment of the torso, between the diaphragm and the sacrum (pelvis). The five vertebra in the lumbar region are the largest and strongest in the spinal column.
Pelvis	The pelvis is the bony structure located at the base of the spine (properly known as the caudal end). The pelvis incorporates the socket portion of the hip joint for each leg (in bipeds) or hind leg (in quadrupeds). It forms the lower limb (or hind-limb) girdle of the skeleton.
Vertebrae	Vertebrae are the individual bones that make up the vertebral column (aka spine) - a flexuous and flexible column.
Spinal cord	The spinal cord is a part of the vertebrate nervous system that is enclosed in and protected by the vertebral column (it passes through the spinal canal). It consists of nerve cells. The spinal cord carries sensory signals and motor innervation to most of the skeletal muscles in the body.
Articular	The articular is a bone in the lower jaw of most tetrapods, including reptiles, birds, and amphibians, but has become a middle ear bone (the malleus) in mammals. It is the site of articulation between the lower jaw and the skull, and is connected to two other lower jaw bones, the suprangular and the angular.
Joint	A joint (articulation) is the location at which two bones make contact (articulate). They are constructed to both allow movement and provide mechanical support.
Transverse	A transverse (also known as axial or horizontal) plane is an X-Y plane, parallel to the ground, which (in humans) separates the superior from the inferior, or put another way, the head from the feet.
Ligament	A ligament is a short band of tough fibrous connective tissue composed mainly of long, stringy collagen fibres. They connect bones to other bones to form a joint. (They do not connect muscles to bones.)
Intervertebral disc	A pad of cartilage between two vertebrae that acts as a shock absorber is called intervertebral disc.
Course	Pattern of development and change of a disorder over time is a course.
Receptor	A receptor is a protein on the cell membrane or within the cytoplasm or cell nucleus that binds to a specific molecule (a ligand), such as a neurotransmitter, hormone, or other substance, and initiates the cellular response to the ligand. Receptor, in immunology, the region of an antibody which shows recognition of an antigen.
Pain	Pain is an unpleasant sensation which may be associated with actual or potential tissue damage and which may have physical and emotional components.
Fibrosis	Replacement of damaged tissue with fibrous scar tissue rather than by the original tissue type is called fibrosis.

Go to **Cram101.com** for the Practice Tests for this Chapter.

Tissue	A collection of interconnected cells that perform a similar function within an organism is called tissue.
Shock	Circulatory shock, a state of cardiac output that is insufficient to meet the body's physiological needs, with consequences ranging from fainting to death is referred to as shock. Insulin shock, a state of severe hypoglycemia caused by administration of insulin.
Fiber	Fibers used by man come from a wide variety of sources: Natural fiber include those made out of plants, animal and mineral sources. Natural fibers can be classified according to their origin.
Connective tissue	Connective tissue is any type of biological tissue with an extensive extracellular matrix and often serves to support, bind together, and protect organs.
Stress	Stress refers to a condition that is a response to factors that change the human systems normal state.
Blood	Blood is a circulating tissue composed of fluid plasma and cells. The main function of blood is to supply nutrients (oxygen, glucose) and constitutional elements to tissues and to remove waste products.
Lordosis	Lordosis is a term used for an anterior curvature of the vertebral column. Two segments of the vertebral column, namely cervical and lumbar, are normally lordotic, that is, they are set in a curve that has its convexity in front and concavity behind, in the context of human anatomy.
Kyphosis	Kyphosis in the sense of a deformity is the pathologic curving of the spine, where parts of the spinal column lose some or all of their lordotic profile. This causes a bowing of the back, seen as a slouching posture.
Activities of daily living	Activities of daily living is a way to describe the functional status of a person.
Risk factor	A risk factor is a variable associated with an increased risk of disease or infection but risk factors are not necessarily causal.
Affect	Affect is the scientific term used to describe a subject's externally displayed mood. This can be assesed by the nurse by observing facial expression, tone of voice, and body language.
Muscle	Muscle is a contractile form of tissue. It is one of the four major tissue types, the other three being epithelium, connective tissue and nervous tissue. Muscle contraction is used to move parts of the body, as well as to move substances within the body.
Flexor	A muscle or tendon which bends a limb, part of a limb, or part of the body is a flexor.
Hip	In anatomy, the hip is the bony projection of the femur, known as the greater trochanter, and the overlying muscle and fat.
Pathology	Pathology is the study of the processes underlying disease and other forms of illness, harmful abnormality, or dysfunction.
Plexus	A plexus is also a network of blood vessels, with the choroid plexuses of the brain being the most commonly mentioned example. A choroid plexus is very thin and vascular roof plates of the most anterior and most posterior cavities of the brain which expand into the interiors of the cavities.
Brachial plexus	The brachial plexus is an arrangement of nerve fibres running from the spine, through the neck, the axilla (armpit region), and into the arm. All nerves of the arm stem from the brachial plexus.
Vertebral column	In human anatomy, the vertebral column is a column of vertebrae situated in the dorsal aspect

Go to **Cram101.com** for the Practice Tests for this Chapter.

of the abdomen. It houses the spinal cord in its spinal canal.

Rotation	Movement turning a body part on its longitudinal axis is rotation.
Flexion	In anatomy, Flexion is movement whereby bones or other parts of the body, including the trunk, are brought closer together by decreasing the joint angle. The opposite term is extention, or straightening.
Extension	Movement increasing the angle between parts at a joint is referred to as extension.
Scoliosis	Scoliosis is a condition that involves a lateral curvature of the spine; that is, the spine is bent sideways. Scoliosis is incurable, but its natural course can be affected with treatments such as surgery or bracing.
Acute	In medicine, an acute disease is a disease with either or both of: a rapid onset; and a short course (as opposed to a chronic course).
Extensor	A muscle or tendon that straightens or extends a limb is called an extensor.
Homeostasis	Homeostasis is the property of an open system, especially living organisms, to regulate its internal environment to maintain a stable, constant condition, by means of multiple dynamic equilibrium adjustments, controlled by interrelated regulation mechanisms.
Intervention	Intervention refers to a planned attempt to break through addicts' or abusers' denial and get them into treatment. Interventions most often occur when legal, workplace, health, relationship, or financial problems have become intolerable.
Lead	Lead is a chemical element in the periodic table that has the symbol Pb and atomic number 82. A soft, heavy, toxic and malleable poor metal, lead is bluish white when freshly cut but tarnishes to dull gray when exposed to air. Lead is used in building construction, lead-acid batteries, bullets and shot, and is part of solder, pewter, and fusible alloys.
Hyperextension	Hyperextension is the movement of a body part beyond the normal range of motion, such as the position of the head when looking upwards into the sky.
Cartilage	Cartilage is a type of dense connective tissue. Cartilage is composed of cells called chondrocytes which are dispersed in a firm gel-like ground substance, called the matrix. Cartilage is avascular (contains no blood vessels) and nutrients are diffused through the matrix.
Sagittal	A sagittal plane is an X-Z plane, perpendicular to the ground and to the coronal plane, which separates left from right. The midsagittal plane is the specific sagittal plane that is exactly in the middle of the body.
Coronal	A coronal (also known as frontal) plane is an Y-Z plane, perpendicular to the ground, which (in humans) separates the anterior from the posterior, the front from the back, the ventral from the dorsal.
Sagittal plane	Sagittal plane refers to any plane that extends from ventral to dorsal and cephalic to caudal and divides the body into right and left portions. Compare with midsagittal plane.
Coronal plane	The frontal or coronal plane essentially separates the body into the forward half and the back half. This plane is perpendicular to the median and also passes from the top to the bottom along the long axis of the body.
Rectus abdominis	The Rectus abdominis is a long flat muscle, which extends along the whole length of the front of the abdomen, and is separated from its fellow of the opposite side by the linea alba.
Diagnosis	In medicine, diagnosis is the process of identifying a medical condition or disease by its signs, symptoms, and from the results of various diagnostic procedures.
Trial	In classical conditioning, any presentation of a stimulus or pair of stimuli is called a

	trial.
Value	Value is worth in general, and it is thought to be connected to reasons for certain practices, policies, actions, beliefs or emotions. Value is "that which one acts to gain and/or keep."
Fascia	Fascia is specialized connective tissue layer which surrounds muscles, bones, and joints, providing support and protection and giving structure to the body. It consists of three layers: the superficial fascia, the deep fascia and the subserous fascia. Fascia is one of the 3 types of dense connective tissue (the other two being ligaments and tendons).
Attachment	Attachment refers to the psychological tendency to seek closeness to another person, to feel secure when that person is present, and to feel anxious when that person is absent.
Variable	A characteristic or aspect in which people, objects, events, or conditions vary is called variable.
Nerve	A nerve is an enclosed, cable-like bundle of nerve fibers or axons, which includes the glia that ensheath the axons in myelin.
Spinal nerve	The spinal nerve is usually a mized nerve, formed from the dorsal and ventral roots that come out of the spinal cord.
Isometric exercise	Isometric exercise is a form of physical exercise in which the muscles flex and hold a stationary position. No movement of a load takes place, and the exercises require little in the way of equipment.
Specificity	A medical diagnostic test for a certain disease, specificity is the proportion of true negatives of all the negative samples tested.
Isometric contraction	A muscle contraction in which there is no movement and the length of the muscle does not change is an isometric contraction.
Symmetry	Symmetry is the balanced distribution of duplicate body parts or shapes from one side of the body to the other.
Medicine	Medicine is the branch of health science and the sector of public life concerned with maintaining or restoring human health through the study, diagnosis and treatment of disease and injury.
Gill	An extension of the body surface of an aquatic animal, specialized for gas exchange and/or suspension feeding is called a gill.
Identical twins	Identical twins occur when a single egg is fertilized to form one zygote (monozygotic) but the zygote then divides into two separate embryos.
Syndrome	Syndrome is the association of several clinically recognizable features, signs, symptoms, phenomena or characteristics which often occur together, so that the presence of one feature alerts the physician to the presence of the others
Protocol	Protocol is a document with the aim of guiding decisions and criteria in specific areas of healthcare, as defined by an authoritative examination of current evidence. It details the activities to be executed in specific situations.
Rehabilitation	Rehabilitation is the restoration of lost capabilities, or the treatment aimed at producing it. Also refers to treatment for dependency on psychoactive substances such as alcohol, prescription drugs, and illicit drugs such as cocaine, heroin or amphetamines.
Assessment	In clinical practice, the process by which a mental health professional gathers and compiles information about a client for the purpose of describing the person's problems or disorder and developing a plan of treatment is an assessment.

Aerobic	An aerobic organism is an organism that has an oxygen based metabolism. Aerobes, in a process known as cellular respiration, use oxygen to oxidize substrates (for example sugars and fats) in order to obtain energy.
Aerobic exercise	Exercise in which oxygen is used to produce ATP is aerobic exercise.
Lifestyle	The culturally, socially, economically, and environmentally conditioned complex of actions characteristic of an individual, group, or community as a pattern of habituated behavior over time that is health related but not necessarily health directed is a lifestyle.
Health	Health is a term that refers to a combination of the absence of illness, the ability to cope with everyday activities, physical fitness, and high quality of life.
Affect	Affect is the scientific term used to describe a subject's externally displayed mood. This can be assesed by the nurse by observing facial expression, tone of voice, and body language.
Relapse prevention	Extending therapeutic progress by teaching the client how to cope with future troubling situations is a relapse prevention technique.
Outcome	Outcome is the impact of care provided to a patient. They can be positive, such as the ability to walk freely as a result of rehabilitation, or negative, such as the occurrence of bedsores as a result of lack of mobility of a patient.
Health outcome	Any medically or epidemiologically defined characteristic of a patient or population that results from health promotion or care provided or required, as measured at one point in time is a health outcome.
Variable	A characteristic or aspect in which people, objects, events, or conditions vary is called variable.
Population	Population refers to all members of a well-defined group of organisms, events, or things.
Lead	Lead is a chemical element in the periodic table that has the symbol Pb and atomic number 82. A soft, heavy, toxic and malleable poor metal, lead is bluish white when freshly cut but tarnishes to dull gray when exposed to air. Lead is used in building construction, lead-acid batteries, bullets and shot, and is part of solder, pewter, and fusible alloys.
Certification	A professional certification, trade certification, or professional designation often called simply certification or qualification is a designation earned by a person to certify that he is qualified to perform a job. Certification indicates that the individual has a specific knowledge, skills, or abilities in the view of the certifying body.
Base	The common definition of a base is a chemical compound that absorbs hydronium ions when dissolved in water (a proton acceptor). An alkali is a special example of a base, where in an aqueous environment, hydroxide ions are donated.
Knowledge base	The general background knowledge a person possesses, which influences most cognitive task performance is called knowledge base.
Rapport	Rapport is one of the most important features or characteristics of unconscious human interaction. It is commonality of perspective, being in "sync", being on the same wavelength as the person you are talking to.
Empathy	Empathy refers to reacting to another's feelings with an emotional response that is similar to the other's response.
Value	Value is worth in general, and it is thought to be connected to reasons for certain practices, policies, actions, beliefs or emotions. Value is "that which one acts to gain and/or keep."
Incentive	Incentive refers to an object, person, or situation perceived as being capable of satisfying

	a need.
Planning	In agreement with the patient, the nurse addresses each of the problems identified in the planning phase. For each problem a measurable goal is set. For example, for the patient discussed above, the goal would be for the patient's skin to remain intact. The result is a nursing care plan. This is the third step.
Stimulus	Stimulus in a nervous system, a factor that triggers sensory transduction.
Individual differences	The stable, consistent ways that people are different from each other are called individual differences.
Adaptation	A biological adaptation is an anatomical structure, physiological process or behavioral trait of an organism that has evolved over a period of time by the process of natural selection such that it increases the expected long-term reproductive success of the organism.
Adjustment	Adjustment is an attempt to cope with a given situation.
Pain	Pain is an unpleasant sensation which may be associated with actual or potential tissue damage and which may have physical and emotional components.
Thrill	Thrill is a vibration felt when the hand is placed flat on the chest; caused by abnormal blood flow through the heart as a result of disease.
Heart rate	Heart rate is a term used to describe the frequency of the cardiac cycle. It is considered one of the four vital signs. Usually it is calculated as the number of contractions of the heart in one minute and expressed as "beats per minute".
Constant	A behavior or characteristic that does not vary from one observation to another is referred to as a constant.
Criterion	Criterion refers to a standard of comparison. For performance appraisal, it is the definition of good performance.
Shock	Circulatory shock, a state of cardiac output that is insufficient to meet the body's physiological needs, with consequences ranging from fainting to death is referred to as shock. Insulin shock, a state of severe hypoglycemia caused by administration of insulin.
Stress	Stress refers to a condition that is a response to factors that change the human systems normal state.
Joint	A joint (articulation) is the location at which two bones make contact (articulate). They are constructed to both allow movement and provide mechanical support.
Hip	In anatomy, the hip is the bony projection of the femur, known as the greater trochanter, and the overlying muscle and fat.
Flexion	In anatomy, Flexion is movement whereby bones or other parts of the body, including the trunk, are brought closer together by decreasing the joint angle. The opposite term is extention, or straightening.
Stroke	A stroke or cerebrovascular accident (CVA) occurs when the blood supply to a part of the brain is suddenly interrupted.
Coronary	Referring to the heart or the blood vessels of the heart is referred to as coronary.
Muscle	Muscle is a contractile form of tissue. It is one of the four major tissue types, the other three being epithelium, connective tissue and nervous tissue. Muscle contraction is used to move parts of the body, as well as to move substances within the body.
Resistance	Resistance refers to a nonspecific ability to ward off infection or disease regardless of whether the body has been previously exposed to it. A force that opposes the flow of a fluid

Go to **Cram101.com** for the Practice Tests for this Chapter.

such as air or blood. Compare with immunity.

Bypass	In medicine, a bypass generally means an alternate or additional route for blood flow, which is created in bypass surgery, e.g. coronary artery bypass surgery by moving blood vessels or implanting synthetic tubing.
Pulse	The rhythmic stretching of the arteries caused by the pressure of blood forced through the arteries by contractions of the ventricles during systole is a pulse.
Interest groups	Groups organized to pursue specific interests in the political arena are referred to as interest groups.
Interest group	Interest group refers to an organization that attempts to affect political decisions by supporting candidates sympathetic to their interests and by influencing those already in positions of authority.
Acute	In medicine, an acute disease is a disease with either or both of: a rapid onset; and a short course (as opposed to a chronic course).
Hypertension	Hypertension is a medical condition where the blood pressure in the arteries is chronically elevated. Persistent hypertension is one of the risk factors for strokes, heart attacks, heart failure and arterial aneurysm, and is a leading cause of chronic renal failure.
Pelvis	The pelvis is the bony structure located at the base of the spine (properly known as the caudal end). The pelvis incorporates the socket portion of the hip joint for each leg (in bipeds) or hind leg (in quadrupeds). It forms the lower limb (or hind-limb) girdle of the skeleton.
Eye	An eye is an organ that detects light. Different kinds of light-sensitive organs are found in a variety of creatures. The simplest eyes do nothing but detect whether the surroundings are light or dark, while more complex eyes can distinguish shapes and colors.
Conditioning	Processes by which behaviors can be learned or modified through interaction with the environment are conditioning.
Fraud	In the broadest sense, a fraud is a deception made for personal gain, although it has a more specific legal meaning, the exact details varying between jurisdictions.
Calorie	Calorie refers to a unit used to measure heat energy and the energy contents of foods.
Rotation	Movement turning a body part on its longitudinal axis is rotation.
Course	Pattern of development and change of a disorder over time is a course.
Case study	A carefully drawn biography that may be obtained through interviews, questionnaires, and psychological tests is called a case study.
Medicine	Medicine is the branch of health science and the sector of public life concerned with maintaining or restoring human health through the study, diagnosis and treatment of disease and injury.
Behavior modification	Behavior Modification is a technique of altering an individual's reactions to stimuli through positive reinforcement and the extinction of maladaptive behavior.

Health	Health is a term that refers to a combination of the absence of illness, the ability to cope with everyday activities, physical fitness, and high quality of life.
Test battery	A group of tests and interviews given to the same individual is a test battery.
Induction	A discipline technique in which a parent uses reason and explanation of the consequences for others of a child's actions is called induction.
Power test	A test without a time limit is referred to as a power test.
Criterion	Criterion refers to a standard of comparison. For performance appraisal, it is the definition of good performance.
Body mass index	Body mass index refers to a number derived from an individual's weight and height used to estimate body fat. The formula is- weight /height' .
Aerobic	An aerobic organism is an organism that has an oxygen based metabolism. Aerobes, in a process known as cellular respiration, use oxygen to oxidize substrates (for example sugars and fats) in order to obtain energy.
Diabetes	Diabetes is a medical disorder characterized by varying or persistent elevated blood sugar levels, especially after eating. All types of diabetes share similar symptoms and complications at advanced stages: dehydration and ketoacidosis, cardiovascular disease, chronic renal failure, retinal damage which can lead to blindness, nerve damage which can lead to erectile dysfunction, gangrene with risk of amputation of toes, feet, and even legs.
Epidemic	An epidemic is a disease that appears as new cases in a given human population, during a given period, at a rate that substantially exceeds what is "expected", based on recent experience.
Obesity	The state of being more than 20 percent above the average weight for a person of one's height is called obesity.
Public health	Public health is concerned with threats to the overall health of a community based on population health analysis.
Hypertension	Hypertension is a medical condition where the blood pressure in the arteries is chronically elevated. Persistent hypertension is one of the risk factors for strokes, heart attacks, heart failure and arterial aneurysm, and is a leading cause of chronic renal failure.
Risk factor	A risk factor is a variable associated with an increased risk of disease or infection but risk factors are not necessarily causal.
Outcome	Outcome is the impact of care provided to a patient. They can be positive, such as the ability to walk freely as a result of rehabilitation, or negative, such as the occurrence of bedsores as a result of lack of mobility of a patient.
Lifestyle	The culturally, socially, economically, and environmentally conditioned complex of actions characteristic of an individual, group, or community as a pattern of habituated behavior over time that is health related but not necessarily health directed is a lifestyle.
Aerobic exercise	Exercise in which oxygen is used to produce ATP is aerobic exercise.
Stress	Stress refers to a condition that is a response to factors that change the human systems normal state.
Muscle	Muscle is a contractile form of tissue. It is one of the four major tissue types, the other three being epithelium, connective tissue and nervous tissue. Muscle contraction is used to move parts of the body, as well as to move substances within the body.
Resistance	Resistance refers to a nonspecific ability to ward off infection or disease regardless of whether the body has been previously exposed to it. A force that opposes the flow of a fluid

Go to **Cram101.com** for the Practice Tests for this Chapter.

such as air or blood. Compare with immunity.

Adolescence	Adolescence is the period of psychological and social transition between childhood and adulthood (gender-specific manhood, or womanhood). As a transitional stage of human development it represents the period of time during which a juvenile matures into adulthood.
Medicine	Medicine is the branch of health science and the sector of public life concerned with maintaining or restoring human health through the study, diagnosis and treatment of disease and injury.
Centers for Disease Control and Prevention	The Centers for Disease Control and Prevention in Atlanta, Georgia, is recognized as the lead United States agency for protecting the public health and safety of people by providing credible information to enhance health decisions, and promoting health through strong partnerships with state health departments and other organizations.
Morbidity	Morbidity refers to any condition that causes illness.
Mortality	The incidence of death in a population is mortality.
Consensus	General agreement is a consensus.
Health promotion	Any planned combination of educational, political, regulatory, and organizational supports for actions and conditions of living conducive to the health of individuals, groups, or communities is called health promotion.
Chronic disease	Disease of long duration often not detected in its early stages and from which the patient will not recover is referred to as a chronic disease.
Human development	The lifelong process of physical, cognitive, and social growth and development is human development.

Go to **Cram101.com** for the Practice Tests for this Chapter.

Population	Population refers to all members of a well-defined group of organisms, events, or things.
Individual differences	The stable, consistent ways that people are different from each other are called individual differences.
Medicine	Medicine is the branch of health science and the sector of public life concerned with maintaining or restoring human health through the study, diagnosis and treatment of disease and injury.
Lead	Lead is a chemical element in the periodic table that has the symbol Pb and atomic number 82. A soft, heavy, toxic and malleable poor metal, lead is bluish white when freshly cut but tarnishes to dull gray when exposed to air. Lead is used in building construction, lead-acid batteries, bullets and shot, and is part of solder, pewter, and fusible alloys.
Health	Health is a term that refers to a combination of the absence of illness, the ability to cope with everyday activities, physical fitness, and high quality of life.
Housework	Unpaid work carried on in and around the home such as cooking, cleaning and shopping, is referred to as a housework.
Activities of daily living	Activities of daily living is a way to describe the functional status of a person.
Chronic disease	Disease of long duration often not detected in its early stages and from which the patient will not recover is referred to as a chronic disease.
Intervention	Intervention refers to a planned attempt to break through addicts' or abusers' denial and get them into treatment. Interventions most often occur when legal, workplace, health, relationship, or financial problems have become intolerable.
Morbidity	Morbidity refers to any condition that causes illness.
Lifestyle	The culturally, socially, economically, and environmentally conditioned complex of actions characteristic of an individual, group, or community as a pattern of habituated behavior over time that is health related but not necessarily health directed is a lifestyle.
Aerobic	An aerobic organism is an organism that has an oxygen based metabolism. Aerobes, in a process known as cellular respiration, use oxygen to oxidize substrates (for example sugars and fats) in order to obtain energy.
Affect	Affect is the scientific term used to describe a subject's externally displayed mood. This can be assesed by the nurse by observing facial expression, tone of voice, and body language.
Oxygen	Oxygen is a chemical element in the periodic table. It has the symbol O and atomic number 8. Oxygen is the second most common element on Earth, composing around 46% of the mass of Earth's crust and 28% of the mass of Earth as a whole, and is the third most common element in the universe.
Cardiac output	Cardiac output is the volume of blood being pumped by the heart in a minute. It is equal to the heart rate multiplied by the stroke volume.
Young adult	An young adult is someone between the ages of 20 and 40 years old.
Capillary	A capillary is the smallest of a body's blood vessels, measuring 5-10 micro meters. They connect arteries and veins, and most closely interact with tissues. Their walls are composed of a single layer of cells, the endothelium. This layer is so thin that molecules such as oxygen, water and lipids can pass through them by diffusion and enter the tissues.
Enzyme	An enzyme is a protein that catalyzes, or speeds up, a chemical reaction. They are essential to sustain life because most chemical reactions in biological cells would occur too slowly, or would lead to different products, without them.

Diabetes	Diabetes is a medical disorder characterized by varying or persistent elevated blood sugar levels, especially after eating. All types of diabetes share similar symptoms and complications at advanced stages: dehydration and ketoacidosis, cardiovascular disease, chronic renal failure, retinal damage which can lead to blindness, nerve damage which can lead to erectile dysfunction, gangrene with risk of amputation of toes, feet, and even legs.
Atrophy	Atrophy is the partial or complete wasting away of a part of the body. Causes of atrophy include poor nourishment, poor circulation, loss of hormonal support, loss of nerve supply to the target organ, disuse or lack of exercise, or disease intrinsic to the tissue itself.
Muscle	Muscle is a contractile form of tissue. It is one of the four major tissue types, the other three being epithelium, connective tissue and nervous tissue. Muscle contraction is used to move parts of the body, as well as to move substances within the body.
Fiber	Fibers used by man come from a wide variety of sources: Natural fiber include those made out of plants, animal and mineral sources. Natural fibers can be classified according to their origin.
Metabolic rate	Energy expended by the body per unit time is called metabolic rate.
Distribution	Distribution in pharmacology is a branch of pharmacokinetics describing reversible transfer of drug from one location to another within the body.
Hypertension	Hypertension is a medical condition where the blood pressure in the arteries is chronically elevated. Persistent hypertension is one of the risk factors for strokes, heart attacks, heart failure and arterial aneurysm, and is a leading cause of chronic renal failure.
Muscle fiber	Cell with myofibrils containing actin and myosin filaments arranged within sarcomeres is a muscle fiber.
Resistance	Resistance refers to a nonspecific ability to ward off infection or disease regardless of whether the body has been previously exposed to it. A force that opposes the flow of a fluid such as air or blood. Compare with immunity.
Motor unit	A motor neuron and all the muscle fibers it controls is called the motor unit.
Skeletal muscle	Skeletal muscle is a type of striated muscle, attached to the skeleton. They are used to facilitate movement, by applying force to bones and joints; via contraction. They generally contract voluntarily (via nerve stimulation), although they can contract involuntarily.
Neural adaptation	Neural adaptation refers to a temporary change of the neural response to a stimulus as the result of preceding stimulation.
Adaptation	A biological adaptation is an anatomical structure, physiological process or behavioral trait of an organism that has evolved over a period of time by the process of natural selection such that it increases the expected long-term reproductive success of the organism.
Elderly	Old age consists of ages nearing the average life span of human beings, and thus the end of the human life cycle. Euphemisms for older people include advanced adult, elderly, and senior or senior citizen.
Conditioning	Processes by which behaviors can be learned or modified through interaction with the environment are conditioning.
Longitudinal study	Longitudinal study refers to a type of developmental study in which the same group of participants is followed and measured at different ages.
Bone mineral density	A bone mineral density test is used to measure bone density and determine fracture risk for osteoporosis.
Cardiovascular	Cardiovascular disease refers to afflictions in the mechanisms, including the heart, blood

Go to **Cram101.com** for the Practice Tests for this Chapter.

disease	vessels, and their controllers, that are responsible for transporting blood to the body's tissues and organs. Psychological factors may play important roles in such diseases and their treatments.
Menopause	Menopause is the physiological cessation of menstrual cycles associated with advancing age in species that experience such cycles. Menopause is sometimes referred to as change of life or climacteric.
Calcium	Calcium is the chemical element in the periodic table that has the symbol Ca and atomic number 20. Calcium is a soft grey alkaline earth metal that is used as a reducing agent in the extraction of thorium, zirconium and uranium. Calcium is also the fifth most abundant element in the Earth's crust.
Estrogen	Estrogen is a steroid that functions as the primary female sex hormone. While present in both men and women, they are found in women in significantly higher quantities.
Hormone	A hormone is a chemical messenger from one cell to another. All multicellular organisms produce hormones. The best known hormones are those produced by endocrine glands of vertebrate animals, but hormones are produced by nearly every organ system and tissue type in a human or animal body. Hormone molecules are secreted directly into the bloodstream, they move by circulation or diffusion to their target cells, which may be nearby cells in the same tissue or cells of a distant organ of the body.
Hormone replacement therapy	Hormone replacement therapy is a system of medical treatment for perimenopausal and postmenopausal women, based on the assumption that it may prevent discomfort and health problems caused by diminished circulating estrogen hormones.
Testosterone	Testosterone is a steroid hormone from the androgen group. Testosterone is secreted in the testes of men and the ovaries of women. It is the principal male sex hormone and the "original" anabolic steroid. In both males and females, it plays key roles in health and well-being.
Research design	A research design tests a hypothesis. The basic typess are: descriptive, correlational, and experimental.
Variability	Statistically, variability refers to how much the scores in a distribution spread out, away from the mean.
Assessment	In clinical practice, the process by which a mental health professional gathers and compiles information about a client for the purpose of describing the person's problems or disorder and developing a plan of treatment is an assessment.
Independence	The condition in which one variable has no effect on another is referred to as independence.
Risk factor	A risk factor is a variable associated with an increased risk of disease or infection but risk factors are not necessarily causal.
Glucose	Glucose, a simple monosaccharide sugar, is one of the most important carbohydrates and is used as a source of energy in animals and plants. Glucose is one of the main products of photosynthesis and starts respiration.
Cancer	Cancer is a class of diseases or disorders characterized by uncontrolled division of cells and the ability of these cells to invade other tissues, either by direct growth into adjacent tissue through invasion or by implantation into distant sites by metastasis.
Atherosclerosis	Process by which a fatty substance or plaque builds up inside arteries to form obstructions is called atherosclerosis.
Lung cancer	Lung cancer is a malignant tumour of the lungs. Most commonly it is bronchogenic carcinoma (about 90%).

Go to **Cram101.com** for the Practice Tests for this Chapter.

Intolerance	Intolerance refers to a type of interaction in which two or more drugs produce extremely uncomfortable symptoms.
Incidence	In epidemiological studies of a particular disorder, the rate at which new cases occur in a given place at a given time is called incidence.
Arthritis	Arthritis is a group of conditions that affect the health of the bone joints in the body. Arthritis can be caused from strains and injuries caused by repetitive motion, sports, overexertion, and falls. Unlike the autoimmune diseases, it largely affects older people and results from the degeneration of joint cartilage.
Hip	In anatomy, the hip is the bony projection of the femur, known as the greater trochanter, and the overlying muscle and fat.
Value	Value is worth in general, and it is thought to be connected to reasons for certain practices, policies, actions, beliefs or emotions. Value is "that which one acts to gain and/or keep."
Steady state	Steady state is a system in which a particular variable is not changing but energy must be continuously added to maintain this variable constant.
Clinician	A health professional authorized to provide services to people suffering from one or more pathologies is a clinician.
Coronary	Referring to the heart or the blood vessels of the heart is referred to as coronary.
Artery	Vessel that takes blood away from the heart to the tissues and organs of the body is called an artery.
Coronary artery	An artery that supplies blood to the wall of the heart is called a coronary artery.
Chronic obstructive pulmonary disease	Chronic obstructive pulmonary disease is an umbrella term for a group of respiratory tract diseases that are characterized by airflow obstruction or limitation. It is usually caused by tobacco smoking.
Coronary artery disease	Coronary artery disease (CAD) is the end result of the accumulation of atheromatous plaques within the walls of the arteries that supply the myocardium (the muscle of the heart).
Socialization	Socialization refers to guidance of people into socially desirable behavior by means of verbal messages, the systematic use of rewards and punishments, and other methods of teaching.
Physical therapy	Physical therapy is a health profession concerned with the assessment, diagnosis, and treatment of disease and disability through physical means. It is based upon principles of medical science, and is generally held to be within the sphere of conventional medicine.
Course	Pattern of development and change of a disorder over time is a course.
Aerobic endurance	The length of time a muscle can continue to contract using aerobic pathways is referred to as aerobic endurance.
Base	The common definition of a base is a chemical compound that absorbs hydronium ions when dissolved in water (a proton acceptor). An alkali is a special example of a base, where in an aqueous environment, hydroxide ions are donated.
Joint	A joint (articulation) is the location at which two bones make contact (articulate). They are constructed to both allow movement and provide mechanical support.
Rehabilitation	Rehabilitation is the restoration of lost capabilities, or the treatment aimed at producing it. Also refers to treatment for dependency on psychoactive substances such as alcohol, prescription drugs, and illicit drugs such as cocaine, heroin or amphetamines.

Go to **Cram101.com** for the Practice Tests for this Chapter.

Articular	The articular is a bone in the lower jaw of most tetrapods, including reptiles, birds, and amphibians, but has become a middle ear bone (the malleus) in mammals. It is the site of articulation between the lower jaw and the skull, and is connected to two other lower jaw bones, the suprangular and the angular.
Cartilage	Cartilage is a type of dense connective tissue. Cartilage is composed of cells called chondrocytes which are dispersed in a firm gel-like ground substance, called the matrix. Cartilage is avascular (contains no blood vessels) and nutrients are diffused through the matrix.
Osteoarthritis	Osteoarthritis is a condition in which low-grade inflammation results in pain in the joints, caused by wearing of the cartilage that covers and acts as a cushion inside joints.
Proprioception	Proprioception is the sense of the position of parts of the body, relative to other parts of the body. Unlike the six exteroception senses of sight, taste, smell, touch, hearing, and balance, that advise us of the outside world, proprioception is a sense that provides feedback solely on the status of the body internally.
Older adult	Older adult is an adult over the age of 65.
Pain	Pain is an unpleasant sensation which may be associated with actual or potential tissue damage and which may have physical and emotional components.
Inflammation	Inflammation is the first response of the immune system to infection or irritation and may be referred to as the innate cascade.
Trauma	Trauma refers to a severe physical injury or wound to the body caused by an external force, or a psychological shock having a lasting effect on mental life.
Quality of life	Quality of life refers to the perception of individuals or groups that their needs are being satisfied and that they are not being denied opportunities to achieve happiness and fulfillment.
Human development	The lifelong process of physical, cognitive, and social growth and development is human development.
Certification	A professional certification, trade certification, or professional designation often called simply certification or qualification is a designation earned by a person to certify that he is qualified to perform a job. Certification indicates that the individual has a specific knowledge, skills, or abilities in the view of the certifying body.
Physiology	The study of the function of cells, tissues, and organs is referred to as physiology.
Hypertrophy	Hypertrophy is the increase of the size of an organ. It should be distinguished from hyperplasia which occurs due to cell division; hypertrophy occurs due to an increase in cell size rather than division. It is most commonly seen in muscle that has been actively stimulated, the most well-known method being exercise.
Public health	Public health is concerned with threats to the overall health of a community based on population health analysis.
Centers for Disease Control and Prevention	The Centers for Disease Control and Prevention in Atlanta, Georgia, is recognized as the lead United States agency for protecting the public health and safety of people by providing credible information to enhance health decisions, and promoting health through strong partnerships with state health departments and other organizations.

Go to **Cram101.com** for the Practice Tests for this Chapter.

Health	Health is a term that refers to a combination of the absence of illness, the ability to cope with everyday activities, physical fitness, and high quality of life.
Cardiovascular disease	Cardiovascular disease refers to afflictions in the mechanisms, including the heart, blood vessels, and their controllers, that are responsible for transporting blood to the body's tissues and organs. Psychological factors may play important roles in such diseases and their treatments.
Rehabilitation	Rehabilitation is the restoration of lost capabilities, or the treatment aimed at producing it. Also refers to treatment for dependency on psychoactive substances such as alcohol, prescription drugs, and illicit drugs such as cocaine, heroin or amphetamines.
Population	Population refers to all members of a well-defined group of organisms, events, or things.
Mental health	Mental health refers to the 'thinking' part of psychosocial health; includes your values, attitudes, and beliefs.
Stress	Stress refers to a condition that is a response to factors that change the human systems normal state.
Secondary prevention	Psychological counseling, psychotropic medications, and other rehabilitation treatment programs designed to prevent repeat offenses are called secondary prevention.
Aerobic	An aerobic organism is an organism that has an oxygen based metabolism. Aerobes, in a process known as cellular respiration, use oxygen to oxidize substrates (for example sugars and fats) in order to obtain energy.
Aerobic exercise	Exercise in which oxygen is used to produce ATP is aerobic exercise.
Coronary	Referring to the heart or the blood vessels of the heart is referred to as coronary.
Coronary heart disease	Coronary heart disease is the end result of the accumulation of atheromatous plaques within the walls of the arteries that supply the myocardium (the muscle of the heart).
Fibrosis	Replacement of damaged tissue with fibrous scar tissue rather than by the original tissue type is called fibrosis.
Artery	Vessel that takes blood away from the heart to the tissues and organs of the body is called an artery.
Lipid	Lipid is one class of aliphatic hydrocarbon-containing organic compounds essential for the structure and function of living cells. They are characterized by being water-insoluble but soluble in nonpolar organic solvents.
Atherosclerosis	Process by which a fatty substance or plaque builds up inside arteries to form obstructions is called atherosclerosis.
Blood	Blood is a circulating tissue composed of fluid plasma and cells. The main function of blood is to supply nutrients (oxygen, glucose) and constitutional elements to tissues and to remove waste products.
Agent	Agent refers to an epidemiological term referring to the organism or object that transmits a disease from the environment to the host.
Coronary arteries	Arteries that directly supply the heart with blood are referred to as coronary arteries.
Endothelial cell	A endothelial cell also controls the passage of materials — and the transit of white blood cells — into and out of the bloodstream. In some organs, there are highly differentiated endothelial cells to perform specialized 'filtering' functions.
Coronary artery	An artery that supplies blood to the wall of the heart is called a coronary artery.

Go to **Cram101.com** for the Practice Tests for this Chapter.

Blood pressure	Blood pressure is the pressure exerted by the blood on the walls of the blood vessels.
Hypertension	Hypertension is a medical condition where the blood pressure in the arteries is chronically elevated. Persistent hypertension is one of the risk factors for strokes, heart attacks, heart failure and arterial aneurysm, and is a leading cause of chronic renal failure.
Lipoprotein	A lipoprotein is a biochemical assembly that contains both proteins and lipids and may be structural or catalytic in function. They may be enzymes, proton pumps, ion pumps, or some combination of these functions.
Occlusion	The term occlusion is often used to refer to blood vessels, arteries or veins which have become totally blocked to any blood flow.
Ischemia	Narrowing of arteries caused by plaque buildup within the arteries is called ischemia.
Stroke	A stroke or cerebrovascular accident (CVA) occurs when the blood supply to a part of the brain is suddenly interrupted.
Lead	Lead is a chemical element in the periodic table that has the symbol Pb and atomic number 82. A soft, heavy, toxic and malleable poor metal, lead is bluish white when freshly cut but tarnishes to dull gray when exposed to air. Lead is used in building construction, lead-acid batteries, bullets and shot, and is part of solder, pewter, and fusible alloys.
Myocardial infarction	Acute myocardial infarction, commonly known as a heart attack, is a serious, sudden heart condition usually characterized by varying degrees of chest pain or discomfort, weakness, sweating, nausea, vomiting, and arrhythmias, sometimes causing loss of consciousness.
Blood vessel	A blood vessel is a part of the circulatory system and function to transport blood throughout the body. The most important types, arteries and veins, are so termed because they carry blood away from or towards the heart, respectively.
Infarction	The sudden death of tissue from a lack of blood perfusion is referred to as an infarction.
Muscle	Muscle is a contractile form of tissue. It is one of the four major tissue types, the other three being epithelium, connective tissue and nervous tissue. Muscle contraction is used to move parts of the body, as well as to move substances within the body.
Pain	Pain is an unpleasant sensation which may be associated with actual or potential tissue damage and which may have physical and emotional components.
Obesity	The state of being more than 20 percent above the average weight for a person of one's height is called obesity.
Calorie	Calorie refers to a unit used to measure heat energy and the energy contents of foods.
Sodium	Sodium is the chemical element in the periodic table that has the symbol Na (Natrium in Latin) and atomic number 11. Sodium is a soft, waxy, silvery reactive metal belonging to the alkali metals that is abundant in natural compounds (especially halite). It is highly reactive.
Congestive heart failure	Congestive heart failure is the inability of the heart to pump a sufficient amount of blood throughout the body, or requiring elevated filling pressures in order to pump effectively.
Coronary artery disease	Coronary artery disease (CAD) is the end result of the accumulation of atheromatous plaques within the walls of the arteries that supply the myocardium (the muscle of the heart).
Heart attack	A heart attack, is a serious, sudden heart condition usually characterized by varying degrees of chest pain or discomfort, weakness, sweating, nausea, vomiting, and arrhythmias, sometimes causing loss of consciousness. It occurs when the blood supply to a part of the heart is interrupted, causing death and scarring of the local heart tissue.
Brain	The part of the central nervous system involved in regulating and controlling body activity

	and interpreting information from the senses transmitted through the nervous system is referred to as the brain.
Angina	Angina pectoris is chest pain due to ischemia (a lack of blood and hence oxygen supply) to the heart muscle, generally due to obstruction or spasm of the coronary arteries (the heart's blood vessels). Coronary artery disease, the main cause of angina, is due to atherosclerosis of the cardiac arteries.
Bypass	In medicine, a bypass generally means an alternate or additional route for blood flow, which is created in bypass surgery, e.g. coronary artery bypass surgery by moving blood vessels or implanting synthetic tubing.
Angina pectoris	Angina pectoris is chest pain due to ischemia (a lack of blood and hence oxygen supply) to the heart muscle, generally due to obstruction or spasm of the coronary arteries (the heart's blood vessels).
Angioplasty	Angioplasty is the mechanical, hydraulic dilation of a narrowed or totally obstructed arterial lumen, generally caused by atheroma (the lesion of atherosclerosis).
Ventricle	In the heart, a ventricle is a heart chamber which collects blood from an atrium (another heart chamber) and pumps it out of the heart.
Oxygen	Oxygen is a chemical element in the periodic table. It has the symbol O and atomic number 8. Oxygen is the second most common element on Earth, composing around 46% of the mass of Earth's crust and 28% of the mass of Earth as a whole, and is the third most common element in the universe.
Value	Value is worth in general, and it is thought to be connected to reasons for certain practices, policies, actions, beliefs or emotions. Value is "that which one acts to gain and/or keep."
Fiber	Fibers used by man come from a wide variety of sources: Natural fiber include those made out of plants, animal and mineral sources. Natural fibers can be classified according to their origin.
Muscle fiber	Cell with myofibrils containing actin and myosin filaments arranged within sarcomeres is a muscle fiber.
Tissue	A collection of interconnected cells that perform a similar function within an organism is called tissue.
Irritability	Irritability is an excessive response to stimuli. Irritability takes many forms, from the contraction of a unicellular organism when touched to complex reactions involving all the senses of higher animals.
Arrhythmias	Arrhythmias refers to abnormal heart rhythms which may be too slow, too early, too rapid, or irregular.
Arrhythmia	Cardiac arrhythmia is a group of conditions in which muscle contraction of the heart is irregular for any reason.
Vein	Vein in animals, is a vessel that returns blood to the heart. In plants, a vascular bundle in a leaf, composed of xylem and phloem.
Coronary artery bypass surgery	Coronary artery bypass surgery is a surgical procedure performed on patients with coronary artery disease (see atherosclerosis) for the relief of angina and possible improved heart muscle function.
Concept	A mental category used to class together objects, relations, events, abstractions, or qualities that have common properties is called concept.

Go to **Cram101.com** for the Practice Tests for this Chapter.

Percutaneous	In surgery, percutaneous pertains to any medical procedure where access to inner organs or other tissue is done via needle-puncture of the skin, rather than by using an "open" approach where inner organs or tissue are exposed (typically with the use of a scalpel).
Stent	In medicine, a stent is either an expandable wire mesh or hollow perforated tube that is inserted into a hollow structure of the body to keep it open.
Catheter	A tubular surgical instrument for withdrawing fluids from a cavity of the body, especially one for introduction into the bladder through the urethra for the withdrawal of urine is referred to as a catheter.
Blood clot	A blood clot is the final product of the blood coagulation step in hemostasis. It is achieved via the aggregation of platelets that form a platelet plug, and the activation of the humoral coagulation system
Mortality	The incidence of death in a population is mortality.
Lifestyle	The culturally, socially, economically, and environmentally conditioned complex of actions characteristic of an individual, group, or community as a pattern of habituated behavior over time that is health related but not necessarily health directed is a lifestyle.
Intervention	Intervention refers to a planned attempt to break through addicts' or abusers' denial and get them into treatment. Interventions most often occur when legal, workplace, health, relationship, or financial problems have become intolerable.
Electrocardi-gram	An electrocardiogram is a graphic produced by an electrocardiograph, which records the electrical voltage in the heart in the form of a continuous strip graph. It is the prime tool in cardiac electrophysiology, and has a prime function in screening and diagnosis of cardiovascular diseases..
Oscilloscope	An oscilloscope is a piece of electronic test equipment that allows signal voltages to be viewed, usually as a two-dimensional graph of one or more electrical potential differences (vertical axis) plotted as a function of time or of some other voltage (horizontal axis).
Advanced cardiac life support	Advanced cardiac life support (ACLS) is a detailed medical protocol for the provision of lifesaving cardiac care in settings ranging from the pre-hospital environment to the hospital setting.
Life support	Life support, in the medical field, refers to a set of therapies for preserving a patient's life when essential body systems are not functioning sufficiently to sustain life unaided.
Protocol	Protocol is a document with the aim of guiding decisions and criteria in specific areas of healthcare, as defined by an authoritative examination of current evidence. It details the activities to be executed in specific situations.
Depression	In everyday language depression refers to any downturn in mood, which may be relatively transitory and perhaps due to something trivial. This is differentiated from Clinical depression which is marked by symptoms that last two weeks or more and are so severe that they interfere with daily living.
Heart rate	Heart rate is a term used to describe the frequency of the cardiac cycle. It is considered one of the four vital signs. Usually it is calculated as the number of contractions of the heart in one minute and expressed as "beats per minute".
Thallium	Thallium is the chemical element in the periodic table that has the symbol Tl and atomic number 81. This soft gray malleable poor metal resembles tin but discolors when exposed to air. Thallium is highly toxic and is used in rat poisons and insecticides but since it might also cause cancer.
Myocardium	Myocardium is the muscular tissue of the heart. The myocardium is composed of specialized

Go to **Cram101.com** for the Practice Tests for this Chapter.

cardiac muscle cells with an ability not possessed by muscle tissue elsewhere in the body.

Potassium	Potassium is a chemical element in the periodic table. It has the symbol K (L. kalium) and atomic number 19. Potassium is a soft silvery-white metallic alkali metal that occurs naturally bound to other elements in seawater and many minerals.
Red blood cells	Red blood cells are the most common type of blood cell and are the vertebrate body's principal means of delivering oxygen from the lungs or gills to body tissues via the blood.
Red blood cell	The red blood cell is the most common type of blood cell and is the vertebrate body's principal means of delivering oxygen from the lungs or gills to body tissues via the blood.
Technetium	Technetium is a chemical element that has the symbol Tc and the atomic number 43. The chemical properties of this silvery grey, radioactive, crystalline transition metal are intermediate between rhenium and manganese. Its short-lived isotope 99mTc is used in nuclear medicine for a wide variety of diagnostic tests. ^{99}Tc is used as a gamma ray-free source of beta particles, and its pertechnetate ion (TcO$_4^-$) could find use as an anodic corrosion inhibitor for steel.
Aorta	The largest artery in the human body, the aorta originates from the left ventricle of the heart and brings oxygenated blood to all parts of the body in the systemic circulation.
Femoral artery	The femoral artery is a large artery of the thigh. It is a continuation of the external iliac artery, which comes from the abdominal aorta. The external iliac artery becomes known as the femoral artery after it passes the inguinal ligament.
Angiography	Angiography is a medical imaging technique in which an X-Ray picture is taken to visualize the inner opening of blood filled structures, including arteries, veins and the heart chambers.
Angiogram	The X-ray film or image of the blood vessels is called an angiograph, or more commonly, an angiogram.
Acute	In medicine, an acute disease is a disease with either or both of: a rapid onset; and a short course (as opposed to a chronic course).
Outpatient	Outpatient refers to a patient who requires treatment but does not need to be admitted into the institution for those sevices.
Conditioning	Processes by which behaviors can be learned or modified through interaction with the environment are conditioning.
Resistance	Resistance refers to a nonspecific ability to ward off infection or disease regardless of whether the body has been previously exposed to it. A force that opposes the flow of a fluid such as air or blood. Compare with immunity.
Triglyceride	Triglyceride is a glyceride in which the glycerol is esterified with three fatty acids. They are the main constituent of vegetable oil and animal fats and play an important role in metabolism as energy sources. They contain a bit more than twice as much energy as carbohydrates and proteins.
Cholesterol	Cholesterol is a steroid, a lipid, and an alcohol, found in the cell membranes of all body tissues, and transported in the blood plasma of all animals. It is an important component of the membranes of cells, providing stability; it makes the membrane's fluidity stable over a bigger temperature interval.
Left heart	Left heart is a term used to refer collectively to the left atrium and left ventricle of the heart; occasionally, this term is intended to reference the left atrium, left ventricle, and the aorta collectively.
Medicine	Medicine is the branch of health science and the sector of public life concerned with

	maintaining or restoring human health through the study, diagnosis and treatment of disease and injury.
Lifestyle changes	Lifestyle changes are changes to the way a person lives which are often called for when treating chronic disease.
Chronic disease	Disease of long duration often not detected in its early stages and from which the patient will not recover is referred to as a chronic disease.

Obesity	The state of being more than 20 percent above the average weight for a person of one's height is called obesity.
Etiology	The apparent causation and developmental history of an illness is an etiology.
Calorie	Calorie refers to a unit used to measure heat energy and the energy contents of foods.
Predisposition	Predisposition refers to an inclination or diathesis to respond in a certain way, either inborn or acquired. In abnormal psychology, it is a factor that lowers the ability to withstand stress and inclines the individual toward pathology.
Body image	A person's body image is their perception of their physical appearance. It is more than what a person thinks they will see in a mirror, it is inextricably tied to their self-esteem and acceptance by peers.
Lifestyle	The culturally, socially, economically, and environmentally conditioned complex of actions characteristic of an individual, group, or community as a pattern of habituated behavior over time that is health related but not necessarily health directed is a lifestyle.
Health	Health is a term that refers to a combination of the absence of illness, the ability to cope with everyday activities, physical fitness, and high quality of life.
Body mass index	Body mass index refers to a number derived from an individual's weight and height used to estimate body fat. The formula is- weight /height' .
Morbidity rate	Measures the number of individuals who become ill as a result of a particular disease within a susceptible population during a specific time period are morbidity rate.
Morbidity	Morbidity refers to any condition that causes illness.
Mortality	The incidence of death in a population is mortality.
Sleep apnea	Sleep apnea refers to a sleep disorder involving periods during sleep when breathing stops and the person must awaken briefly in order to breathe; major symptoms are excessive daytime sleepiness and loud snoring.
Diabetes	Diabetes is a medical disorder characterized by varying or persistent elevated blood sugar levels, especially after eating. All types of diabetes share similar symptoms and complications at advanced stages: dehydration and ketoacidosis, cardiovascular disease, chronic renal failure, retinal damage which can lead to blindness, nerve damage which can lead to erectile dysfunction, gangrene with risk of amputation of toes, feet, and even legs.
Cancer	Cancer is a class of diseases or disorders characterized by uncontrolled division of cells and the ability of these cells to invade other tissues, either by direct growth into adjacent tissue through invasion or by implantation into distant sites by metastasis.
Stroke	A stroke or cerebrovascular accident (CVA) occurs when the blood supply to a part of the brain is suddenly interrupted.
Apnea	Apnea is the absence of external breathing. During apnea there is no movement of the muscles of respiration and the volume of the lungs initially remains unchanged. .
Colon	The colon is the part of the intestine from the cecum to the rectum. Its primary purpose is to extract water from feces.
Osteoarthritis	Osteoarthritis is a condition in which low-grade inflammation results in pain in the joints, caused by wearing of the cartilage that covers and acts as a cushion inside joints.
Congestive heart failure	Congestive heart failure is the inability of the heart to pump a sufficient amount of blood throughout the body, or requiring elevated filling pressures in order to pump effectively.
Hypertension	Hypertension is a medical condition where the blood pressure in the arteries is chronically

elevated. Persistent hypertension is one of the risk factors for strokes, heart attacks, heart failure and arterial aneurysm, and is a leading cause of chronic renal failure.

Gallbladder

The gallbladder is a pear-shaped organ that stores bile until the body needs it for digestion. It is connected to the liver and the duodenum by the biliary tract.

Comorbidity

Comorbidity refers to the presence of more than one mental disorder occurring in an individual at the same time.

Prospective study

Prospective study is a long-term study of a group of people, beginning before the onset of a common disorder. It allows investigators to see how the disorder develops.

Population

Population refers to all members of a well-defined group of organisms, events, or things.

Trial

In classical conditioning, any presentation of a stimulus or pair of stimuli is called a trial.

Aerobic

An aerobic organism is an organism that has an oxygen based metabolism. Aerobes, in a process known as cellular respiration, use oxygen to oxidize substrates (for example sugars and fats) in order to obtain energy.

Aerobic exercise

Exercise in which oxygen is used to produce ATP is aerobic exercise.

Insight

Insight refers to a sudden awareness of the relationships among various elements that had previously appeared to be independent of one another.

Resistance

Resistance refers to a nonspecific ability to ward off infection or disease regardless of whether the body has been previously exposed to it. A force that opposes the flow of a fluid such as air or blood. Compare with immunity.

Ephedrine

Ephedrine (EPH) is a sympathomimetic amine commonly used as a decongestant and to treat hypotension associated with regional anaesthesia. Chemically, it is an alkaloid derived from various plants in the genus Ephedra (family Ephedraceae).

Protocol

Protocol is a document with the aim of guiding decisions and criteria in specific areas of healthcare, as defined by an authoritative examination of current evidence. It details the activities to be executed in specific situations.

Digestive system

The organ system that ingests food, breaks it down into smaller chemical units, and absorbs the nutrient molecules is referred to as the digestive system.

Absorption

Absorption is a physical or chemical phenomenon or a process in which atoms, molecules, or ions enter some bulk phase - gas, liquid or solid material. In nutrition, amino acids are broken down through digestion, which begins in the stomach.

Urgency

Urgency is an intense and sudden desire to urinate.

Brain

The part of the central nervous system involved in regulating and controlling body activity and interpreting information from the senses transmitted through the nervous system is referred to as the brain.

Neurotransmitter

A neurotransmitter is a chemical that is used to relay, amplify and modulate electrical signals between a neuron and another cell.

Norepinephrine

Norepinephrine is a catecholamine and a phenethylamine with chemical formula $C_8H_{11}NO_3$. It is released from the adrenal glands as a hormone into the blood, but it is also a neurotransmitter in the nervous system where it is released from noradrenergic neurons during synaptic transmission.

Serotonin

Serotonin is a monoamine neurotransmitter synthesized in serotonergic neurons in the central nervous system and enterochromaffin cells in the gastrointestinal tract. It is believed to play an important part in the biochemistry of depression, migraine, bipolar disorder and

anxiety.

Metabolic rate Energy expended by the body per unit time is called metabolic rate.

Conditioning Processes by which behaviors can be learned or modified through interaction with the environment are conditioning.

Thermoregulation Thermoregulation is the ability of an organism to keep its body temperature within certain boundaries, even when temperature surrounding is very different.

Tissue A collection of interconnected cells that perform a similar function within an organism is called tissue.

Muscle Muscle is a contractile form of tissue. It is one of the four major tissue types, the other three being epithelium, connective tissue and nervous tissue. Muscle contraction is used to move parts of the body, as well as to move substances within the body.

Minerals Minerals refer to inorganic chemical compounds found in nature; salts.

Planning In agreement with the patient, the nurse addresses each of the problems identified in the planning phase. For each problem a measurable goal is set. For example, for the patient discussed above, the goal would be for the patient's skin to remain intact. The result is a nursing care plan. This is the third step.

Vitamin An organic compound other than a carbohydrate, lipid, or protein that is needed for normal metabolism but that the body cannot synthesize in adequate amounts is called a vitamin.

Macronutrients Macrominerals are macronutrients that are chemical elements. They include calcium, magnesium, sodium, potassium, phosphorus and chlorine. They are dietary minerals needed by the human body in high quantities (generally more than 100 mg/day) as opposed to microminerals (trace elements) which are only required in very small amounts.

Macronutrient A chemical substance that an organism must obtain in relatively large amounts is referred to as macronutrient.

Saturated fat Saturated fat is fat that consists of triglycerides containing only fatty acids that have no double bonds between the carbon atoms of the fatty acid chain (hence, they are fully saturated with hydrogen atoms).

Distribution Distribution in pharmacology is a branch of pharmacokinetics describing reversible transfer of drug from one location to another within the body.

Lipid Lipid is one class of aliphatic hydrocarbon-containing organic compounds essential for the structure and function of living cells. They are characterized by being water-insoluble but soluble in nonpolar organic solvents.

Blood Blood is a circulating tissue composed of fluid plasma and cells. The main function of blood is to supply nutrients (oxygen, glucose) and constitutional elements to tissues and to remove waste products.

Stress Stress refers to a condition that is a response to factors that change the human systems normal state.

Stress management Stress management encompasses techniques intended to equip a person with effective coping mechanisms for dealing with psychological stress.

Outcome Outcome is the impact of care provided to a patient. They can be positive, such as the ability to walk freely as a result of rehabilitation, or negative, such as the occurrence of bedsores as a result of lack of mobility of a patient.

Menopause Menopause is the physiological cessation of menstrual cycles associated with advancing age in species that experience such cycles. Menopause is sometimes referred to as change of life or

Go to **Cram101.com** for the Practice Tests for this Chapter.

	climacteric.
Medicine	Medicine is the branch of health science and the sector of public life concerned with maintaining or restoring human health through the study, diagnosis and treatment of disease and injury.
Intervention	Intervention refers to a planned attempt to break through addicts' or abusers' denial and get them into treatment. Interventions most often occur when legal, workplace, health, relationship, or financial problems have become intolerable.
Consensus	General agreement is a consensus.
Public health	Public health is concerned with threats to the overall health of a community based on population health analysis.
Epidemic	An epidemic is a disease that appears as new cases in a given human population, during a given period, at a rate that substantially exceeds what is "expected", based on recent experience.
Evaluation	The fifth step of the nursing process where nursing care and the patient's goal achievement are measured is the evaluation.
Chronic disease	Disease of long duration often not detected in its early stages and from which the patient will not recover is referred to as a chronic disease.

Diabetes	Diabetes is a medical disorder characterized by varying or persistent elevated blood sugar levels, especially after eating. All types of diabetes share similar symptoms and complications at advanced stages: dehydration and ketoacidosis, cardiovascular disease, chronic renal failure, retinal damage which can lead to blindness, nerve damage which can lead to erectile dysfunction, gangrene with risk of amputation of toes, feet, and even legs.
Glucose	Glucose, a simple monosaccharide sugar, is one of the most important carbohydrates and is used as a source of energy in animals and plants. Glucose is one of the main products of photosynthesis and starts respiration.
Blood	Blood is a circulating tissue composed of fluid plasma and cells. The main function of blood is to supply nutrients (oxygen, glucose) and constitutional elements to tissues and to remove waste products.
Diabetes mellitus	Diabetes mellitus is a medical disorder characterized by varying or persistent hyperglycemia (elevated blood sugar levels), especially after eating. All types of diabetes mellitus share similar symptoms and complications at advanced stages.
Hyperglycemia	Hyperglycemia is a condition in which an excessive amount of glucose circulates in the blood plasma.
Pancreas	The pancreas is a retroperitoneal organ that serves two functions: exocrine - it produces pancreatic juice containing digestive enzymes, and endocrine - it produces several important hormones, namely insulin.
Insulin	Insulin is a polypeptide hormone that regulates carbohydrate metabolism. Apart from being the primary effector in carbohydrate homeostasis, it also has a substantial effect on small vessel muscle tone, controls storage and release of fat (triglycerides) and cellular uptake of both amino acids and some electrolytes.
Autoimmune	Autoimmune refers to immune reactions against normal body cells; self against self.
Receptor	A receptor is a protein on the cell membrane or within the cytoplasm or cell nucleus that binds to a specific molecule (a ligand), such as a neurotransmitter, hormone, or other substance, and initiates the cellular response to the ligand. Receptor, in immunology, the region of an antibody which shows recognition of an antigen.
Gestational diabetes	A form of diabetes that develops during pregnancy and typically disappears after the baby is delivered is gestational diabetes.
Obesity	The state of being more than 20 percent above the average weight for a person of one's height is called obesity.
Impaired glucose tolerance	Impaired glucose tolerance is a pre-diabetic state, associated with insulin resistance and increased risk cardiovascular pathology. It may precede type 2 diabetes mellitus by many years.
Hypertension	Hypertension is a medical condition where the blood pressure in the arteries is chronically elevated. Persistent hypertension is one of the risk factors for strokes, heart attacks, heart failure and arterial aneurysm, and is a leading cause of chronic renal failure.
Risk factor	A risk factor is a variable associated with an increased risk of disease or infection but risk factors are not necessarily causal.
Tolerance	Drug tolerance occurs when a subject's reaction to a drug decreases so that larger doses are required to achieve the same effect.
Intervention	Intervention refers to a planned attempt to break through addicts' or abusers' denial and get them into treatment. Interventions most often occur when legal, workplace, health, relationship, or financial problems have become intolerable.

Go to **Cram101.com** for the Practice Tests for this Chapter.

Carbohydrate	Carbohydrate is a chemical compound that contains oxygen, hydrogen, and carbon atoms. They consist of monosaccharide sugars of varying chain lengths and that have the general chemical formula $C_n(H_2O)_n$ or are derivatives of such.
Insulin resistance	In medicine, insulin resistance denotes a decompenzation of glucose homeostasis where the tissues appear to be less responsive to insulin.
Resistance	Resistance refers to a nonspecific ability to ward off infection or disease regardless of whether the body has been previously exposed to it. A force that opposes the flow of a fluid such as air or blood. Compare with immunity.
Plasma	Fluid portion of circulating blood is called plasma.
Injection	A method of rapid drug delivery that puts the substance directly in the bloodstream, in a muscle, or under the skin is called injection.
Agent	Agent refers to an epidemiological term referring to the organism or object that transmits a disease from the environment to the host.
Lifestyle	The culturally, socially, economically, and environmentally conditioned complex of actions characteristic of an individual, group, or community as a pattern of habituated behavior over time that is health related but not necessarily health directed is a lifestyle.
Cardiovascular disease	Cardiovascular disease refers to afflictions in the mechanisms, including the heart, blood vessels, and their controllers, that are responsible for transporting blood to the body's tissues and organs. Psychological factors may play important roles in such diseases and their treatments.
Coronary	Referring to the heart or the blood vessels of the heart is referred to as coronary.
Artery	Vessel that takes blood away from the heart to the tissues and organs of the body is called an artery.
Coronary artery	An artery that supplies blood to the wall of the heart is called a coronary artery.
Coronary artery disease	Coronary artery disease (CAD) is the end result of the accumulation of atheromatous plaques within the walls of the arteries that supply the myocardium (the muscle of the heart).
Health	Health is a term that refers to a combination of the absence of illness, the ability to cope with everyday activities, physical fitness, and high quality of life.
Quality of life	Quality of life refers to the perception of individuals or groups that their needs are being satisfied and that they are not being denied opportunities to achieve happiness and fulfillment.
Lipid	Lipid is one class of aliphatic hydrocarbon-containing organic compounds essential for the structure and function of living cells. They are characterized by being water-insoluble but soluble in nonpolar organic solvents.
Nerve	A nerve is an enclosed, cable-like bundle of nerve fibers or axons, which includes the glia that ensheath the axons in myelin.
Lead	Lead is a chemical element in the periodic table that has the symbol Pb and atomic number 82. A soft, heavy, toxic and malleable poor metal, lead is bluish white when freshly cut but tarnishes to dull gray when exposed to air. Lead is used in building construction, lead-acid batteries, bullets and shot, and is part of solder, pewter, and fusible alloys.
Sensory nerves	Sensory nerves bring impulses toward the central nervous system.
Blood vessel	A blood vessel is a part of the circulatory system and function to transport blood throughout the body. The most important types, arteries and veins, are so termed because they carry blood away from or towards the heart, respectively.

Go to **Cram101.com** for the Practice Tests for this Chapter.

Protocol	Protocol is a document with the aim of guiding decisions and criteria in specific areas of healthcare, as defined by an authoritative examination of current evidence. It details the activities to be executed in specific situations.
Aerobic	An aerobic organism is an organism that has an oxygen based metabolism. Aerobes, in a process known as cellular respiration, use oxygen to oxidize substrates (for example sugars and fats) in order to obtain energy.
Autonomic neuropathy	Autonomic neuropathy is a disease of the non-voluntary, non-sensory nervous system affecting mostly the internal organs such as the bladder muscles, the cardiovascular system, the digestive tract, and the genital organs.
Neuropathy	Any condition that affects any segment of the nervous system is called neuropathy. Many people with diabetes eventually develop nerve damage.
Hypoglycemia	An abnormally low level of glucose in the blood that results when the pancreas secretes too much insulin into the blood is called hypoglycemia.
Adjustment	Adjustment is an attempt to cope with a given situation.
Kidney	The kidney is a bean-shaped excretory organ in vertebrates. Part of the urinary system, the kidneys filter wastes (especially urea) from the blood and excrete them, along with water, as urine.
Ketone bodies	Ketone bodies are three chemicals that are produced as by-products when fatty acids are broken down for energy. Any production of ketone bodies is called ketogenesis, and this is necessary in small amounts. But when excess ketone bodies accumulate, this abnormal state is called ketosis.
Elevation	Elevation refers to upward movement of a part of the body.
Peripheral neuropathy	Impaired sensory, motor, and reflex actions affecting arms and legs, and causing calf muscle tenderness and difficulty in rising from a squatting position is referred to as peripheral neuropathy.
Aerobic exercise	Exercise in which oxygen is used to produce ATP is aerobic exercise.
Muscle	Muscle is a contractile form of tissue. It is one of the four major tissue types, the other three being epithelium, connective tissue and nervous tissue. Muscle contraction is used to move parts of the body, as well as to move substances within the body.
Peripheral nerve	A nerve that links the brain and spinal cord to the rest of the body peripheral nervous system- in vertebrates, the part of the nervous system that connects the central nervous system to the rest of the body is a peripheral nerve.
Cholesterol	Cholesterol is a steroid, a lipid, and an alcohol, found in the cell membranes of all body tissues, and transported in the blood plasma of all animals. It is an important component of the membranes of cells, providing stability; it makes the membrane's fluidity stable over a bigger temperature interval.
Ischemia	Narrowing of arteries caused by plaque buildup within the arteries is called ischemia.
Stress	Stress refers to a condition that is a response to factors that change the human systems normal state.
Lipoprotein	A lipoprotein is a biochemical assembly that contains both proteins and lipids and may be structural or catalytic in function. They may be enzymes, proton pumps, ion pumps, or some combination of these functions.
Medicine	Medicine is the branch of health science and the sector of public life concerned with maintaining or restoring human health through the study, diagnosis and treatment of disease

Go to **Cram101.com** for the Practice Tests for this Chapter.

	and injury.
Chronic disease	Disease of long duration often not detected in its early stages and from which the patient will not recover is referred to as a chronic disease.

Emphysema	Emphysema is a chronic lung disease. It is often caused by exposure to toxic chemicals or long-term exposure to tobacco smoke..
Fibrosis	Replacement of damaged tissue with fibrous scar tissue rather than by the original tissue type is called fibrosis.
Asthma	Asthma is a complex disease characterized by bronchial hyperresponsiveness (BHR), inflammation, mucus production and intermittent airway obstruction.
Cystic fibrosis	Cystic fibrosis is an autosomal recessive hereditary disease of the exocrine glands. It affects the lungs, sweat glands and the digestive system. It causes chronic respiratory and digestive problems.
Bronchitis	Bronchitis is an obstructive pulmonary disease characterized by inflammation of the bronchi of the lungs.
Health	Health is a term that refers to a combination of the absence of illness, the ability to cope with everyday activities, physical fitness, and high quality of life.
Mental health	Mental health refers to the 'thinking' part of psychosocial health; includes your values, attitudes, and beliefs.
Dyspnea	Dyspnea or shortness of breath (SOB) is perceived difficulty breathing or pain on breathing. It is a common symptom of numerous medical disorders.
Aerobic	An aerobic organism is an organism that has an oxygen based metabolism. Aerobes, in a process known as cellular respiration, use oxygen to oxidize substrates (for example sugars and fats) in order to obtain energy.
Aerobic exercise	Exercise in which oxygen is used to produce ATP is aerobic exercise.
Rehabilitation	Rehabilitation is the restoration of lost capabilities, or the treatment aimed at producing it. Also refers to treatment for dependency on psychoactive substances such as alcohol, prescription drugs, and illicit drugs such as cocaine, heroin or amphetamines.
Hypoxemia	Hypoxemia refers to a deficiency of oxygen in the bloodstream.
Oxygen	Oxygen is a chemical element in the periodic table. It has the symbol O and atomic number 8. Oxygen is the second most common element on Earth, composing around 46% of the mass of Earth's crust and 28% of the mass of Earth as a whole, and is the third most common element in the universe.
Chronic obstructive pulmonary disease	Chronic obstructive pulmonary disease is an umbrella term for a group of respiratory tract diseases that are characterized by airflow obstruction or limitation. It is usually caused by tobacco smoking.
Lungs	Lungs are the essential organs of respiration in air-breathing vertebrates. Their principal function is to transport oxygen from the atmosphere into the bloodstream, and to excrete carbon dioxide from the bloodstream into the atmosphere.
Tissue	A collection of interconnected cells that perform a similar function within an organism is called tissue.
Parenchyma	The parenchyma are the functional parts of an organ in the body (i.e. the nephrons of the kidney, the alveoli of the lungs). In plants parenchyma cells are thin-walled cells of the ground tissue that make up the bulk of most nonwoody structures, although sometimes their cell walls can be lignified.
Capillary	A capillary is the smallest of a body's blood vessels, measuring 5-10 micro meters. They connect arteries and veins, and most closely interact with tissues. Their walls are composed

Go to **Cram101.com** for the Practice Tests for this Chapter.

	of a single layer of cells, the endothelium. This layer is so thin that molecules such as oxygen, water and lipids can pass through them by diffusion and enter the tissues.
Blood	Blood is a circulating tissue composed of fluid plasma and cells. The main function of blood is to supply nutrients (oxygen, glucose) and constitutional elements to tissues and to remove waste products.
Affect	Affect is the scientific term used to describe a subject's externally displayed mood. This can be assesed by the nurse by observing facial expression, tone of voice, and body language.
Sputum	The mucous secretion from the lungs, bronchi, and trachea that is ejected through the mouth is sputum.
Chronic bronchitis	A persistent lung infection characterized by coughing, swelling of the lining of the respiratory tract, an increase in mucus production, a decrease in the number and activity of cilia, and produces sputum for at least three months in two consecutive years is called chronic bronchitis.
Alveoli	Alveoli are anatomical structures that have the form of a hollow cavity. In the lung, the pulmonary alveoli are spherical outcroppings of the respiratory bronchioles and are the primary sites of gas exchange with the blood.
Bronchioles	The bronchioles are the first airway branches that no longer contain cartilage. They are branches of the bronchi, and are smaller than one millimetre in diameter.
Bronchiole	The bronchiole is the first airway branch that no longer contains cartilage. They are branches of the bronchi, and are smaller than one millimetre in diameter.
Mortality rate	Mortality rate is the number of deaths (from a disease or in general) per 1000 people and typically reported on an annual basis.
Statistics	Statistics is a type of data analysis which practice includes the planning, summarizing, and interpreting of observations of a system possibly followed by predicting or forecasting of future events based on a mathematical model of the system being observed.
Mortality	The incidence of death in a population is mortality.
Statistic	A statistic is an observable random variable of a sample.
Wheezing	Wheezing is a continuous, coarse, whistling sound produced in the respiratory airways during breathing. For wheezing to occur, some part of the respiratory tree must be narrowed or obstructed, or airflow velocity within the respiratory tree must be heightened.
Antigen	An antigen is a substance that stimulates an immune response, especially the production of antibodies. They are usually proteins or polysaccharides, but can be any type of molecule, including small molecules (haptens) coupled to a protein (carrier).
Infection	The invasion and multiplication of microorganisms in body tissues is called an infection.
Tonsils	The tonsils are areas of lymphoid tissue on either side of the throat. As with other organs of the lymphatic system, the tonsils act as part of the immune system to help protect against infection.
Tonsil	Tonsil refers to a patch of lymphatic tissue consisting of connective tissue that contains many lymphocytes; located in the pharynx and throat.
Stress	Stress refers to a condition that is a response to factors that change the human systems normal state.
Viral	Viral phenomena are objects or patterns able to replicate themselves or convert other objects into copies of themselves when these objects are exposed to them.

Go to **Cram101.com** for the Practice Tests for this Chapter.

Genetic disorder	A genetic disorder is a disease caused by abnormal expression of one or more genes in a person causing a clinical phenotype.
Bronchodilator	A bronchodilator is a medication intended to improve bronchial airflow. Treatment of bronchial asthma is the most common application of these drugs.
Expectorant	Dry coughs are treated with cough suppressants (antitussives) that suppress the body's urge to cough, while productive coughs (coughs that produce phlegm) are treated with a expectorant that loosen mucus from the respiratory tract.
Exocrine gland	Exocrine gland refers to glands that secrete their products via a duct. Typically, they include sweat glands, salivary glands, mammary glands and many glands of the digestive system.
Gland	A gland is an organ in an animal's body that synthesizes a substance for release such as hormones, often into the bloodstream or into cavities inside the body or its outer surface.
Inflammation	Inflammation is the first response of the immune system to infection or irritation and may be referred to as the innate cascade.
Antibiotic	Antibiotic refers to substance such as penicillin or streptomycin that is toxic to microorganisms. Usually a product of a particular microorvanism or plant.
Embolism	An embolism occurs when an object (the embolus) migrates from one part of the body and causes a blockage of a blood vessel in another part of the body.
Edema	Edema is swelling of any organ or tissue due to accumulation of excess fluid. Edema has many root causes, but its common mechanism is accumulation of fluid into the tissues.
Pulmonary embolism	A pulmonary embolism occurs when a blood clot, generally a venous thrombus, becomes dislodged from its site of formation and embolizes to the arterial blood supply of one of the lungs.
Radiation therapy	Treatment for cancer in which parts of the body that have cancerous tumors are exposed to high-energy radiation to disrupt cell division of the cancer cells is called radiation therapy.
Pulmonary edema	Pulmonary edema is swelling and/or fluid accumulation in the lungs. It leads to impaired gas exchange and may cause respiratory failure.
Chemotherapy	Chemotherapy is the use of chemical substances to treat disease. In its modern-day use, it refers almost exclusively to cytostatic drugs used to treat cancer.In its non-oncological use, the term may also refer to antibiotics.
Radiation	The emission of electromagnetic waves by all objects warmer than absolute zero is referred to as radiation.
Syndrome	Syndrome is the association of several clinically recognizable features, signs, symptoms, phenomena or characteristics which often occur together, so that the presence of one feature alerts the physician to the presence of the others
Tetanus	Tetanus is a serious and often fatal disease caused by the neurotoxin tetanospasmin which is produced by the Gram-positive, obligate anaerobic bacterium Clostridium tetani. Tetanus also refers to a state of muscle tension.
Myasthenia gravis	Myasthenia gravis is a neuromuscular disease leading to fluctuating weakness and fatiguability.
Amyotrophic lateral sclerosis	Amyotrophic lateral sclerosis is a progressive, invariably fatal motor neurone disease. In ALS, both the upper motor neurons and the lower motor neurons degenerate or die, ceasing to send messages to muscles.
Spinal cord	The spinal cord is a part of the vertebrate nervous system that is enclosed in and protected

by the vertebral column (it passes through the spinal canal). It consists of nerve cells. The spinal cord carries sensory signals and motor innervation to most of the skeletal muscles in the body.

Obesity | The state of being more than 20 percent above the average weight for a person of one's height is called obesity.

Abdomen | The abdomen is a part of the body. In humans, and in many other vertebrates, it is the region between the thorax and the pelvis. In fully developed insects, the abdomen is the third (or posterior) segment, after the head and thorax.

Thoracic cavity | The thoracic cavity is the chamber of the human body (and other animal bodies) that is protected by the thoracic wall (thoracic cage and associated skin, muscle, and fascia).

Muscle | Muscle is a contractile form of tissue. It is one of the four major tissue types, the other three being epithelium, connective tissue and nervous tissue. Muscle contraction is used to move parts of the body, as well as to move substances within the body.

Residual volume | Residual volume is the amount of air left in the lungs after a maximal exhalation. This averages about 1.5 L..

Vital capacity | Vital capacity is the total amount of air that a person can expire after a complete inspiration.

Inspiratory reserve volume | Volume of air that can be forcibly inhaled after normal inhalation is referred to as inspiratory reserve volume.

Expiratory reserve volume | Expiratory reserve volume is the amount of additional air that can be breathed out after normal expiration. This is about 1.5 L.

Tidal volume | Tidal volume (TV) is the amount of air breathed in or out during normal human respiration. It is normally from 450 to 500 mL.

Assess | Assess is to systematically and continuously collect, validate, and communicate patient data.

Evaluation | The fifth step of the nursing process where nursing care and the patient's goal achievement are measured is the evaluation.

Ratio | In number and more generally in algebra, a ratio is the linear relationship between two quantities.

Inhalation | Inhalation is the movement of air from the external environment, through the airways, into the alveoli during breathing.

Value | Value is worth in general, and it is thought to be connected to reasons for certain practices, policies, actions, beliefs or emotions. Value is "that which one acts to gain and/or keep."

Cardiovascular system | The circulatory system or cardiovascular system is the organ system which circulates blood around the body of most animals.

Diffusion | Random movement of molecules from a region of higher concentration toward one of lower concentration is referred to as diffusion.

Pulse | The rhythmic stretching of the arteries caused by the pressure of blood forced through the arteries by contractions of the ventricles during systole is a pulse.

Pulse oximeter | A pulse oximeter is a medical device that indirectly measures the amount of oxygen in a patient's blood. It is often attached to a medical monitor so staff can directly read a patient's oxygenation at all times.

Ventilation | Ventilation refers to a mechanism that provides contact between an animal's respiratory

Go to **Cram101.com** for the Practice Tests for this Chapter.

surface and the air or water to which it is exposed. It is also called breathing.

Hemoglobin	Hemoglobin is the iron-containing oxygen-transport metalloprotein in the red cells of the blood in mammals and other animals. Hemoglobin transports oxygen from the lungs to the rest of the body, such as to the muscles, where it releases the oxygen load.
Heart rate	Heart rate is a term used to describe the frequency of the cardiac cycle. It is considered one of the four vital signs. Usually it is calculated as the number of contractions of the heart in one minute and expressed as "beats per minute".
Activities of daily living	Activities of daily living is a way to describe the functional status of a person.
Partial pressure	The partial pressure of a gas in a mixture or solution is what the pressure of that gas would be if all other components of the mixture or solution suddenly vanished without its temperature changing.
Population	Population refers to all members of a well-defined group of organisms, events, or things.
Smooth muscle	Smooth muscle is a type of non-striated muscle, found within the "walls" of hollow organs; such as blood vessels, the bladder, the uterus, and the gastrointestinal tract. Smooth muscle is used to move matter within the body, via contraction; it generally operates "involuntarily", without nerve stimulation.
Acute	In medicine, an acute disease is a disease with either or both of: a rapid onset; and a short course (as opposed to a chronic course).
Receptor	A receptor is a protein on the cell membrane or within the cytoplasm or cell nucleus that binds to a specific molecule (a ligand), such as a neurotransmitter, hormone, or other substance, and initiates the cellular response to the ligand. Receptor, in immunology, the region of an antibody which shows recognition of an antigen.
Seizure	A seizure is a temporary alteration in brain function expressed as a changed mental state, tonic or clonic movements and various other symptoms. They are due to temporary abnormal electrical activity of a group of brain cells.
Nervous system	The nervous system of an animal coordinates the activity of the muscles, monitors the organs, constructs and processes input from the senses, and initiates actions.
Central nervous system	The central nervous system comprized of the brain and spinal cord, represents the largest part of the nervous system. Together with the peripheral nervous system, it has a fundamental role in the control of behavior.
Tachycardia	Tachycardia is an abnormally rapid beating of the heart, defined as a resting heart rate of over 100 beats per minute. Common causes are autonomic nervous system or endocrine system activity, hemodynamic responses, and various forms of cardiac arrhythmia.
Arrhythmias	Arrhythmias refers to abnormal heart rhythms which may be too slow, too early, too rapid, or irregular.
Arrhythmia	Cardiac arrhythmia is a group of conditions in which muscle contraction of the heart is irregular for any reason.
Medicine	Medicine is the branch of health science and the sector of public life concerned with maintaining or restoring human health through the study, diagnosis and treatment of disease and injury.
Diuretic	A diuretic is any drug that elevates the rate of bodily urine excretion.
Pulmonary hypertension	Pulmonary hypertension (PH) is an increase in blood pressure in the pulmonary artery or lung vasculature.

Hypertension	Hypertension is a medical condition where the blood pressure in the arteries is chronically elevated. Persistent hypertension is one of the risk factors for strokes, heart attacks, heart failure and arterial aneurysm, and is a leading cause of chronic renal failure.
Hypertrophy	Hypertrophy is the increase of the size of an organ. It should be distinguished from hyperplasia which occurs due to cell division; hypertrophy occurs due to an increase in cell size rather than division. It is most commonly seen in muscle that has been actively stimulated, the most well-known method being exercise.
Excretion	Excretion is the biological process by which an organism chemically separates waste products from its body. The waste products are then usually expelled from the body by elimination.
Agent	Agent refers to an epidemiological term referring to the organism or object that transmits a disease from the environment to the host.
Antihistamine	An antihistamine is a drug which serves to reduce or eliminate effects mediated by histamine, an endogenous chemical mediator released during allergic reactions, through action at the histamine receptor.
Right heart	Right heart is a term used to refer collectively to the right atrium and right ventricle of the heart; occasionally, this term is intended to reference the right atrium, right ventricle, and the pulmonary trunk collectively.
Potassium	Potassium is a chemical element in the periodic table. It has the symbol K (L. kalium) and atomic number 19. Potassium is a soft silvery-white metallic alkali metal that occurs naturally bound to other elements in seawater and many minerals.
Pain	Pain is an unpleasant sensation which may be associated with actual or potential tissue damage and which may have physical and emotional components.
Coronary	Referring to the heart or the blood vessels of the heart is referred to as coronary.
Artery	Vessel that takes blood away from the heart to the tissues and organs of the body is called an artery.
Coronary artery	An artery that supplies blood to the wall of the heart is called a coronary artery.
Coronary artery disease	Coronary artery disease (CAD) is the end result of the accumulation of atheromatous plaques within the walls of the arteries that supply the myocardium (the muscle of the heart).
Physical therapy	Physical therapy is a health profession concerned with the assessment, diagnosis, and treatment of disease and disability through physical means. It is based upon principles of medical science, and is generally held to be within the sphere of conventional medicine.
Leach	To dissolve and filter through soil is to leach.
Thorax	The thorax is a division of an animal's body that lies between the head and the abdomen. In humans, the thorax is the region of the body that extends from the neck to the diaphragm, not including the upper limbs.

Go to **Cram101.com** for the Practice Tests for this Chapter.

Health	Health is a term that refers to a combination of the absence of illness, the ability to cope with everyday activities, physical fitness, and high quality of life.
Osteoporosis	Osteoporosis is a disease of bone in which bone mineral density (BMD) is reduced, bone microarchitecture is disrupted, the amount and variety of non-collagenous proteins in bone is changed, and a concomitantly fracture risk is increased.
Risk factor	A risk factor is a variable associated with an increased risk of disease or infection but risk factors are not necessarily causal.
Diabetes	Diabetes is a medical disorder characterized by varying or persistent elevated blood sugar levels, especially after eating. All types of diabetes share similar symptoms and complications at advanced stages: dehydration and ketoacidosis, cardiovascular disease, chronic renal failure, retinal damage which can lead to blindness, nerve damage which can lead to erectile dysfunction, gangrene with risk of amputation of toes, feet, and even legs.
Obesity	The state of being more than 20 percent above the average weight for a person of one's height is called obesity.
Cardiovascular disease	Cardiovascular disease refers to afflictions in the mechanisms, including the heart, blood vessels, and their controllers, that are responsible for transporting blood to the body's tissues and organs. Psychological factors may play important roles in such diseases and their treatments.
Fetus	Fetus refers to a developing human from the ninth week of gestation until birth; has all the major structures of an adult.
Lead	Lead is a chemical element in the periodic table that has the symbol Pb and atomic number 82. A soft, heavy, toxic and malleable poor metal, lead is bluish white when freshly cut but tarnishes to dull gray when exposed to air. Lead is used in building construction, lead-acid batteries, bullets and shot, and is part of solder, pewter, and fusible alloys.
Critical period	A period of time when an instinctive response can be elicited by a particular stimulus is referred to as critical period.
First trimester	The first trimester is the period of time from the first day of the last menstrual period through 12 weeks of gestation. It is during this period that the embryo undergoes most of its early structural development. Most miscarriages occur during this period.
Trimester	In human development, one of three 3-mnonth-long periods of pregnancy is called trimester.
Core temperature	Core temperature is the operating temperature of an organism, specifically in deep structures of the body such as the liver, in comparison to temperatures of peripheral tissues.
Blood	Blood is a circulating tissue composed of fluid plasma and cells. The main function of blood is to supply nutrients (oxygen, glucose) and constitutional elements to tissues and to remove waste products.
Skin	Skin is an organ of the integumentary system composed of a layer of tissues that protect underlying muscles and organs.
Ventilation	Ventilation refers to a mechanism that provides contact between an animal's respiratory surface and the air or water to which it is exposed. It is also called breathing.
Oxygen	Oxygen is a chemical element in the periodic table. It has the symbol O and atomic number 8. Oxygen is the second most common element on Earth, composing around 46% of the mass of Earth's crust and 28% of the mass of Earth as a whole, and is the third most common element in the universe.
Cardiac output	Cardiac output is the volume of blood being pumped by the heart in a minute. It is equal to the heart rate multiplied by the stroke volume.

Go to **Cram101.com** for the Practice Tests for this Chapter.

Resistance	Resistance refers to a nonspecific ability to ward off infection or disease regardless of whether the body has been previously exposed to it. A force that opposes the flow of a fluid such as air or blood. Compare with immunity.
Uterus	The uterus is the major female reproductive organ of most mammals. One end, the cervix, opens into the vagina; the other is connected on both sides to the fallopian tubes. The main function is to accept a fertilized ovum which becomes implanted into the endometrium, and derives nourishment from blood vessels which develop exclusively for this purpose.
Blood vessel	A blood vessel is a part of the circulatory system and function to transport blood throughout the body. The most important types, arteries and veins, are so termed because they carry blood away from or towards the heart, respectively.
Hyperthermia	Hyperthermia is an acute condition which occurs when the body produces or absorbs more heat than it can dissipate. It is usually due to excessive exposure to heat.
Hydration	Hydration can create a hydrate from which water can be reextracted. When hydration occurs in a chemical reaction it is called a hydration reaction, in which water is permanently and chemically combined with a reactant in a way that it can no longer be reextracted.
Trauma	Trauma refers to a severe physical injury or wound to the body caused by an external force, or a psychological shock having a lasting effect on mental life.
Elimination	Elimination refers to the physiologic excretion of drugs and other substances from the body.
Center of gravity	In physics, the center of gravity (CG) of an object is a point at which the object's mass can be assumed, for many purposes, to be concentrated.
Joint	A joint (articulation) is the location at which two bones make contact (articulate). They are constructed to both allow movement and provide mechanical support.
Pelvis	The pelvis is the bony structure located at the base of the spine (properly known as the caudal end). The pelvis incorporates the socket portion of the hip joint for each leg (in bipeds) or hind leg (in quadrupeds). It forms the lower limb (or hind-limb) girdle of the skeleton.
Planning	In agreement with the patient, the nurse addresses each of the problems identified in the planning phase. For each problem a measurable goal is set. For example, for the patient discussed above, the goal would be for the patient's skin to remain intact. The result is a nursing care plan. This is the third step.
Hip	In anatomy, the hip is the bony projection of the femur, known as the greater trochanter, and the overlying muscle and fat.
Osteopenia	Decreased bone mass caused by cancer, hyperthyroidism, or other reasons is called osteopenia.
Vertebrae	Vertebrae are the individual bones that make up the vertebral column (aka spine) - a flexuous and flexible column.
Bone mineral density	A bone mineral density test is used to measure bone density and determine fracture risk for osteoporosis.
Diagnosis	In medicine, diagnosis is the process of identifying a medical condition or disease by its signs, symptoms, and from the results of various diagnostic procedures.
Assess	Assess is to systematically and continuously collect, validate, and communicate patient data.
Standard deviation	In probability and statistics, the standard deviation is the most commonly used measure of statistical dispersion. Simply put, it measures how spread out the values in a data set are.
World Health Organization	The World Health Organization (WHO) is a specialized agency of the United Nations, acting as a coordinating authority on international public health, headquartered in Geneva,

Switzerland.

Estrogen

Estrogen is a steroid that functions as the primary female sex hormone. While present in both men and women, they are found in women in significantly higher quantities.

Receptor

A receptor is a protein on the cell membrane or within the cytoplasm or cell nucleus that binds to a specific molecule (a ligand), such as a neurotransmitter, hormone, or other substance, and initiates the cellular response to the ligand. Receptor, in immunology, the region of an antibody which shows recognition of an antigen.

Hormone

A hormone is a chemical messenger from one cell to another. All multicellular organisms produce hormones. The best known hormones are those produced by endocrine glands of vertebrate animals, but hormones are produced by nearly every organ system and tissue type in a human or animal body. Hormone molecules are secreted directly into the bloodstream, they move by circulation or diffusion to their target cells, which may be nearby cells in the same tissue or cells of a distant organ of the body.

Ethnicity

While ethnicity and race are related concepts, the concept of ethnicity is rooted in the idea of social groups, marked especially by shared nationality, tribal affiliation, religious faith, shared language, or cultural and traditional origins and backgrounds, whereas race is rooted in the idea of biological classification of Homo sapiens to subspecies according to chosen genotypic and/or phenotypic traits.

Arthritis

Arthritis is a group of conditions that affect the health of the bone joints in the body. Arthritis can be caused from strains and injuries caused by repetitive motion, sports, overexertion, and falls. Unlike the autoimmune diseases, it largely affects older people and results from the degeneration of joint cartilage.

Affect

Affect is the scientific term used to describe a subject's externally displayed mood. This can be assesed by the nurse by observing facial expression, tone of voice, and body language.

Menopause

Menopause is the physiological cessation of menstrual cycles associated with advancing age in species that experience such cycles. Menopause is sometimes referred to as change of life or climacteric.

Vitamin

An organic compound other than a carbohydrate, lipid, or protein that is needed for normal metabolism but that the body cannot synthesize in adequate amounts is called a vitamin.

Calcium

Calcium is the chemical element in the periodic table that has the symbol Ca and atomic number 20. Calcium is a soft grey alkaline earth metal that is used as a reducing agent in the extraction of thorium, zirconium and uranium. Calcium is also the fifth most abundant element in the Earth's crust.

Adolescence

Adolescence is the period of psychological and social transition between childhood and adulthood (gender-specific manhood, or womanhood). As a transitional stage of human development it represents the period of time during which a juvenile matures into adulthood.

Protocol

Protocol is a document with the aim of guiding decisions and criteria in specific areas of healthcare, as defined by an authoritative examination of current evidence. It details the activities to be executed in specific situations.

Muscle

Muscle is a contractile form of tissue. It is one of the four major tissue types, the other three being epithelium, connective tissue and nervous tissue. Muscle contraction is used to move parts of the body, as well as to move substances within the body.

Aerobic

An aerobic organism is an organism that has an oxygen based metabolism. Aerobes, in a process known as cellular respiration, use oxygen to oxidize substrates (for example sugars and fats) in order to obtain energy.

Lifestyle

The culturally, socially, economically, and environmentally conditioned complex of actions

characteristic of an individual, group, or community as a pattern of habituated behavior over time that is health related but not necessarily health directed is a lifestyle.

Glycogen
Glycogen refers to a complex, extensively branched polysaccharide of many glucose monomers; serves as an energy-storage molecule in liver and muscle cells.

Anemia
Anemia is a deficiency of red blood cells and/or hemoglobin. This results in a reduced ability of blood to transfer oxygen to the tissues, and this causes hypoxia; since all human cells depend on oxygen for survival, varying degrees of anemia can have a wide range of clinical consequences.

Electrolyte
An electrolyte is a substance that dissociates into free ions when dissolved (or molten), to produce an electrically conductive medium. Because they generally consist of ions in solution, they are also known as ionic solutions.

Amenorrhea
Amenorrhea is the absence of a menstrual period in a woman of reproductive age. Physiologic states of amenorrhea are seen during pregnancy and lactation (breastfeeding).

Anorexia
Anorexia nervosa is an eating disorder characterized by voluntary starvation and exercise stress.

Bulimia
Bulimia refers to a disorder in which a person binges on incredibly large quantities of food, then purges by vomiting or by using laxatives. Bulimia is often less about food, and more to do with deep psychological issues and profound feelings of lack of control.

Anorexia nervosa
Anorexia nervosa is an eating disorder characterized by voluntary starvation and exercise stress.

Eating disorders
Psychological disorders characterized by distortion of the body image and gross disturbances in eating patterns are called eating disorders.

Bulimia nervosa
Bulimia nervosa is a psychological condition in which the subject engages in recurrent binge eating followed by intentionally; vomiting, misuse of laxatives or other medication, excessive exercising, and fasting, in order to compensate for the intake of the food and prevent weight gain:

Calorie
Calorie refers to a unit used to measure heat energy and the energy contents of foods.

Population
Population refers to all members of a well-defined group of organisms, events, or things.

Menarche
Menarche is the first menstrual period as a girl's body progresses through the changes of puberty. Menarche usually occurs about two years after the first changes of breast development.

Ovaries
Ovaries are egg-producing reproductive organs found in female organisms.

Ovary
The primary reproductive organ of a female is called an ovary.

Gland
A gland is an organ in an animal's body that synthesizes a substance for release such as hormones, often into the bloodstream or into cavities inside the body or its outer surface.

Pituitary gland
The pituitary gland or hypophysis is an endocrine gland about the size of a pea that sits in the small, bony cavity (sella turcica) at the base of the brain. Its posterior lobe is connected to a part of the brain called the hypothalamus via the infundibulum (or stalk), giving rise to the tuberoinfundibular pathway.

Hypothalamus
Located below the thalamus, the hypothalamus links the nervous system to the endocrine system by synthesizing and secreting neurohormones often called releasing hormones because they function by stimulating the secretion of hormones from the anterior pituitary gland.

Progesterone
Progesterone is a C-21 steroid hormone involved in the female menstrual cycle, pregnancy (supports gestation) and embryogenesis of humans and other species.

Go to **Cram101.com** for the Practice Tests for this Chapter.

189

Menstruation	Loss of blood and tissue from the uterine lining at the end of a female reproductive cycle are referred to as menstruation.
Intervention	Intervention refers to a planned attempt to break through addicts' or abusers' denial and get them into treatment. Interventions most often occur when legal, workplace, health, relationship, or financial problems have become intolerable.
Endogenous	Originating internally, such as the endogenous cholesterol synthesized in the body in contrast to the exogenous cholesterol coming from the diet is referred to as endogenous. Compare with exogenous.
Medicine	Medicine is the branch of health science and the sector of public life concerned with maintaining or restoring human health through the study, diagnosis and treatment of disease and injury.
Chronic disease	Disease of long duration often not detected in its early stages and from which the patient will not recover is referred to as a chronic disease.
Nurse Practitioner	A Nurse Practitioner is a Registered Nurse who has completed advanced education (generally a minimum of a master's degree) and training in the diagnosis and management of common medical conditions, including chronic illnesses.
Consensus	General agreement is a consensus.
Assessment	In clinical practice, the process by which a mental health professional gathers and compiles information about a client for the purpose of describing the person's problems or disorder and developing a plan of treatment is an assessment.
Electrocardi-gram	An electrocardiogram is a graphic produced by an electrocardiograph, which records the electrical voltage in the heart in the form of a continuous strip graph. It is the prime tool in cardiac electrophysiology, and has a prime function in screening and diagnosis of cardiovascular diseases..

Relapse prevention	Extending therapeutic progress by teaching the client how to cope with future troubling situations is a relapse prevention technique.
Health	Health is a term that refers to a combination of the absence of illness, the ability to cope with everyday activities, physical fitness, and high quality of life.
Behavior modification	Behavior Modification is a technique of altering an individual's reactions to stimuli through positive reinforcement and the extinction of maladaptive behavior.
Lifestyle	The culturally, socially, economically, and environmentally conditioned complex of actions characteristic of an individual, group, or community as a pattern of habituated behavior over time that is health related but not necessarily health directed is a lifestyle.
Aerobic	An aerobic organism is an organism that has an oxygen based metabolism. Aerobes, in a process known as cellular respiration, use oxygen to oxidize substrates (for example sugars and fats) in order to obtain energy.
Theory	Theory refers to an explanatory statement, or set of statements, that concisely summarizes the state of knowledge on a phenomenon and provides direction for further study.
Antecedents	In behavior modification, events that typically precede the target response are called antecedents.
Punishment	An unpleasant stimulus that suppresses the behavior it follows is a punishment.
Intervention	Intervention refers to a planned attempt to break through addicts' or abusers' denial and get them into treatment. Interventions most often occur when legal, workplace, health, relationship, or financial problems have become intolerable.
Concept	A mental category used to class together objects, relations, events, abstractions, or qualities that have common properties is called concept.
Affect	Affect is the scientific term used to describe a subject's externally displayed mood. This can be assesed by the nurse by observing facial expression, tone of voice, and body language.
Matching	In connection with experiments, the procedure whereby pairs of subjects are matched on the basis of their similarities on one or more variables, and one member of the pair is assigned to the experimental group and the other to the control group, is referred to as matching.
Stimulus	Stimulus in a nervous system, a factor that triggers sensory transduction.
Value	Value is worth in general, and it is thought to be connected to reasons for certain practices, policies, actions, beliefs or emotions. Value is "that which one acts to gain and/or keep."
Values clarification	The process by which people come to realize their own values and value system is values clarification.
Behavioral contract	A written agreement outlining a promise to adhere to the contingencies of a behavior modification program is a behavioral contract.
Assessment	In clinical practice, the process by which a mental health professional gathers and compiles information about a client for the purpose of describing the person's problems or disorder and developing a plan of treatment is an assessment.
Evaluation	The fifth step of the nursing process where nursing care and the patient's goal achievement are measured is the evaluation.
Variable	A characteristic or aspect in which people, objects, events, or conditions vary is called variable.
Consciousness	Consciousness refers to the ability to perceive, communicate, remember, understand,

Go to **Cram101.com** for the Practice Tests for this Chapter.

	appreciate, and initiate voluntary movements; a functioning sensorium.
Planning	In agreement with the patient, the nurse addresses each of the problems identified in the planning phase. For each problem a measurable goal is set. For example, for the patient discussed above, the goal would be for the patient's skin to remain intact. The result is a nursing care plan. This is the third step.
Obesity	The state of being more than 20 percent above the average weight for a person of one's height is called obesity.
Outcome	Outcome is the impact of care provided to a patient. They can be positive, such as the ability to walk freely as a result of rehabilitation, or negative, such as the occurrence of bedsores as a result of lack of mobility of a patient.
Stress	Stress refers to a condition that is a response to factors that change the human systems normal state.
Stress management	Stress management encompasses techniques intended to equip a person with effective coping mechanisms for dealing with psychological stress.
Intrinsic motivation	Internal motivational factors such as self-determination, curiosity, challenge, and effort are referred to as intrinsic motivation.
Older adult	Older adult is an adult over the age of 65.
Control group	A group that does not receive the treatment effect in an experiment is referred to as the control group or sometimes as the comparison group.
Base	The common definition of a base is a chemical compound that absorbs hydronium ions when dissolved in water (a proton acceptor). An alkali is a special example of a base, where in an aqueous environment, hydroxide ions are donated.
Insight	Insight refers to a sudden awareness of the relationships among various elements that had previously appeared to be independent of one another.
Cognitive restructuring	Cognitive restructuring refers to any behavior therapy procedure that attempts to alter the manner in which a client thinks about life so that he or she changes overt behavior and emotions.
Behavioral rehearsal	Behavior therapy technique in which the client practices coping with troublesome or anxiety arousing situations in a safe and supervised situation is a behavioral rehearsal.
Anxiety	Anxiety is a complex combination of the feeling of fear, apprehension and worry often accompanied by physical sensations such as palpitations, chest pain and/or shortness of breath.
Muscle	Muscle is a contractile form of tissue. It is one of the four major tissue types, the other three being epithelium, connective tissue and nervous tissue. Muscle contraction is used to move parts of the body, as well as to move substances within the body.
Incentive	Incentive refers to an object, person, or situation perceived as being capable of satisfying a need.
Competency	Ability of legal defendants to participate in their own defense and understand the charges and the roles of the trial participants is referred to as competency.
Criterion	Criterion refers to a standard of comparison. For performance appraisal, it is the definition of good performance.
Initial assessment	A initial assessment is a comprehensive nursing assessment resulting in baseline data that enables the nurse to make a judgment about a patient's health status, ability to manage his or her own healthcare, and need for nursing, and to plan individualized, holistic healthcare

for the patient.

Population	Population refers to all members of a well-defined group of organisms, events, or things.
Adjustment	Adjustment is an attempt to cope with a given situation.
Contingency	Contingency refers to a close relationship, especially of a causal nature, between two events, one of which regularly follows the other.
Alcohol	Alcohol is a general term, applied to any organic compound in which a hydroxyl group (-OH) is bound to a carbon atom, which in turn is bound to other hydrogen and/or carbon atoms. The general formula for a simple acyclic alcohol is $C_nH_{2n+1}OH$.
Drug abuse	Drug abuse has a wide range of definitions, all of them relating either to the misuse or overuse of a psychoactive drug or performance enhancing drug for a non-therapeutic or non-medical effect, or referring to any use of illegal drug in the absence of a required, yet practically impossible to get, license from a government authority.
Denial	Denial is a psychological defense mechanism in which a person faced with a fact that is uncomfortable or painful to accept rejects it instead, insisting that it is not true despite what may be overwhelming evidence.
Lead	Lead is a chemical element in the periodic table that has the symbol Pb and atomic number 82. A soft, heavy, toxic and malleable poor metal, lead is bluish white when freshly cut but tarnishes to dull gray when exposed to air. Lead is used in building construction, lead-acid batteries, bullets and shot, and is part of solder, pewter, and fusible alloys.
Abstinence	Abstinence has diverse forms. In its oldest sense it is sexual, as in the practice of continence, chastity, and celibacy.
Loss of control	The point in drug use where the user becomes unable to limit or stop use is referred to as loss of control.
Perceived loss	A perceived loss is a loss tangible only to the person sustaining it.
Relaxation training	Relaxation training is an intervention technique used for tics. The person is taught to relax the muscles involved in the tics.
Assertiveness	Asking for what one wants while demonstrating respect for others is refered to as assertiveness.
Assertiveness training	In behavior therapy, a direct method of training people to express their own desires and feelings and to maintain their own rights in interactions with others, while at the same time respecting the others' rights is called assertiveness training.
Loudness	Loudness refers to the quality of the psychological experience of a sound that is most directly related to the amplitude of the physical sound stimulus.
Humor	In traditional medicine practiced before the advent of modern technology, the four humours (or four humors) were four fluids that were thought to permeate the body and influence its health. A humor is any fluid substance in the body.
Counselor	A counselor is a mental health professional who specializes in helping people with problems not involving serious mental disorders.
Empathy	Empathy refers to reacting to another's feelings with an emotional response that is similar to the other's response.
Informed consent	The term used by psychologists to indicate that a person has agreed to participate in research after receiving information about the purposes of the study and the nature of the treatments is informed consent. Even with informed consent, subjects may withdraw from any experiment at any time.

Confidentiality	Confidentiality refers to an ethical principle associated with several professions (eg, medicine, law, religion, journalism,...). In ethics, and in law, some types of communication between a person and one of these professionals are "privileged" and may not be discussed or divulged to third parties. In those jurisdictions in which the law makes provision for such confidentiality, there are usually penalties for its violation.
Affective disorder	Affective disorder refers to any mood or emotional disorder, e.g., depression, bipolar affective disorder.
Eating disorders	Psychological disorders characterized by distortion of the body image and gross disturbances in eating patterns are called eating disorders.
Depression	In everyday language depression refers to any downturn in mood, which may be relatively transitory and perhaps due to something trivial. This is differentiated from Clinical depression which is marked by symptoms that last two weeks or more and are so severe that they interfere with daily living.
Medicine	Medicine is the branch of health science and the sector of public life concerned with maintaining or restoring human health through the study, diagnosis and treatment of disease and injury.
Behavioral medicine	Behavioral medicine refers to an interdisciplinary field that focuses on developing and integrating behavioral and biomedical knowledge to promote health and reduce illness.
Management techniques	Combining praise, recognition, approval, rules, and reasoning to enforce child discipline are referred to as management techniques.
Inventory	A paper-and-pencil test with questions about a person's thoughts, feelings, and behaviors, which can be scored according to a standard procedure is referred to as inventory.
Validity	The extent to which a test measures what it is intended to measure is called validity.
Health psychology	The field of psychology that studies the relationships between psychological factors and the prevention and treatment of physical illness is called health psychology.
Individual differences	The stable, consistent ways that people are different from each other are called individual differences.
Clinical psychology	Clinical psychology is involved in the diagnosis, assessment, and treatment of patients with mental or behavioral disorders, and conducts research in these various areas.
Health promotion	Any planned combination of educational, political, regulatory, and organizational supports for actions and conditions of living conducive to the health of individuals, groups, or communities is called health promotion.
Public health	Public health is concerned with threats to the overall health of a community based on population health analysis.

Go to **Cram101.com** for the Practice Tests for this Chapter.

Stressor	A factor capable of stimulating a stress response is a stressor.
Affect	Affect is the scientific term used to describe a subject's externally displayed mood. This can be assesed by the nurse by observing facial expression, tone of voice, and body language.
Stress	Stress refers to a condition that is a response to factors that change the human systems normal state.
Catecholamine	Catecholamine is a chemical compound derived from the amino acid tyrosine that acts as a hormone or neurotransmitter. They are examples of phenethylamines.
Health	Health is a term that refers to a combination of the absence of illness, the ability to cope with everyday activities, physical fitness, and high quality of life.
Criterion	Criterion refers to a standard of comparison. For performance appraisal, it is the definition of good performance.
Course	Pattern of development and change of a disorder over time is a course.
Lead	Lead is a chemical element in the periodic table that has the symbol Pb and atomic number 82. A soft, heavy, toxic and malleable poor metal, lead is bluish white when freshly cut but tarnishes to dull gray when exposed to air. Lead is used in building construction, lead-acid batteries, bullets and shot, and is part of solder, pewter, and fusible alloys.
Value	Value is worth in general, and it is thought to be connected to reasons for certain practices, policies, actions, beliefs or emotions. Value is "that which one acts to gain and/or keep."
Acute	In medicine, an acute disease is a disease with either or both of: a rapid onset; and a short course (as opposed to a chronic course).
Stimulus	Stimulus in a nervous system, a factor that triggers sensory transduction.
Anxiety	Anxiety is a complex combination of the feeling of fear, apprehension and worry often accompanied by physical sensations such as palpitations, chest pain and/or shortness of breath.
Muscle	Muscle is a contractile form of tissue. It is one of the four major tissue types, the other three being epithelium, connective tissue and nervous tissue. Muscle contraction is used to move parts of the body, as well as to move substances within the body.
Interaction with others	Interaction with others refers to in forming attitudes, the influence of discussions with others who hold particular attitudes.
Physiological changes	Alterations in heart rate, blood pressure, perspiration, and other involuntary responses are physiological changes.
Concept	A mental category used to class together objects, relations, events, abstractions, or qualities that have common properties is called concept.
Heart attack	A heart attack, is a serious, sudden heart condition usually characterized by varying degrees of chest pain or discomfort, weakness, sweating, nausea, vomiting, and arrhythmias, sometimes causing loss of consciousness. It occurs when the blood supply to a part of the heart is interrupted, causing death and scarring of the local heart tissue.
Depression	In everyday language depression refers to any downturn in mood, which may be relatively transitory and perhaps due to something trivial. This is differentiated from Clinical depression which is marked by symptoms that last two weeks or more and are so severe that they interfere with daily living.
Constant	A behavior or characteristic that does not vary from one observation to another is referred to as a constant.

Go to **Cram101.com** for the Practice Tests for this Chapter.

Arousal	Arousal is a physiological and psychological state involving the activation of the reticular activating system in the brain stem, the autonomic nervous system and the endocrine system, leading to increased heart rate and blood pressure and a condition of alertness and readiness to respond.
Nervous system	The nervous system of an animal coordinates the activity of the muscles, monitors the organs, constructs and processes input from the senses, and initiates actions.
Sympathetic nervous system	The sympathetic nervous system activates what is often termed the "fight or flight response". Messages travel through in a bidirectional flow. Efferent messages can trigger changes in different parts of the body simultaneously.
Sympathetic	The sympathetic nervous system activates what is often termed the "fight or flight response". It is an automatic regulation system, that is, one that operates without the intervention of conscious thought.
Parasympathetic nervous system	The parasympathetic nervous system is one of two divisions of the autonomic nervous system. It conserves energy as it slows the heart rate, increases intestinal and gland activity, and relaxes sphincter muscles in the gastro-intestinal tract. In other words, it acts to reverse the effects of the sympathetic nervous system.
Conditioning	Processes by which behaviors can be learned or modified through interaction with the environment are conditioning.
Adaptation	A biological adaptation is an anatomical structure, physiological process or behavioral trait of an organism that has evolved over a period of time by the process of natural selection such that it increases the expected long-term reproductive success of the organism.
Aerobic	An aerobic organism is an organism that has an oxygen based metabolism. Aerobes, in a process known as cellular respiration, use oxygen to oxidize substrates (for example sugars and fats) in order to obtain energy.
Quality of life	Quality of life refers to the perception of individuals or groups that their needs are being satisfied and that they are not being denied opportunities to achieve happiness and fulfillment.
Cancer	Cancer is a class of diseases or disorders characterized by uncontrolled division of cells and the ability of these cells to invade other tissues, either by direct growth into adjacent tissue through invasion or by implantation into distant sites by metastasis.
Ulcer	An ulcer is an open sore of the skin, eyes or mucous membrane, often caused by an initial abrasion and generally maintained by an inflammation and/or an infection.
Pain	Pain is an unpleasant sensation which may be associated with actual or potential tissue damage and which may have physical and emotional components.
Predisposition	Predisposition refers to an inclination or diathesis to respond in a certain way, either inborn or acquired. In abnormal psychology, it is a factor that lowers the ability to withstand stress and inclines the individual toward pathology.
Hypertension	Hypertension is a medical condition where the blood pressure in the arteries is chronically elevated. Persistent hypertension is one of the risk factors for strokes, heart attacks, heart failure and arterial aneurysm, and is a leading cause of chronic renal failure.
Risk factor	A risk factor is a variable associated with an increased risk of disease or infection but risk factors are not necessarily causal.
Withdrawal symptoms	Withdrawal symptoms are physiological changes that occur when the use of a drug is stopped or dosage decreased.
Obsession	An obsession is a thought or idea that the sufferer cannot stop thinking about. Common

Go to **Cram101.com** for the Practice Tests for this Chapter.

examples include fears of acquiring disease, getting hurt, or causing harm to someone. They are typically automatic, frequent, distressing, and difficult to control or put an end to by themselves.

Lifestyle	The culturally, socially, economically, and environmentally conditioned complex of actions characteristic of an individual, group, or community as a pattern of habituated behavior over time that is health related but not necessarily health directed is a lifestyle.
Population	Population refers to all members of a well-defined group of organisms, events, or things.
Elderly	Old age consists of ages nearing the average life span of human beings, and thus the end of the human life cycle. Euphemisms for older people include advanced adult, elderly, and senior or senior citizen.
Coping mechanism	Coping mechanism is a pattern of behavior used to neutralize, deny, or counteract anxiety, a way to adapt to environmental stress.
Behavior modification	Behavior Modification is a technique of altering an individual's reactions to stimuli through positive reinforcement and the extinction of maladaptive behavior.
Plexus	A plexus is also a network of blood vessels, with the choroid plexuses of the brain being the most commonly mentioned example. A choroid plexus is very thin and vascular roof plates of the most anterior and most posterior cavities of the brain which expand into the interiors of the cavities.
Autogenic training	Autogenic training is a term for a relaxation technique developed by the German psychiatrist Johannes Schultz. It usually involves a series of sessions in which the patients learn to relax their limbs, heart, and breathing. The goal is to induce a pleasant, warm feeling throughout most of the body but induce a feeling of coolness in the forehead. The technique is used against stress-induced psychosomatic disorders.
Solar plexus	The solar plexus is an autonomous cluster of nerve cells in the human body behind the stomach and below the diaphragm near the celiac artery in the abdominal cavity. The solar plexus consists of two ganglia, called celiac ganglia, and a nerve network connecting the two ganglia. The solar plexus controls functions of the internal organs as for example adrenal secretion and the contraction in the intestines.
Pelvis	The pelvis is the bony structure located at the base of the spine (properly known as the caudal end). The pelvis incorporates the socket portion of the hip joint for each leg (in bipeds) or hind leg (in quadrupeds). It forms the lower limb (or hind-limb) girdle of the skeleton.
Abdomen	The abdomen is a part of the body. In humans, and in many other vertebrates, it is the region between the thorax and the pelvis. In fully developed insects, the abdomen is the third (or posterior) segment, after the head and thorax.
Conscious	Conscious refers to the thoughts, feelings, sensations, or memories of which a person is aware at any given moment.
Cognitive restructuring	Cognitive restructuring refers to any behavior therapy procedure that attempts to alter the manner in which a client thinks about life so that he or she changes overt behavior and emotions.
Eye	An eye is an organ that detects light. Different kinds of light-sensitive organs are found in a variety of creatures. The simplest eyes do nothing but detect whether the surroundings are light or dark, while more complex eyes can distinguish shapes and colors.
Biofeedback	Biofeedback is the process of measuring and quantifying an aspect of a subject's physiology, analyzing the data, and then feeding back the information to the subject in a form that allows the subject to enact physiological change.

Go to **Cram101.com** for the Practice Tests for this Chapter.

Relaxation response	Relaxation response refers to the pattern of internal bodily changes that occurs at times of relaxation. This is achieved by decreasing the arousal of the sympathetic nervous system through meditation or other forms of relaxation.
Mental health	Mental health refers to the 'thinking' part of psychosocial health; includes your values, attitudes, and beliefs.
Consensus	General agreement is a consensus.

Heart attack	A heart attack, is a serious, sudden heart condition usually characterized by varying degrees of chest pain or discomfort, weakness, sweating, nausea, vomiting, and arrhythmias, sometimes causing loss of consciousness. It occurs when the blood supply to a part of the heart is interrupted, causing death and scarring of the local heart tissue.
Atrium	The atrium is the blood collection chamber of a heart. It has a thin-walled structure that allows blood to return to the heart. There is at least one atrium in an animal with a closed circulatory system
Blood	Blood is a circulating tissue composed of fluid plasma and cells. The main function of blood is to supply nutrients (oxygen, glucose) and constitutional elements to tissues and to remove waste products.
Superior vena cava	The superior vena cava is a large but short vein that carries de-oxygenated blood from the upper half of the body to the heart's right atrium. It is formed by the left and right brachiocephalic veins (also referred to as the innominate veins) which receive blood from the upper limbs and the head and neck.
Venous blood	In the circulatory system, venous blood or peripheral blood is blood returning to the heart. With one exception (the pulmonary vein) this blood is deoxygenated and high in carbon dioxide, having released oxygen and absorbed CO_2 in the tissues.
Tricuspid valve	The tricuspid valve is on the right side of the heart, between the right atrium and the right ventricle. Being the first valve after the venae cavae, and thus the whole venous system, it is the most common valve to be infected (endocarditis) in IV drug users.
Right ventricle	The right ventricle is one of four chambers (two atria and two ventricles) in the human heart. It receives de-oxygenated blood from the right atrium via the tricuspid valve, and pumps it into the pulmonary artery via the pulmonary valve.
Ventricle	In the heart, a ventricle is a heart chamber which collects blood from an atrium (another heart chamber) and pumps it out of the heart.
Artery	Vessel that takes blood away from the heart to the tissues and organs of the body is called an artery.
Lungs	Lungs are the essential organs of respiration in air-breathing vertebrates. Their principal function is to transport oxygen from the atmosphere into the bloodstream, and to excrete carbon dioxide from the bloodstream into the atmosphere.
Pulmonary artery	The pulmonary artery carrys blood from the heart to the lungs. They are the only arteries (other than umbilical arteries in the fetus) that carry deoxygenated blood.
Carbon	Carbon is a chemical element in the periodic table that has the symbol C and atomic number 6. An abundant nonmetallic, tetravalent element, carbon has several allotropic forms.
Oxygen	Oxygen is a chemical element in the periodic table. It has the symbol O and atomic number 8. Oxygen is the second most common element on Earth, composing around 46% of the mass of Earth's crust and 28% of the mass of Earth as a whole, and is the third most common element in the universe.
Carbon dioxide	Carbon dioxide is an atmospheric gas comprized of one carbon and two oxygen atoms. A very widely known chemical compound, it is frequently called by its formula CO_2. In its solid state, it is commonly known as dry ice.
Veins	Blood vessels that return blood toward the heart from the circulation are referred to as veins.
Vein	Vein in animals, is a vessel that returns blood to the heart. In plants, a vascular bundle in a leaf, composed of xylem and phloem.

Go to **Cram101.com** for the Practice Tests for this Chapter.

Pulmonary vein	The pulmonary vein carries oxygen rich blood from the lungs to the left atrium of the heart. They are the only veins in the adult human body that carry oxygenated blood.
Left atrium	The left atrium is one of four chambers (two atria and two ventricles) in the human heart. It receives oxygenated blood from the pulmonary veins, and pumps it into the left ventricle.
Left ventricle	The left ventricle is one of four chambers (two atria and two ventricles) in the human heart. It receives oxygenated blood from the left atrium via the mitral valve, and pumps it into the aorta via the aortic valve.
Mitral valve	The mitral valve, also known as the bicuspid valve, is a valve in the heart that lies between the left atrium (LA) and the left ventricle (LV). The mitral valve and the tricuspid valve are known as the atrioventricular valves because they lie between the atria and the ventricles of the heart.
Coronary	Referring to the heart or the blood vessels of the heart is referred to as coronary.
Aorta	The largest artery in the human body, the aorta originates from the left ventricle of the heart and brings oxygenated blood to all parts of the body in the systemic circulation.
Coronary arteries	Arteries that directly supply the heart with blood are referred to as coronary arteries.
Coronary artery	An artery that supplies blood to the wall of the heart is called a coronary artery.
Aortic valve	The aortic valve lies between the left ventricle and the aorta. The most common congenital abnormality of the heart is the bicuspid aortic valve. In this condition, instead of three cusps, the aortic valve has two cusps.
Muscle	Muscle is a contractile form of tissue. It is one of the four major tissue types, the other three being epithelium, connective tissue and nervous tissue. Muscle contraction is used to move parts of the body, as well as to move substances within the body.
Inferior vena cava	The inferior vena cava is a large vein that carries de-oxygenated blood from the lower half of the body into the heart. It is formed by the left and right common iliac veins and transports blood to the right atrium of the heart.
Myocardium	Myocardium is the muscular tissue of the heart. The myocardium is composed of specialized cardiac muscle cells with an ability not possessed by muscle tissue elsewhere in the body.
Sinus	A sinus is a pouch or cavity in any organ or tissue, or an abnormal cavity or passage caused by the destruction of tissue.
Left coronary artery	The left coronary artery arises from the aorta above the left cusp of the aortic valve as the left main (LM) artery.
Course	Pattern of development and change of a disorder over time is a course.
Septum	A septum, in general, is a wall separating two cavities or two spaces containing a less dense material. The muscle wall that divides the heart chambers.
Anterior surface	The anterior surface of the body presents, in the middle line, a vertical crest, the sphenoidal crest, which articulates with the perpendicular plate of the ethmoid, and forms part of the septum of the nose.
Interventric-lar septum	Interventricular septum is the stout wall separating the lower chambers (the ventricles) of the heart from one another.
Right coronary artery	The right coronary artery originates above the right cusp of the aortic valve. It travels down the right atrioventricular groove, towards the crux of the heart. At the origin of the RCA is the conus artery.

Go to **Cram101.com** for the Practice Tests for this Chapter.

Capillary	A capillary is the smallest of a body's blood vessels, measuring 5-10 micro meters. They connect arteries and veins, and most closely interact with tissues. Their walls are composed of a single layer of cells, the endothelium. This layer is so thin that molecules such as oxygen, water and lipids can pass through them by diffusion and enter the tissues.
Gas exchange	In humans and other mammals, respiratory gas exchange or ventilation is carried out by mechanisms of the lungs. The actual gas exchange occurs in the alveoli.
Capillaries	Capillaries refer to the smallest of the blood vessels and the sites of exchange between the blood and tissue cells.
Ischemia	Narrowing of arteries caused by plaque buildup within the arteries is called ischemia.
Myocardial infarction	Acute myocardial infarction, commonly known as a heart attack, is a serious, sudden heart condition usually characterized by varying degrees of chest pain or discomfort, weakness, sweating, nausea, vomiting, and arrhythmias, sometimes causing loss of consciousness.
Infarction	The sudden death of tissue from a lack of blood perfusion is referred to as an infarction.
Adenosine	Adenosine is a nucleoside comprized of adenine attached to a ribose (ribofuranose) moiety via a β-N_9-glycosidic bond. Adenosine plays an important role in biochemical processes, such as energy transfer - as adenosine triphosphate (ATP) and adenosine diphosphate (ADP) - as well as in signal transduction as cyclic adenosine monophosphate, cAMP.
Adenosine triphosphate	Organic molecule that stores energy and releases energy for use in cellular processes is adenosine triphosphate.
Mitochondria	Cytoplasmic organelles responsible for ATP generation for cellular activities are referred to as mitochondria.
Organelle	Organelle refers to any structure within a cell that carries out one of its metabolic roles, such as mitochondria, centrioles, endoplasmic reticulum, and the nucleus.
Limited capacity	Limited capacity refers to the concept that one's information processing ability is restricted. Metaphors for capacity include mental space, mental energy or effort, and time.
Blood vessel	A blood vessel is a part of the circulatory system and function to transport blood throughout the body. The most important types, arteries and veins, are so termed because they carry blood away from or towards the heart, respectively.
Organ	Organ refers to a structure consisting of several tissues adapted as a group to perform specific functions.
Depolarization	Depolarization is a decrease in the absolute value of a cell's membrane potential. Thus, changes in membrane voltage in which the membrane potential becomes less positive or less negative are both depolarizations.
Repolarization	In neuroscience, repolarization refers to the change in membrane potential that returns the membrane potential to a negative value after the depolarization phase of an action potential has just previously changed the membrane potential to a positive value.
Conduction system	Special muscle fibers that conduct electrical impulses throughout the muscle of the heart is the conduction system.
Tissue	A collection of interconnected cells that perform a similar function within an organism is called tissue.
Fiber	Fibers used by man come from a wide variety of sources: Natural fiber include those made out of plants, animal and mineral sources. Natural fibers can be classified according to their origin.
Purkinje fiber	A purkinje fiber is located in the inner ventricular walls of the heart, just beneath the

	endocardium. These fibers are specialized myocardial fibers that conduct an electrical stimulus or impulse that enables the heart to contract in a coordinated fashion.
Muscle fiber	Cell with myofibrils containing actin and myosin filaments arranged within sarcomeres is a muscle fiber.
Intercalated disc	An intercalated disc is an undulating double membrane separating adjacent cells in cardiac muscle fibers. They support synchronized contraction of cardiac tissue.
Cardiac muscle	Cardiac muscle is a type of striated muscle found within the heart. Its function is to "pump" blood through the circulatory system. Unlike skeletal muscle, which contracts in response to nerve stimulation, and like smooth muscle, cardiac muscle is myogenic, meaning that it stimulates its own contraction without a requisite electrical impulse.
Electrocardi-gram	An electrocardiogram is a graphic produced by an electrocardiograph, which records the electrical voltage in the heart in the form of a continuous strip graph. It is the prime tool in cardiac electrophysiology, and has a prime function in screening and diagnosis of cardiovascular diseases..
Chordae tendinae	The chordae tendinae are cord-like tendons that connect the papillary muscles to the tricuspid valve and the mitral valve in the heart.
Sinoatrial node	Sinoatrial node refers to a small mass of specialized muscle in the wall of the right atrium; generates electrical signals rhythmically and spontaneously and serves as the heart's pacemaker.
Evaluation	The fifth step of the nursing process where nursing care and the patient's goal achievement are measured is the evaluation.
Lead	Lead is a chemical element in the periodic table that has the symbol Pb and atomic number 82. A soft, heavy, toxic and malleable poor metal, lead is bluish white when freshly cut but tarnishes to dull gray when exposed to air. Lead is used in building construction, lead-acid batteries, bullets and shot, and is part of solder, pewter, and fusible alloys.
Skin	Skin is an organ of the integumentary system composed of a layer of tissues that protect underlying muscles and organs.
Systole	The contraction stage of the heart cycle, when the heart chambers actively pump blood is systole.
Ventricular systole	Ventricular systole is the contraction of the muscles (myocardia) of the left and right ventricles.
Heart rate	Heart rate is a term used to describe the frequency of the cardiac cycle. It is considered one of the four vital signs. Usually it is calculated as the number of contractions of the heart in one minute and expressed as "beats per minute".
Tachycardia	Tachycardia is an abnormally rapid beating of the heart, defined as a resting heart rate of over 100 beats per minute. Common causes are autonomic nervous system or endocrine system activity, hemodynamic responses, and various forms of cardiac arrhythmia.
Bradycardia	Bradycardia, as applied in adult medicine, is defined as a heart rate of under 60 beats per minute, though it is seldom symptomatic until the rate drops below 50 beat/min.
Infection	The invasion and multiplication of microorganisms in body tissues is called an infection.
Quinidine	Quinidine is a pharmaceutical agent that acts as a class I antiarrhythmic agent in the heart. It is a stereoisomer of quinine, originally derived from the bark of the cinchona tree.
Constant	A behavior or characteristic that does not vary from one observation to another is referred to as a constant.

215

Atrioventric-lar node	The atrioventricular node is the tissue between the atria and the ventricles of the heart, which conducts the normal electrical impulse from the atria to the ventricles.
Arrhythmias	Arrhythmias refers to abnormal heart rhythms which may be too slow, too early, too rapid, or irregular.
Arrhythmia	Cardiac arrhythmia is a group of conditions in which muscle contraction of the heart is irregular for any reason.
Stimulant	A stimulant is a drug which increases the activity of the sympathetic nervous system and produces a sense of euphoria or awakeness.
Blocking	A sudden break or interuption in the flow of thinking or speech that is seen as an absence in thought is refered to as blocking.
Receptor	A receptor is a protein on the cell membrane or within the cytoplasm or cell nucleus that binds to a specific molecule (a ligand), such as a neurotransmitter, hormone, or other substance, and initiates the cellular response to the ligand. Receptor, in immunology, the region of an antibody which shows recognition of an antigen.
Inspiration	Inspiration begins with the onset of contraction of the diaphragm, which results in expansion of the intrapleural space and an increase in negative pressure according to Boyle's Law.
Expiration	In respiration, expiration is initiated by a decrease in volume and positive pressure exerted upon the intrapleural space upon diaphragm relaxation.
Ephedrine	Ephedrine (EPH) is a sympathomimetic amine commonly used as a decongestant and to treat hypotension associated with regional anaesthesia. Chemically, it is an alkaloid derived from various plants in the genus Ephedra (family Ephedraceae).
Nicotine	Nicotine is an organic compound, an alkaloid found naturally throughout the tobacco plant, with a high concentration in the leaves. It is a potent nerve poison and is included in many insecticides. In lower concentrations, the substance is a stimulant and is one of the main factors leading to the pleasure and habit-forming qualities of tobacco smoking.
Antihistamine	An antihistamine is a drug which serves to reduce or eliminate effects mediated by histamine, an endogenous chemical mediator released during allergic reactions, through action at the histamine receptor.
Atrial fibrillation	Atrial fibrillation (AF or afib) is an abnormal heart rhythm (cardiac arrhythmia) which involves the two small, upper heart chambers (the atria).
Fibrillation	Fibrillation is the rapid, irregular, and unsynchronized contraction of the muscle fibers of the heart. There are two major classes of fibrillation, atrial fibrillation and ventricular fibrillation.
Cardiac output	Cardiac output is the volume of blood being pumped by the heart in a minute. It is equal to the heart rate multiplied by the stroke volume.
Baseline	Measure of a particular behavior or process taken before the introduction of the independent variable or treatment is called the baseline.
Refractory phase	Refractory phase refers to the brief period after stimulation of a nerve, muscle, or other irritable element during which it is unresponsive to a second stimulus. Similarly, it is the period after intercourse during which the male cannot have another orgasm.
Catecholamine	Catecholamine is a chemical compound derived from the amino acid tyrosine that acts as a hormone or neurotransmitter. They are examples of phenethylamines.
Prognosis	Prognosis refers to the prospects for the future or outcome of a disease.
Depression	In everyday language depression refers to any downturn in mood, which may be relatively

transitory and perhaps due to something trivial. This is differentiated from Clinical depression which is marked by symptoms that last two weeks or more and are so severe that they interfere with daily living.

Incidence
In epidemiological studies of a particular disorder, the rate at which new cases occur in a given place at a given time is called incidence.

Pulse
The rhythmic stretching of the arteries caused by the pressure of blood forced through the arteries by contractions of the ventricles during systole is a pulse.

Ventricular fibrillation
Ventricular fibrillation is a cardiac condition that consists of a lack of coordination of the contraction of the muscle tissue of the large chambers of the heart that eventually leads to the heart stopping altogether.

Cardiopulmonary resuscitation
Cardiopulmonary resuscitation is an emergency first aid protocol for an unconscious person on whom both breathing and pulse cannot be detected.

Shock
Circulatory shock, a state of cardiac output that is insufficient to meet the body's physiological needs, with consequences ranging from fainting to death is referred to as shock. Insulin shock, a state of severe hypoglycemia caused by administration of insulin.

Angina
Angina pectoris is chest pain due to ischemia (a lack of blood and hence oxygen supply) to the heart muscle, generally due to obstruction or spasm of the coronary arteries (the heart's blood vessels). Coronary artery disease, the main cause of angina, is due to atherosclerosis of the cardiac arteries.

Angina pectoris
Angina pectoris is chest pain due to ischemia (a lack of blood and hence oxygen supply) to the heart muscle, generally due to obstruction or spasm of the coronary arteries (the heart's blood vessels).

Pain
Pain is an unpleasant sensation which may be associated with actual or potential tissue damage and which may have physical and emotional components.

Bypass
In medicine, a bypass generally means an alternate or additional route for blood flow, which is created in bypass surgery, e.g. coronary artery bypass surgery by moving blood vessels or implanting synthetic tubing.

Coronary artery bypass surgery
Coronary artery bypass surgery is a surgical procedure performed on patients with coronary artery disease (see atherosclerosis) for the relief of angina and possible improved heart muscle function.

Adverse impact
Adverse impact refers to potential unfairness in the treatment of minority group or protected class members. In hiring it occurs if the protected class's selection ratio is less than four-fifths of the nonprotected class's selection ratio.

Elevation
Elevation refers to upward movement of a part of the body.

Aneurysm
An aneurysm is a localized dilation or ballooning of a blood vessel by more than 50% of the diameter of the vessel. Aneurysms most commonly occur in the arteries at the base of the brain and in the aorta (the main artery coming out of the heart) - this is an aortic aneurysm.

Scar
A scar results from the biologic process of wound repair in the skin and other tissues of the body. It is a connective tissue that fills the wound.

Acute
In medicine, an acute disease is a disease with either or both of: a rapid onset; and a short course (as opposed to a chronic course).

Enzyme
An enzyme is a protein that catalyzes, or speeds up, a chemical reaction. They are essential to sustain life because most chemical reactions in biological cells would occur too slowly, or would lead to different products, without them.

Serum	Serum is the same as blood plasma except that clotting factors (such as fibrin) have been removed. Blood plasma contains fibrinogen.
Sublingual	Area beneath the tongue is called sublingual.
Affect	Affect is the scientific term used to describe a subject's externally displayed mood. This can be assesed by the nurse by observing facial expression, tone of voice, and body language.
Blood pressure	Blood pressure is the pressure exerted by the blood on the walls of the blood vessels.
Migraine	Migraine is a neurologic disease, of which the most common symptom is an intense and disabling headache. Migraine is the most common type of vascular headache.
Hypertension	Hypertension is a medical condition where the blood pressure in the arteries is chronically elevated. Persistent hypertension is one of the risk factors for strokes, heart attacks, heart failure and arterial aneurysm, and is a leading cause of chronic renal failure.
Norepinephrine	Norepinephrine is a catecholamine and a phenethylamine with chemical formula $C_8H_{11}NO_3$. It is released from the adrenal glands as a hormone into the blood, but it is also a neurotransmitter in the nervous system where it is released from noradrenergic neurons during synaptic transmission.
Epinephrine	Epinephrine is a hormone and a neurotransmitter. Epinephrine plays a central role in the short-term stress reaction—the physiological response to threatening or exciting conditions (fight-or-flight response). It is secreted by the adrenal medulla.
Intestine	The intestine is the portion of the alimentary canal extending from the stomach to the anus and, in humans and mammals, consists of two segments, the small intestine and the large intestine. The intestine is the part of the body responsible for extracting nutrition from food.
Arteriole	An arteriole is a blood vessel that extends and branches out from an artery and leads to capillaries. They have thick muscular walls and are the primary site of vascular resistance.
Bladder	A hollow muscular storage organ for storing urine is a bladder.
Uterus	The uterus is the major female reproductive organ of most mammals. One end, the cervix, opens into the vagina; the other is connected on both sides to the fallopian tubes. The main function is to accept a fertilized ovum which becomes implanted into the endometrium, and derives nourishment from blood vessels which develop exclusively for this purpose.
Smooth muscle	Smooth muscle is a type of non-striated muscle, found within the "walls" of hollow organs; such as blood vessels, the bladder, the uterus, and the gastrointestinal tract. Smooth muscle is used to move matter within the body, via contraction; it generally operates "involuntarily", without nerve stimulation.
Asthma	Asthma is a complex disease characterized by bronchial hyperresponsiveness (BHR), inflammation, mucus production and intermittent airway obstruction.
Bronchitis	Bronchitis is an obstructive pulmonary disease characterized by inflammation of the bronchi of the lungs.
Insulin	Insulin is a polypeptide hormone that regulates carbohydrate metabolism. Apart from being the primary effector in carbohydrate homeostasis, it also has a substantial effect on small vessel muscle tone, controls storage and release of fat (triglycerides) and cellular uptake of both amino acids and some electrolytes.
Hypoglycemia	An abnormally low level of glucose in the blood that results when the pancreas secretes too much insulin into the blood is called hypoglycemia.
Regression	A regression equation refers to a mathematical relationship where one variable is predictable

Go to **Cram101.com** for the Practice Tests for this Chapter.

equation	from another.
Regression	Return to a form of behavior characteristic of an earlier stage of development is a regression.
Medicine	Medicine is the branch of health science and the sector of public life concerned with maintaining or restoring human health through the study, diagnosis and treatment of disease and injury.
Placebo	A placebo is an inactive substance (pill, liquid, etc.), which is administered as if it were a therapy, but which has no therapeutic value other than the placebo effect.
Nitrate	Nitrate refers to a salt of nitric acid; a compound containing the radical NO_3; biologically, the final form of nitrogen from the oxidation of organic nitrogen compounds.
Vascular smooth muscle	Vascular smooth muscle refers to the particular type of smooth muscle found within, and composing the majority of the wall of blood vessels.
Resistance	Resistance refers to a nonspecific ability to ward off infection or disease regardless of whether the body has been previously exposed to it. A force that opposes the flow of a fluid such as air or blood. Compare with immunity.
Calcium	Calcium is the chemical element in the periodic table that has the symbol Ca and atomic number 20. Calcium is a soft grey alkaline earth metal that is used as a reducing agent in the extraction of thorium, zirconium and uranium. Calcium is also the fifth most abundant element in the Earth's crust.
Channel	Channel, in communications (sometimes called communications channel), refers to the medium used to convey information from a sender (or transmitter) to a receiver.
Hypotension	In physiology and medicine, hypotension refers to an abnormally low blood pressure. It is often associated with shock, though not necessarily indicative of it.
Antagonist	A antagonist is a drug that interacts with the target cell of a receptor site to inhibit or prevent the action of an agonist.
Inpatient	Inpatient refers to a person who enters a healthcare setting for a stay ranging from 24 hours to many years.
Trade name	A drug company's name for their patented medication is called a trade name.
Excretion	Excretion is the biological process by which an organism chemically separates waste products from its body. The waste products are then usually expelled from the body by elimination.
Diuretic	A diuretic is any drug that elevates the rate of bodily urine excretion.
Electrolytes	Electrolytes refers to compounds that separate into ions in water and, in turn, are able to conduct an electrical current. These include sodium, chloride, and potassium.
Electrolyte	An electrolyte is a substance that dissociates into free ions when dissolved (or molten), to produce an electrically conductive medium. Because they generally consist of ions in solution, they are also known as ionic solutions.
Hypokalemia	Hypokalemia is a potentially fatal condition in which the body fails to retain sufficient potassium to maintain health.
Potassium	Potassium is a chemical element in the periodic table. It has the symbol K (L. kalium) and atomic number 19. Potassium is a soft silvery-white metallic alkali metal that occurs naturally bound to other elements in seawater and many minerals.
Glucose	Glucose, a simple monosaccharide sugar, is one of the most important carbohydrates and is used as a source of energy in animals and plants. Glucose is one of the main products of

Go to **Cram101.com** for the Practice Tests for this Chapter.

photosynthesis and starts respiration.

Triglyceride	Triglyceride is a glyceride in which the glycerol is esterified with three fatty acids. They are the main constituent of vegetable oil and animal fats and play an important role in metabolism as energy sources. They contain a bit more than twice as much energy as carbohydrates and proteins.
Cholesterol	Cholesterol is a steroid, a lipid, and an alcohol, found in the cell membranes of all body tissues, and transported in the blood plasma of all animals. It is an important component of the membranes of cells, providing stability; it makes the membrane's fluidity stable over a bigger temperature interval.
Metabolism	Metabolism is the biochemical modification of chemical compounds in living organisms and cells. This includes the biosynthesis of complex organic molecules (anabolism) and their breakdown (catabolism).
Solution	Solution refers to homogenous mixture formed when a solute is dissolved in a solvent.
Inhibitor	An inhibitor is a type of effector (biology) that decreases or prevents the rate of a chemical reaction. They are often called negative catalysts.
Lipid	Lipid is one class of aliphatic hydrocarbon-containing organic compounds essential for the structure and function of living cells. They are characterized by being water-insoluble but soluble in nonpolar organic solvents.
Acid	An acid is a water-soluble, sour-tasting chemical compound that when dissolved in water, gives a solution with a pH of less than 7.
Triglycerides	Triglycerides refer to fats and oils composed of fatty acids and glycerol; are the body's most concentrated source of energy fuel; also known as neutral fats.
Liver	The liver is an organ in vertebrates, including humans. It plays a major role in metabolism and has a number of functions in the body including drug detoxification, glycogen storage, and plasma protein synthesis. It also produces bile, which is important for digestion.
Agent	Agent refers to an epidemiological term referring to the organism or object that transmits a disease from the environment to the host.
Anticoagulant	A biochemical that inhibits blood clotting is referred to as an anticoagulant.
Trauma	Trauma refers to a severe physical injury or wound to the body caused by an external force, or a psychological shock having a lasting effect on mental life.
Craving	Craving refers to the powerful desire to use a psychoactive drug or engage in a compulsive behavior. It is manifested in physiological changes, such as raised heart rate, sweating, anxiety, drop in body temperature, pupil dilation, and stomach muscle movements.
Mucosa	The mucosa is a lining of ectodermic origin, covered in epithelium, and involved in absorption and secretion. They line various body cavities that are exposed to the external environment and internal organs.
Plasma	Fluid portion of circulating blood is called plasma.
Cardiac arrhythmia	Cardiac arrhythmia is a group of conditions in which the muscle contraction of the heart is irregular or is faster or slower than normal.
Bronchodilator	A bronchodilator is a medication intended to improve bronchial airflow. Treatment of bronchial asthma is the most common application of these drugs.
Hyperglycemia	Hyperglycemia is a condition in which an excessive amount of glucose circulates in the blood plasma.

Go to **Cram101.com** for the Practice Tests for this Chapter.

Pancreas	The pancreas is a retroperitoneal organ that serves two functions: exocrine - it produces pancreatic juice containing digestive enzymes, and endocrine - it produces several important hormones, namely insulin.
Sugar	A sugar is the simplest molecule that can be identified as a carbohydrate. These include monosaccharides and disaccharides, trisaccharides and the oligosaccharides. The term "glyco-" indicates the presence of a sugar in an otherwise non-carbohydrate substance.
Carbohydrate	Carbohydrate is a chemical compound that contains oxygen, hydrogen, and carbon atoms. They consist of monosaccharide sugars of varying chain lengths and that have the general chemical formula $C_n(H_2O)_n$ or are derivatives of such.
Diabetes	Diabetes is a medical disorder characterized by varying or persistent elevated blood sugar levels, especially after eating. All types of diabetes share similar symptoms and complications at advanced stages: dehydration and ketoacidosis, cardiovascular disease, chronic renal failure, retinal damage which can lead to blindness, nerve damage which can lead to erectile dysfunction, gangrene with risk of amputation of toes, feet, and even legs.
Diabetes mellitus	Diabetes mellitus is a medical disorder characterized by varying or persistent hyperglycemia (elevated blood sugar levels), especially after eating. All types of diabetes mellitus share similar symptoms and complications at advanced stages.
Injection	A method of rapid drug delivery that puts the substance directly in the bloodstream, in a muscle, or under the skin is called injection.
Protein	A protein is a complex, high-molecular-weight organic compound that consists of amino acids joined by peptide bonds. They are essential to the structure and function of all living cells and viruses. Many are enzymes or subunits of enzymes.
Anxiety	Anxiety is a complex combination of the feeling of fear, apprehension and worry often accompanied by physical sensations such as palpitations, chest pain and/or shortness of breath.
Tranquilizer	A sedative, or tranquilizer, is a drug that depresses the central nervous system (CNS), which causes calmness, relaxation, reduction of anxiety, sleepiness, slowed breathing, slurred speech, staggering gait, poor judgment, and slow, uncertain reflexes.
Minor tranquilizers	Drugs that produce relaxation or reduce anxiety are referred to as minor tranquilizers.
Alcohol	Alcohol is a general term, applied to any organic compound in which a hydroxyl group (-OH) is bound to a carbon atom, which in turn is bound to other hydrogen and/or carbon atoms. The general formula for a simple acyclic alcohol is $C_nH_{2n+1}OH$.
Major tranquilizer	Antipsychotic drug is referred to as major tranquilizer.
Reaction time	The amount of time required to respond to a stimulus is referred to as reaction time.
Joint	A joint (articulation) is the location at which two bones make contact (articulate). They are constructed to both allow movement and provide mechanical support.
Pharmacist	A pharmacist takes requests for medicines from a physician in the form of a medical prescription and dispense the medication to the patient and counsel them on the proper use and adverse effects of that medication.
Variable	A characteristic or aspect in which people, objects, events, or conditions vary is called variable.
Rehabilitation	Rehabilitation is the restoration of lost capabilities, or the treatment aimed at producing it. Also refers to treatment for dependency on psychoactive substances such as alcohol,

	prescription drugs, and illicit drugs such as cocaine, heroin or amphetamines.
Stress	Stress refers to a condition that is a response to factors that change the human systems normal state.
Cardiology	Cardiology is the branch of medicine dealing with disorders of the heart and blood vessels. The field is commonly divided in the branches of congenital heart defects, coronary artery disease, heart failure, valvular heart disease and electrophysiology.
Marijuana	Marijuana refers to the dried vegetable matter of the Cannabis sativa plant.

Contusion	Brain contusion, a form of traumatic brain injury, is a bruise of the brain tissue. Like bruises in other tissues, cerebral contusion can be caused by multiple microhemorrhages, small blood vessel leaks into brain tissue.
Wound	A wound is type of physical trauma wherein the skin is torn, cut or punctured, or where blunt force trauma causes a contusion.
Skin	Skin is an organ of the integumentary system composed of a layer of tissues that protect underlying muscles and organs.
Hypothermia	Hypothermia is a low core body temperature, defined clinically as a temperature of less than 35 degrees celsius.
Insulin	Insulin is a polypeptide hormone that regulates carbohydrate metabolism. Apart from being the primary effector in carbohydrate homeostasis, it also has a substantial effect on small vessel muscle tone, controls storage and release of fat (triglycerides) and cellular uptake of both amino acids and some electrolytes.
Shock	Circulatory shock, a state of cardiac output that is insufficient to meet the body's physiological needs, with consequences ranging from fainting to death is referred to as shock. Insulin shock, a state of severe hypoglycemia caused by administration of insulin.
Planning	In agreement with the patient, the nurse addresses each of the problems identified in the planning phase. For each problem a measurable goal is set. For example, for the patient discussed above, the goal would be for the patient's skin to remain intact. The result is a nursing care plan. This is the third step.
Aerobic	An aerobic organism is an organism that has an oxygen based metabolism. Aerobes, in a process known as cellular respiration, use oxygen to oxidize substrates (for example sugars and fats) in order to obtain energy.
Solution	Solution refers to homogenous mixture formed when a solute is dissolved in a solvent.
Sharps container	A sharps container is a single use container that is filled with used medical needles then disposed of. It is normal practice world wide for used needles to be placed immediately into a sharps container after a single use. Needles are never to be reused.
Antiseptic	An antiseptic is a substance that prevents the growth and reproduction of various microorganisms (such as bacteria, fungi, protozoa, and viruses) on the external surfaces of the body. Some are true germicides, capable of destroying the bacteria, whilst others merely prevent or inhibit their growth.
Blood	Blood is a circulating tissue composed of fluid plasma and cells. The main function of blood is to supply nutrients (oxygen, glucose) and constitutional elements to tissues and to remove waste products.
Acute	In medicine, an acute disease is a disease with either or both of: a rapid onset; and a short course (as opposed to a chronic course).
Muscle	Muscle is a contractile form of tissue. It is one of the four major tissue types, the other three being epithelium, connective tissue and nervous tissue. Muscle contraction is used to move parts of the body, as well as to move substances within the body.
Lead	Lead is a chemical element in the periodic table that has the symbol Pb and atomic number 82. A soft, heavy, toxic and malleable poor metal, lead is bluish white when freshly cut but tarnishes to dull gray when exposed to air. Lead is used in building construction, lead-acid batteries, bullets and shot, and is part of solder, pewter, and fusible alloys.
Adaptation	A biological adaptation is an anatomical structure, physiological process or behavioral trait of an organism that has evolved over a period of time by the process of natural selection

Go to **Cram101.com** for the Practice Tests for this Chapter.

	such that it increases the expected long-term reproductive success of the organism.
Stress	Stress refers to a condition that is a response to factors that change the human systems normal state.
Joint	A joint (articulation) is the location at which two bones make contact (articulate). They are constructed to both allow movement and provide mechanical support.
Diabetes	Diabetes is a medical disorder characterized by varying or persistent elevated blood sugar levels, especially after eating. All types of diabetes share similar symptoms and complications at advanced stages: dehydration and ketoacidosis, cardiovascular disease, chronic renal failure, retinal damage which can lead to blindness, nerve damage which can lead to erectile dysfunction, gangrene with risk of amputation of toes, feet, and even legs.
Asthma	Asthma is a complex disease characterized by bronchial hyperresponsiveness (BHR), inflammation, mucus production and intermittent airway obstruction.
Health	Health is a term that refers to a combination of the absence of illness, the ability to cope with everyday activities, physical fitness, and high quality of life.
Implementation	The methods by which the goal will be achieved is also recorded at this fourth stage. The methods of implementation must be recorded in an explicit and tangible format in a way that the patient can understand should he wish to read it. Clarity is essential as it will aid communication between those tasked with carrying out patient care.
Pain	Pain is an unpleasant sensation which may be associated with actual or potential tissue damage and which may have physical and emotional components.
Pathogen	A pathogen or infectious agent is a biological agent that causes disease or illness to its host. The term is most often used for agents that disrupt the normal physiology of a multicellular animal or plant.
Elevation	Elevation refers to upward movement of a part of the body.
Concept	A mental category used to class together objects, relations, events, abstractions, or qualities that have common properties is called concept.
Tissue	A collection of interconnected cells that perform a similar function within an organism is called tissue.
Vasoconstriction	Vasoconstriction refers to a decrease in the diameter of a blood vessel.
Blood vessel	A blood vessel is a part of the circulatory system and function to transport blood throughout the body. The most important types, arteries and veins, are so termed because they carry blood away from or towards the heart, respectively.
Vasodilation	An increase in the diameter of superficial blood vessels triggered by nerve signals that relax the smooth muscles of the vessel walls is referred to as vasodilation.
Referred pain	Referred pain is an unpleasant senzation localised to an area separate from the site of the causative injury or other painful stimulation. Often, referred pain arises when a nerve is compressed or damaged at or near its origin.
Trauma	Trauma refers to a severe physical injury or wound to the body caused by an external force, or a psychological shock having a lasting effect on mental life.
Friction	Friction is the force that opposes the relative motion or tendency of such motion of two surfaces in contact. The resulting injury to skin resembles an abrasion and can also damage superficial blood vessels directly under the skin.
Infection	The invasion and multiplication of microorganisms in body tissues is called an infection.

Go to **Cram101.com** for the Practice Tests for this Chapter.

Traction	Traction refers to the set of mechanisms for straightening broken bones or relieving pressure on the skeletal system. It is largely replaced now by more modern techniques, but certain approaches are still used today for hip fractures.
Hydrogen	Hydrogen is a chemical element in the periodic table that has the symbol H and atomic number 1. At standard temperature and pressure it is a colorless, odorless, nonmetallic, univalent, tasteless, highly flammable diatomic gas.
Lymph	Lymph originates as blood plasma lost from the circulatory system, which leaks out into the surrounding tissues. The lymphatic system collects this fluid by diffusion into lymph capillaries, and returns it to the circulatory system.
Gland	A gland is an organ in an animal's body that synthesizes a substance for release such as hormones, often into the bloodstream or into cavities inside the body or its outer surface.
Fever	Fever (also known as pyrexia, or a febrile response, and archaically known as ague) is a medical symptom that describes an increase in internal body temperature to levels that are above normal (37°C, 98.6°F).
Hydrogen peroxide	Hydrogen peroxide is a clear liquid, slightly more viscous than water, that has strong oxidizing properties and is therefore a powerful bleaching agent that has found use as a disinfectant, as an oxidizer, and in rocketry (particularly in high concentrations as high-test peroxide (HTP) as a monopropellant, and in bipropellant systems.
Tetanus	Tetanus is a serious and often fatal disease caused by the neurotoxin tetanospasmin which is produced by the Gram-positive, obligate anaerobic bacterium Clostridium tetani. Tetanus also refers to a state of muscle tension.
Suture	Suture refers to an immovable joint, such as that between flat bones of the skull. Also the stitches used to hold tissue together or to close a wound.
Agent	Agent refers to an epidemiological term referring to the organism or object that transmits a disease from the environment to the host.
Pulse	The rhythmic stretching of the arteries caused by the pressure of blood forced through the arteries by contractions of the ventricles during systole is a pulse.
Pupil	Pupil refers to the opening in the iris that admits light into the interior of the vertebrate eye. Muscles in the iris regulate its size.
Eye	An eye is an organ that detects light. Different kinds of light-sensitive organs are found in a variety of creatures. The simplest eyes do nothing but detect whether the surroundings are light or dark, while more complex eyes can distinguish shapes and colors.
Blood pressure	Blood pressure is the pressure exerted by the blood on the walls of the blood vessels.
Vital signs	Vital signs include pulse, blood pressure, respiratory rate, and body temperature measurements.
Carbohydrate	Carbohydrate is a chemical compound that contains oxygen, hydrogen, and carbon atoms. They consist of monosaccharide sugars of varying chain lengths and that have the general chemical formula $C_n(H_2O)_n$ or are derivatives of such.
Fluid balance	Fluid balance refers to equilibrium between fluid intake and output or between the amounts of fluid contained in the body's different fluid compartments.
Syncope	Syncope is also the medical term for fainting.
Cramp	A cramp is an unpleasant sensation caused by contraction, usually of a muscle. It can be caused by cold or overexertion.
Sweat gland	Gland responsible for the loss of a watery fluid, consisting mainly of sodium chloride

234

Go to **Cram101.com** for the Practice Tests for this Chapter.

(commonly known as salt) and urea in solution, that is secreted through the skin is a sweat gland.

Stroke   A stroke or cerebrovascular accident (CVA) occurs when the blood supply to a part of the brain is suddenly interrupted.

Diuretic   A diuretic is any drug that elevates the rate of bodily urine excretion.

Alcohol   Alcohol is a general term, applied to any organic compound in which a hydroxyl group (-OH) is bound to a carbon atom, which in turn is bound to other hydrogen and/or carbon atoms. The general formula for a simple acyclic alcohol is $C_nH_{2n+1}OH$.

Salt   Salt is a term used for ionic compounds composed of positively charged cations and negatively charged anions, so that the product is neutral and without a net charge.

Contamination   The introduction of microorganisms or particulate matter into a normally sterile environment is called contamination.

Inflammation   Inflammation is the first response of the immune system to infection or irritation and may be referred to as the innate cascade.

Wart   A wart is a generally small, rough, cauliflower-like growth, of viral origin, typically on hands and feet.

Hydration   Hydration can create a hydrate from which water can be reextracted. When hydration occurs in a chemical reaction it is called a hydration reaction, in which water is permanently and chemically combined with a reactant in a way that it can no longer be reextracted.

Minerals   Minerals refer to inorganic chemical compounds found in nature; salts.

Sodium   Sodium is the chemical element in the periodic table that has the symbol Na (Natrium in Latin) and atomic number 11. Sodium is a soft, waxy, silvery reactive metal belonging to the alkali metals that is abundant in natural compounds (especially halite). It is highly reactive.

Glucose   Glucose, a simple monosaccharide sugar, is one of the most important carbohydrates and is used as a source of energy in animals and plants. Glucose is one of the main products of photosynthesis and starts respiration.

Electrolyte   An electrolyte is a substance that dissociates into free ions when dissolved (or molten), to produce an electrically conductive medium. Because they generally consist of ions in solution, they are also known as ionic solutions.

Sugar   A sugar is the simplest molecule that can be identified as a carbohydrate. These include monosaccharides and disaccharides, trisaccharides and the oligosaccharides. The term "glyco-" indicates the presence of a sugar in an otherwise non-carbohydrate substance.

Dehydration   Dehydration is the removal of water from an object. Medically, dehydration is a serious and potentially life-threatening condition in which the body contains an insufficient volume of water for normal functioning.

Freezing   Freezing is the process in which blood is frozen and all of the plasma and 99% of the WBCs are eliminated when thawing takes place and the nontransferable cryoprotectant is removed.

Hyperglycemia   Hyperglycemia is a condition in which an excessive amount of glucose circulates in the blood plasma.

Hypoglycemia   An abnormally low level of glucose in the blood that results when the pancreas secretes too much insulin into the blood is called hypoglycemia.

Brain   The part of the central nervous system involved in regulating and controlling body activity and interpreting information from the senses transmitted through the nervous system is

Go to **Cram101.com** for the Practice Tests for this Chapter.

referred to as the brain.

Hypotension	In physiology and medicine, hypotension refers to an abnormally low blood pressure. It is often associated with shock, though not necessarily indicative of it.
Heart attack	A heart attack, is a serious, sudden heart condition usually characterized by varying degrees of chest pain or discomfort, weakness, sweating, nausea, vomiting, and arrhythmias, sometimes causing loss of consciousness. It occurs when the blood supply to a part of the heart is interrupted, causing death and scarring of the local heart tissue.
Hyperthermia	Hyperthermia is an acute condition which occurs when the body produces or absorbs more heat than it can dissipate. It is usually due to excessive exposure to heat.
Tachycardia	Tachycardia is an abnormally rapid beating of the heart, defined as a resting heart rate of over 100 beats per minute. Common causes are autonomic nervous system or endocrine system activity, hemodynamic responses, and various forms of cardiac arrhythmia.
Bradycardia	Bradycardia, as applied in adult medicine, is defined as a heart rate of under 60 beats per minute, though it is seldom symptomatic until the rate drops below 50 beat/min.
Apnea	Apnea is the absence of external breathing. During apnea there is no movement of the muscles of respiration and the volume of the lungs initially remains unchanged. .
Dyspnea	Dyspnea or shortness of breath (SOB) is perceived difficulty breathing or pain on breathing. It is a common symptom of numerous medical disorders.
Hyperventilation	Hyperventilation is the state of breathing faster or deeper (hyper) than necessary, and thereby reducing the carbon dioxide concentration of the blood below normal. This causes various symptoms such as numbness or tingling in the hands, feet and lips, lightheadedness, dizziness, headache, chest pain and sometimes fainting.
Tachypnea	A related symptom of hyperventilation, tachypnea is characterized by rapid breathing and is not identical with hyperventilation - tachypnea may be necessary for a sufficient gas-exchange of the body,
Consciousness	Consciousness refers to the ability to perceive, communicate, remember, understand, appreciate, and initiate voluntary movements; a functioning sensorium.
Conscious	Conscious refers to the thoughts, feelings, sensations, or memories of which a person is aware at any given moment.
Delirium	Delirium is a medical term used to describe an acute decline in attention and cognition. Delirium is probably the single most common acute disorder affecting adults in general hospitals. It affects 10-20% of all adults in hospital, and 30-40% of older patients.
Double vision	Diplopia, colloquially known as double vision, is the perception of two images from a single object. The images may be horizontal, vertical, or diagonal.
Carbon	Carbon is a chemical element in the periodic table that has the symbol C and atomic number 6. An abundant nonmetallic, tetravalent element, carbon has several allotropic forms.
Carbon dioxide	Carbon dioxide is an atmospheric gas comprized of one carbon and two oxygen atoms. A very widely known chemical compound, it is frequently called by its formula CO_2. In its solid state, it is commonly known as dry ice.
Wheeze	A wheeze is a continuous, coarse, whistling sound produced in the respiratory airways during breathing. For this to occur some part of the respiratory tree must be narrowed or obstructed, or airflow velocity within the respiratory tree must be heightened.
Blocking	A sudden break or interuption in the flow of thinking or speech that is seen as an absence in thought is refered to as blocking.

Go to **Cram101.com** for the Practice Tests for this Chapter.

Heimlich maneuver	Procedure in which the air in a person's own lungs is used to expel an obstructing piece of food is referred to as the Heimlich maneuver.
Rescue breathing	Rescue Breathing is a specific first aid protocol which refers to the delivery of air from a person (the rescuer) into a patient.
Oxygen	Oxygen is a chemical element in the periodic table. It has the symbol O and atomic number 8. Oxygen is the second most common element on Earth, composing around 46% of the mass of Earth's crust and 28% of the mass of Earth as a whole, and is the third most common element in the universe.
Lungs	Lungs are the essential organs of respiration in air-breathing vertebrates. Their principal function is to transport oxygen from the atmosphere into the bloodstream, and to excrete carbon dioxide from the bloodstream into the atmosphere.
Cyanosis	Bluish skin coloration due to decreased blood oxygen concentration is called cyanosis.
Fecal incontinence	Fecal incontinence is the inability to control one's bowels. When one feels the urge to have a bowel movement, they may not be able to hold it until they can get to a toilet, or stool may leak from the rectum unexpectedly.
Urinary retention	Urinary retention is a lack of ability to urinate eventhough urine is produced by the kidneys and enters the bladder.
Irritability	Irritability is an excessive response to stimuli. Irritability takes many forms, from the contraction of a unicellular organism when touched to complex reactions involving all the senses of higher animals.
Cardiopulmonary resuscitation	Cardiopulmonary resuscitation is an emergency first aid protocol for an unconscious person on whom both breathing and pulse cannot be detected.
Diagnosis	In medicine, diagnosis is the process of identifying a medical condition or disease by its signs, symptoms, and from the results of various diagnostic procedures.
Medial	In anatomical terms of location toward or near the midline is called medial.
Bursa	A bursa is a fluid filled sac located between a bone and tendon which normally serves to reduce friction between the two moving surfaces.
A band	A band is a dark band corresponding to an area where actin and myosin filaments overlap in cardiac or skeletal muscle.
Tendon	A tendon or sinew is a tough band of fibrous connective tissue that connects muscle to bone. They are similar to ligaments except that ligaments join one bone to another.
Connective tissue	Connective tissue is any type of biological tissue with an extensive extracellular matrix and often serves to support, bind together, and protect organs.
Extensor	A muscle or tendon that straightens or extends a limb is called an extensor.
Flexor	A muscle or tendon which bends a limb, part of a limb, or part of the body is a flexor.
Affect	Affect is the scientific term used to describe a subject's externally displayed mood. This can be assesed by the nurse by observing facial expression, tone of voice, and body language.
Acute pain	Acute pain refers to pain that typically follows an injury and that disappears once the injury heals or is effectively treated.
Evaluation	The fifth step of the nursing process where nursing care and the patient's goal achievement are measured is the evaluation.
Direct observation	Direct observation refers to assessing behavior through direct surveillance.

Outcome	Outcome is the impact of care provided to a patient. They can be positive, such as the ability to walk freely as a result of rehabilitation, or negative, such as the occurrence of bedsores as a result of lack of mobility of a patient.
Course	Pattern of development and change of a disorder over time is a course.
Individual differences	The stable, consistent ways that people are different from each other are called individual differences.
Palpation	Palpation is a method of examination in which the examiner feels the size or shape or firmness or location of something.
Artery	Vessel that takes blood away from the heart to the tissues and organs of the body is called an artery.
Assess	Assess is to systematically and continuously collect, validate, and communicate patient data.
Rectum	The rectum is the final straight portion of the large intestine in some mammals, and the gut in others, terminating in the anus.
Spinal cord	The spinal cord is a part of the vertebrate nervous system that is enclosed in and protected by the vertebral column (it passes through the spinal canal). It consists of nerve cells. The spinal cord carries sensory signals and motor innervation to most of the skeletal muscles in the body.
Paralysis	Paralysis is the complete loss of muscle function for one or more muscle groups. Paralysis may be localized, or generalized, or it may follow a certain pattern.
Tourniquet	A tourniquet is a tightly tied band applied around a body part (an arm or a leg) sometimes used in an attempt to stop severe traumatic bleeding, but also during venipuncture, and other medical procedures.
Cardiac arrest	A cardiac arrest is the ceszation of normal circulation of the blood due to failure of the ventricles of the heart to contract effectively during systole.
Ventricular fibrillation	Ventricular fibrillation is a cardiac condition that consists of a lack of coordination of the contraction of the muscle tissue of the large chambers of the heart that eventually leads to the heart stopping altogether.
Fibrillation	Fibrillation is the rapid, irregular, and unsynchronized contraction of the muscle fibers of the heart. There are two major classes of fibrillation, atrial fibrillation and ventricular fibrillation.
Sinus	A sinus is a pouch or cavity in any organ or tissue, or an abnormal cavity or passage caused by the destruction of tissue.
Myocardial infarction	Acute myocardial infarction, commonly known as a heart attack, is a serious, sudden heart condition usually characterized by varying degrees of chest pain or discomfort, weakness, sweating, nausea, vomiting, and arrhythmias, sometimes causing loss of consciousness.
Infarction	The sudden death of tissue from a lack of blood perfusion is referred to as an infarction.
Sternum	Sternum or breastbone is a long, flat bone located in the center of the thorax (chest). It connects to the rib bones via cartilage, forming the rib cage with them, and thus helps to protect the lungs and heart from physical trauma.
Medicine	Medicine is the branch of health science and the sector of public life concerned with maintaining or restoring human health through the study, diagnosis and treatment of disease and injury.
Reid	Reid was the founder of the Scottish School of Common Sense, and played an integral role in the Scottish Enlightenment. He advocated direct realism, or common sense realism, and argued

strongly against the Theory of Ideas advocated by John Locke and René Descartes.

Rehabilitation	Rehabilitation is the restoration of lost capabilities, or the treatment aimed at producing it. Also refers to treatment for dependency on psychoactive substances such as alcohol, prescription drugs, and illicit drugs such as cocaine, heroin or amphetamines.
Assessment	In clinical practice, the process by which a mental health professional gathers and compiles information about a client for the purpose of describing the person's problems or disorder and developing a plan of treatment is an assessment.

Planning	In agreement with the patient, the nurse addresses each of the problems identified in the planning phase. For each problem a measurable goal is set. For example, for the patient discussed above, the goal would be for the patient's skin to remain intact. The result is a nursing care plan. This is the third step.
Concept	A mental category used to class together objects, relations, events, abstractions, or qualities that have common properties is called concept.
Evaluation	The fifth step of the nursing process where nursing care and the patient's goal achievement are measured is the evaluation.
Lead	Lead is a chemical element in the periodic table that has the symbol Pb and atomic number 82. A soft, heavy, toxic and malleable poor metal, lead is bluish white when freshly cut but tarnishes to dull gray when exposed to air. Lead is used in building construction, lead-acid batteries, bullets and shot, and is part of solder, pewter, and fusible alloys.
Rapport	Rapport is one of the most important features or characteristics of unconscious human interaction. It is commonality of perspective, being in "sync", being on the same wavelength as the person you are talking to.
Health	Health is a term that refers to a combination of the absence of illness, the ability to cope with everyday activities, physical fitness, and high quality of life.
Informed consent	The term used by psychologists to indicate that a person has agreed to participate in research after receiving information about the purposes of the study and the nature of the treatments is informed consent. Even with informed consent, subjects may withdraw from any experiment at any time.
Heart attack	A heart attack, is a serious, sudden heart condition usually characterized by varying degrees of chest pain or discomfort, weakness, sweating, nausea, vomiting, and arrhythmias, sometimes causing loss of consciousness. It occurs when the blood supply to a part of the heart is interrupted, causing death and scarring of the local heart tissue.
Lifestyle changes	Lifestyle changes are changes to the way a person lives which are often called for when treating chronic disease.
Lifestyle	The culturally, socially, economically, and environmentally conditioned complex of actions characteristic of an individual, group, or community as a pattern of habituated behavior over time that is health related but not necessarily health directed is a lifestyle.
Carrier	Person in apparent health whose chromosomes contain a pathologic mutant gene that may be transmitted to his or her children is a carrier.
Negligence	Under law, negligence is usually defined in the context of jury instructions wherein a judge instructs the jury that a party is to be considered negligent if they failed to exercise the standard of care that a reasonable person would have exercised under the same circumstances.
Malpractice	Medical malpractice is an act or omission by a health care provider which deviates from accepted standards of practice in the medical community and which causes injury to the patient.
Eye	An eye is an organ that detects light. Different kinds of light-sensitive organs are found in a variety of creatures. The simplest eyes do nothing but detect whether the surroundings are light or dark, while more complex eyes can distinguish shapes and colors.
Implementation	The methods by which the goal will be achieved is also recorded at this fourth stage. The methods of implementation must be recorded in an explicit and tangible format in a way that the patient can understand should he wish to read it. Clarity is essential as it will aid communication between those tasked with carrying out patient care.

Go to **Cram101.com** for the Practice Tests for this Chapter.

Inventory	A paper-and-pencil test with questions about a person's thoughts, feelings, and behaviors, which can be scored according to a standard procedure is referred to as inventory.
Assessment	In clinical practice, the process by which a mental health professional gathers and compiles information about a client for the purpose of describing the person's problems or disorder and developing a plan of treatment is an assessment.
Pulse	The rhythmic stretching of the arteries caused by the pressure of blood forced through the arteries by contractions of the ventricles during systole is a pulse.
Rehabilitation	Rehabilitation is the restoration of lost capabilities, or the treatment aimed at producing it. Also refers to treatment for dependency on psychoactive substances such as alcohol, prescription drugs, and illicit drugs such as cocaine, heroin or amphetamines.
Incentive	Incentive refers to an object, person, or situation perceived as being capable of satisfying a need.
Extension	Movement increasing the angle between parts at a joint is referred to as extension.
Base	The common definition of a base is a chemical compound that absorbs hydronium ions when dissolved in water (a proton acceptor). An alkali is a special example of a base, where in an aqueous environment, hydroxide ions are donated.
Job satisfaction	A person's attitudes and feelings about his or her job and facets of the job are called job satisfaction.
Wellness	A dimension of health beyond the absence of disease or infirmity, including social, emotional, and spiritual aspects of health is called wellness.
Electrocardigram	An electrocardiogram is a graphic produced by an electrocardiograph, which records the electrical voltage in the heart in the form of a continuous strip graph. It is the prime tool in cardiac electrophysiology, and has a prime function in screening and diagnosis of cardiovascular diseases..
Oxygen	Oxygen is a chemical element in the periodic table. It has the symbol O and atomic number 8. Oxygen is the second most common element on Earth, composing around 46% of the mass of Earth's crust and 28% of the mass of Earth as a whole, and is the third most common element in the universe.
Lipid	Lipid is one class of aliphatic hydrocarbon-containing organic compounds essential for the structure and function of living cells. They are characterized by being water-insoluble but soluble in nonpolar organic solvents.
Blood	Blood is a circulating tissue composed of fluid plasma and cells. The main function of blood is to supply nutrients (oxygen, glucose) and constitutional elements to tissues and to remove waste products.
Blood pressure	Blood pressure is the pressure exerted by the blood on the walls of the blood vessels.
Case study	A carefully drawn biography that may be obtained through interviews, questionnaires, and psychological tests is called a case study.
Medicine	Medicine is the branch of health science and the sector of public life concerned with maintaining or restoring human health through the study, diagnosis and treatment of disease and injury.

Go to **Cram101.com** for the Practice Tests for this Chapter.

Skeletal system	Skeletal systems are commonly divided into three types - external (an exoskeleton), internal (an endoskeleton), and fluid based (a hydrostatic skeleton), though hydrostatic skeletal systems may be classified separately from the other two since they lack hardened support structures.
Ossification	Ossification is the process of bone formation, in which connective tissues, such as cartilage are turned to bone or bone-like tissue.
Joint	A joint (articulation) is the location at which two bones make contact (articulate). They are constructed to both allow movement and provide mechanical support.
Muscle	Muscle is a contractile form of tissue. It is one of the four major tissue types, the other three being epithelium, connective tissue and nervous tissue. Muscle contraction is used to move parts of the body, as well as to move substances within the body.
Vertebral column	In human anatomy, the vertebral column is a column of vertebrae situated in the dorsal aspect of the abdomen. It houses the spinal cord in its spinal canal.
Base	The common definition of a base is a chemical compound that absorbs hydronium ions when dissolved in water (a proton acceptor). An alkali is a special example of a base, where in an aqueous environment, hydroxide ions are donated.
Anatomy	Anatomy is the branch of biology that deals with the structure and organization of living things. It can be divided into animal anatomy (zootomy) and plant anatomy (phytonomy).
Tissue	A collection of interconnected cells that perform a similar function within an organism is called tissue.
Stress	Stress refers to a condition that is a response to factors that change the human systems normal state.
Cancellous	Cancellous bone is a spongy type of bone with a very high surface area, found at the ends of long bones. The spongy bone contains red bone marrow which leads to the production of red blood cells.
Epiphyses	Epiphyses refers to ends of long bones. The epiphyseal plate-sometimes referred to as the growth plate-is made of cartilage and allows growth of the bone to occur. During childhood, the cartilage cells multiply and absorb calcium, to develop into bone.
Epiphysis	Epiphysis refers to the end of a long bone.
Articular	The articular is a bone in the lower jaw of most tetrapods, including reptiles, birds, and amphibians, but has become a middle ear bone (the malleus) in mammals. It is the site of articulation between the lower jaw and the skull, and is connected to two other lower jaw bones, the suprangular and the angular.
Cartilage	Cartilage is a type of dense connective tissue. Cartilage is composed of cells called chondrocytes which are dispersed in a firm gel-like ground substance, called the matrix. Cartilage is avascular (contains no blood vessels) and nutrients are diffused through the matrix.
Friction	Friction is the force that opposes the relative motion or tendency of such motion of two surfaces in contact. The resulting injury to skin resembles an abrasion and can also damage superficial blood vessels directly under the skin.
Shock	Circulatory shock, a state of cardiac output that is insufficient to meet the body's physiological needs, with consequences ranging from fainting to death is referred to as shock. Insulin shock, a state of severe hypoglycemia caused by administration of insulin.
Femur	The femur or thigh bone is the longest, most voluminous and strongest bone of the human body. It forms part of the hip and part of the knee.

Go to **Cram101.com** for the Practice Tests for this Chapter.

Hyaline cartilage	Hyaline cartilage is the most abundant type of cartilage. Hyaline cartilage is a translucent matrix or ground substance found lining bones in joints. It is also present inside bones, serving as a center of ossification or bone growth
Compact bone	Type of bone that contains osteons consisting of concentric layers of matrix and osteocytes in lacunae is called compact bone. It forms the stout walls of the diaphysis of long bones and a thin wall of the epiphysis of long bones
Spongy bone	Type of bone that has an irregular meshlike arrangement of thin plates of bone filled with red marrow is spongy bone.
Attachment	Attachment refers to the psychological tendency to seek closeness to another person, to feel secure when that person is present, and to feel anxious when that person is absent.
Periosteum	The periosteum is an envelope of fibrous connective tissue that is wrapped around the bone in all places except at joints.
Skeleton	In biology, the skeleton or skeletal system is the biological system providing physical support in living organisms.
Carpal	In human anatomy, the carpal bones are the bones of the human wrist.There are eight of them altogether, and they can be thought of as forming two rows of four.
Organ	Organ refers to a structure consisting of several tissues adapted as a group to perform specific functions.
Ischium	The ischium forms the lower and back part of the hip bone. It is divisible into three portions—a body and two rami.
Pubis	The pubis, the anterior part of the hip bone, is divisible into a body, a superior and an inferior ramus.
Vertebrae	Vertebrae are the individual bones that make up the vertebral column (aka spine) - a flexuous and flexible column.
Puberty	A time in the life of a developing individual characterized by the increasing production of sex hormones, which cause it to reach sexual maturity is called puberty.
Fusion	Fusion refers to the combination of two atoms into a single atom as a result of a collision, usually accompanied by the release of energy.
Trauma	Trauma refers to a severe physical injury or wound to the body caused by an external force, or a psychological shock having a lasting effect on mental life.
Malnutrition	Malnutrition is a general term for the medical condition in a person or animal caused by an unbalanced diet—either too little or too much food, or a diet missing one or more important nutrients.
Fibrocartilage	Fibrocartilage, as its name implies, is a type of cartilage arranged in a fibrous matrix that is similar to fibrous connective tissues. It is found in areas that require tensile strength, such as intervertebral disks.
Ligament	A ligament is a short band of tough fibrous connective tissue composed mainly of long, stringy collagen fibres. They connect bones to other bones to form a joint. (They do not connect muscles to bones.)
Connective tissue	Connective tissue is any type of biological tissue with an extensive extracellular matrix and often serves to support, bind together, and protect organs.
Articular capsule	The joint capsule or articular capsule form complete envelopes for the freely movable bone joints. Each capsule consists of two layers — a outer layer (stratum fibrosum) composed of white fibrous tissue, and an inner layer (stratum synoviale) which is a secreting layer.

Synovial membrane	Membrane that forms the inner lining of the capsule of a freely movable joint is called synovial membrane. The membrane contains a fibrous outer layer, as well as an inner layer that is responsible for the production of specific components of synovial fluid, which nourishes and lubricates the joint.
Synovial joint	Synovial joint refers to freely moving joint in which two bones are separated by a cavity.
Absorption	Absorption is a physical or chemical phenomenon or a process in which atoms, molecules, or ions enter some bulk phase - gas, liquid or solid material. In nutrition, amino acids are broken down through digestion, which begins in the stomach.
Radioulnar	The sides of the forearm are named after its bones: Structures closer to the radius are radial, structures closer to the ulna are ulnar, and structures relating to both bones are referred to as radioulnar.
Tibia	The Tibia or shin bone, in human anatomy, is the larger of the two bones in the leg below the knee. It is found medial (towards the middle) and anterior (towards the front) to the other such bone, the fibula. It is the second-longest bone in the human body.
Tendon	A tendon or sinew is a tough band of fibrous connective tissue that connects muscle to bone. They are similar to ligaments except that ligaments join one bone to another.
Hip	In anatomy, the hip is the bony projection of the femur, known as the greater trochanter, and the overlying muscle and fat.
Bursitis	Bursitis is the inflammation of one or more bursae, or small sacks of oil, in the body. Bursitis is commonly caused by repetition of movement or excessive pressure.
Bursa	A bursa is a fluid filled sac located between a bone and tendon which normally serves to reduce friction between the two moving surfaces.
Inflammation	Inflammation is the first response of the immune system to infection or irritation and may be referred to as the innate cascade.
Range of motion	Range of motion is a measurement of movement through a particular joint or muscle range.
Hinge joint	Hinge joint refers to a joint that allows movement in only one plane. In humans, examples include the elbow and knee.
Anatomical position	A body posture with the body erect, the face forward, the arms at the sides with the palms facing forward, and the toes pointing straight ahead is referred to as the anatomical position.
Extension	Movement increasing the angle between parts at a joint is referred to as extension.
Flexion	In anatomy, Flexion is movement whereby bones or other parts of the body, including the trunk, are brought closer together by decreasing the joint angle. The opposite term is extention, or straightening.
Hyperextension	Hyperextension is the movement of a body part beyond the normal range of motion, such as the position of the head when looking upwards into the sky.
Abduction	Abduction is movement of a limb away from the body's midline, or of a digit away from the long axis of a limb.
Adduction	Adduction is where there is a reduction in the angle between bones or parts of the body. This only applies to movement along the coronal plane.
Rotation	Movement turning a body part on its longitudinal axis is rotation.
Clavicle	In human anatomy, the clavicle or collar bone is a bone that makes up part of the shoulder girdle (pectoral girdle). It is a doubly-curved long bone that connects the arm (upper limb)

Go to **Cram101.com** for the Practice Tests for this Chapter.

	to the body (trunk), located directly above the first rib.
Scapula	In anatomy, the scapula, or shoulder blade, is the bone that connects the humerus (arm bone) with the clavicle (collar bone).
Sternum	Sternum or breastbone is a long, flat bone located in the center of the thorax (chest). It connects to the rib bones via cartilage, forming the rib cage with them, and thus helps to protect the lungs and heart from physical trauma.
Elevation	Elevation refers to upward movement of a part of the body.
Depression	In everyday language depression refers to any downturn in mood, which may be relatively transitory and perhaps due to something trivial. This is differentiated from Clinical depression which is marked by symptoms that last two weeks or more and are so severe that they interfere with daily living.
Humerus	The humerus is a long bone in the arm or fore-legs (animals) that runs from the shoulder to the elbow. On a skeleton, it fits between the scapula and the radius and ulna.
Medial	In anatomical terms of location toward or near the midline is called medial.
Circumduction	Movement of a body part, such as a limb, so that the end follows a circular path is referred to as circumduction.
Radius	The radius is the bone of the forearm that extends from the inside of the elbow to the thumb side of the wrist. The radius is situated on the lateral side of the ulna, which exceeds it in length and size.
Ulna	The ulna (Elbow Bone) is a long bone, prismatic in form, placed at the medial side of the forearm, parallel with the radius.
Supination	Supination is the opposite of pronation, the rotation of the forearm so that the palm faces anteriorly, or palm facing up. The hand is supine (facing anteriorly) in the anatomical position.
Pronation	Pronation is a rotation of the forearm that moves the palm from an anterior-facing position to a posterior-facing position, or palm facing down. This is not medial rotation as this must be performed when the arm is half flexed.
Metacarpopha-angeal joint	The Metacarpophalangeal joint is of the condyloid kind, formed by the reception of the rounded heads of the metacarpal bones into shallow cavities on the proximal ends of the first phalanges, with the exception of that of the thumb, which presents more of the characters of a ginglymoid joint.
Lumbar	In anatomy, lumbar is an adjective that means of or pertaining to the abdominal segment of the torso, between the diaphragm and the sacrum (pelvis). The five vertebra in the lumbar region are the largest and strongest in the spinal column.
Pelvis	The pelvis is the bony structure located at the base of the spine (properly known as the caudal end). The pelvis incorporates the socket portion of the hip joint for each leg (in bipeds) or hind leg (in quadrupeds). It forms the lower limb (or hind-limb) girdle of the skeleton.
Iliac	In human anatomy, iliac artery refers to several anatomical structures located in the pelvis.
Lumbar vertebrae	The lumbar vertebrae are the largest segments of the movable part of the vertebral column, and can be distinguished by the absence of a foramen (hole) in the transverse process, and by the absence of facets on the sides of the body.
Dorsiflexion	Dorsiflexion is the flexion of the entire foot superiorly, or upwards as when decelerating in an automibile.

Go to **Cram101.com** for the Practice Tests for this Chapter.

Resistance	Resistance refers to a nonspecific ability to ward off infection or disease regardless of whether the body has been previously exposed to it. A force that opposes the flow of a fluid such as air or blood. Compare with immunity.
Fiber	Fibers used by man come from a wide variety of sources: Natural fiber include those made out of plants, animal and mineral sources. Natural fibers can be classified according to their origin.
Skeletal muscle	Skeletal muscle is a type of striated muscle, attached to the skeleton. They are used to facilitate movement, by applying force to bones and joints; via contraction. They generally contract voluntarily (via nerve stimulation), although they can contract involuntarily.
Brachioradialis	Brachioradialis is a muscle located in the forearm, that acts to flex the forearm.
Muscle fiber	Cell with myofibrils containing actin and myosin filaments arranged within sarcomeres is a muscle fiber.
Fascia	Fascia is specialized connective tissue layer which surrounds muscles, bones, and joints, providing support and protection and giving structure to the body. It consists of three layers: the superficial fascia, the deep fascia and the subserous fascia. Fascia is one of the 3 types of dense connective tissue (the other two being ligaments and tendons).
Supraspinatus	The supraspinatus is a relatively small muscle. It is one of the four rotator cuff muscles and also abducts the arm at the shoulder. The spine of the scapula separates the supraspinatus muscle from the infraspinatus muscle, which originates below the spine.
Infraspinatus	The Infraspinatus muscle is a lateral rotator of the glenohumeral joint and adductor of the arm. It attaches medially to the infraspinous fossa of the scapula and laterally to the greater tubercle of the humerus.
Deltoid	The deltoid muscle is the muscle forming the rounded contour of the human shoulder.
Flexor	A muscle or tendon which bends a limb, part of a limb, or part of the body is a flexor.
Rectus abdominis	The Rectus abdominis is a long flat muscle, which extends along the whole length of the front of the abdomen, and is separated from its fellow of the opposite side by the linea alba.
Pectoralis major	The Pectoralis major is a thick, fan-shaped muscle, situated at the upper front (anterior) of the chest wall. It makes up the bulk of the chest muscles in the male and lies under the breast in the female.
Adductor longus	The Adductor longus muscle is a part of the adductor group of the thigh, that as the name suggests adduct the thigh. It originates on the pubic body just below the pubic crest and inserts into the middle third of linea aspera. Its nerve supply is the obturator nerve, branch of anterior division L2, L3, and L4.
Biceps brachii	The biceps brachii is a muscle on the upper arm that acts as a flex to the elbow, but more namely as a muscle to aid simple tasks, such as several types of reciprocal or Radioulnar movement. . It is arguably the best known muscle, as it lies fairly superficially, and is often well-defined even in non-athletes.
Brachialis	Brachialis is a flexor muscle in the upper arm. It lies deep to biceps brachii, and is a more powerful flexor of the elbow.
Stimulus	Stimulus in a nervous system, a factor that triggers sensory transduction.
Neuron	The neuron is a major class of cells in the nervous system. In vertebrates, they are found in the brain, the spinal cord and in the nerves and ganglia of the peripheral nervous system, and their primary role is to process and transmit neural information.
Motor unit	A motor neuron and all the muscle fibers it controls is called the motor unit.

Agonist	Agonist refers to a drug that mimics or increases a neurotransmitter's effects.
Antagonist	A antagonist is a drug that interacts with the target cell of a receptor site to inhibit or prevent the action of an agonist.
Aerobic	An aerobic organism is an organism that has an oxygen based metabolism. Aerobes, in a process known as cellular respiration, use oxygen to oxidize substrates (for example sugars and fats) in order to obtain energy.
Extensor	A muscle or tendon that straightens or extends a limb is called an extensor.
Rehabilitation	Rehabilitation is the restoration of lost capabilities, or the treatment aimed at producing it. Also refers to treatment for dependency on psychoactive substances such as alcohol, prescription drugs, and illicit drugs such as cocaine, heroin or amphetamines.
Trapezius	In human anatomy, the trapezius is a large superficial muscle on a person's back. Trapezius gets its name from its trapezium-like shape; the corners being the neck, the two shoulders, and the thoracic vertebra, T12.
Conscious	Conscious refers to the thoughts, feelings, sensations, or memories of which a person is aware at any given moment.
Affect	Affect is the scientific term used to describe a subject's externally displayed mood. This can be assesed by the nurse by observing facial expression, tone of voice, and body language.
Abductor	An abductor is any muscle that when activated, normally moves a limb or body part away from the body.
Gluteus maximus	The gluteus maximus muscle is the largest of the gluteal muscles which are located in each buttock. By some definitions, the gluteus maxima are the most powerful muscles of the human body.
Thoracic vertebrae	The thoracic vertebrae compose the middle segment of the vertebral column, between the cervical vertebrae and the lumbar vertebrae. They are intermediate in size between those of the cervical and lumbar regions; they increase in size as one proceeds down the spine, the upper vertebrae being much smaller than those in the lower part of the region.
Concept	A mental category used to class together objects, relations, events, abstractions, or qualities that have common properties is called concept.
Center of gravity	In physics, the center of gravity (CG) of an object is a point at which the object's mass can be assumed, for many purposes, to be concentrated.
Distribution	Distribution in pharmacology is a branch of pharmacokinetics describing reversible transfer of drug from one location to another within the body.
Angular	The angular is a large bone in the lower jaw of amphibians, birds and reptiles, which is connected to all other lower jaw bones: the dentary (which is the entire lower jaw in mammals), the splenial, the suprangular, and the articular.
Reid	Reid was the founder of the Scottish School of Common Sense, and played an integral role in the Scottish Enlightenment. He advocated direct realism, or common sense realism, and argued strongly against the Theory of Ideas advocated by John Locke and René Descartes.

Go to **Cram101.com** for the Practice Tests for this Chapter.

Muscle contraction	A muscle contraction occurs when a muscle cell (called a muscle fiber) shortens. There are three general types: skeletal, heart, and smooth.
Theory	Theory refers to an explanatory statement, or set of statements, that concisely summarizes the state of knowledge on a phenomenon and provides direction for further study.
Muscle	Muscle is a contractile form of tissue. It is one of the four major tissue types, the other three being epithelium, connective tissue and nervous tissue. Muscle contraction is used to move parts of the body, as well as to move substances within the body.
Skeletal muscle	Skeletal muscle is a type of striated muscle, attached to the skeleton. They are used to facilitate movement, by applying force to bones and joints; via contraction. They generally contract voluntarily (via nerve stimulation), although they can contract involuntarily.
Fiber	Fibers used by man come from a wide variety of sources: Natural fiber include those made out of plants, animal and mineral sources. Natural fibers can be classified according to their origin.
Muscle fiber	Cell with myofibrils containing actin and myosin filaments arranged within sarcomeres is a muscle fiber.
Metabolism	Metabolism is the biochemical modification of chemical compounds in living organisms and cells. This includes the biosynthesis of complex organic molecules (anabolism) and their breakdown (catabolism).
Tetanus	Tetanus is a serious and often fatal disease caused by the neurotoxin tetanospasmin which is produced by the Gram-positive, obligate anaerobic bacterium Clostridium tetani. Tetanus also refers to a state of muscle tension.
Ratio	In number and more generally in algebra, a ratio is the linear relationship between two quantities.
Heredity	Heredity refers to the transmission of genetic information from parent to offspring.
Carbon	Carbon is a chemical element in the periodic table that has the symbol C and atomic number 6. An abundant nonmetallic, tetravalent element, carbon has several allotropic forms.
Stroke	A stroke or cerebrovascular accident (CVA) occurs when the blood supply to a part of the brain is suddenly interrupted.
Oxygen	Oxygen is a chemical element in the periodic table. It has the symbol O and atomic number 8. Oxygen is the second most common element on Earth, composing around 46% of the mass of Earth's crust and 28% of the mass of Earth as a whole, and is the third most common element in the universe.
Cardiac output	Cardiac output is the volume of blood being pumped by the heart in a minute. It is equal to the heart rate multiplied by the stroke volume.
Stroke volume	The amount of blood pumped by the left ventricle in each contraction is called stroke volume.
Population	Population refers to all members of a well-defined group of organisms, events, or things.
Isometric exercise	Isometric exercise is a form of physical exercise in which the muscles flex and hold a stationary position. No movement of a load takes place, and the exercises require little in the way of equipment.
Resistance	Resistance refers to a nonspecific ability to ward off infection or disease regardless of whether the body has been previously exposed to it. A force that opposes the flow of a fluid such as air or blood. Compare with immunity.
Physiology	The study of the function of cells, tissues, and organs is referred to as physiology.

Go to **Cram101.com** for the Practice Tests for this Chapter.

Nerve	A nerve is an enclosed, cable-like bundle of nerve fibers or axons, which includes the glia that ensheath the axons in myelin.
Chemical energy	Chemical energy refers to energy stored in the chemical bonds of molecules; a form of potential energy.
Carbohydrate	Carbohydrate is a chemical compound that contains oxygen, hydrogen, and carbon atoms. They consist of monosaccharide sugars of varying chain lengths and that have the general chemical formula $C_n(H_2O)_n$ or are derivatives of such.
Protein	A protein is a complex, high-molecular-weight organic compound that consists of amino acids joined by peptide bonds. They are essential to the structure and function of all living cells and viruses. Many are enzymes or subunits of enzymes.
Atom	An atom is the smallest possible particle of a chemical element that retains its chemical properties.
Chemical bond	Chemical bond refers to an attraction between two atoms resulting from a sharing of outer-shell electrons or the presence of opposite charges on the atoms. The bonded atoms gain complete outer electron shells.
Phosphate	A phosphate is a polyatomic ion or radical consisting of one phosphorus atom and four oxygen. In the ionic form, it carries a -3 formal charge, and is denoted PO_4^{3-}.
Adenosine	Adenosine is a nucleoside comprized of adenine attached to a ribose (ribofuranose) moiety via a β-N_9-glycosidic bond. Adenosine plays an important role in biochemical processes, such as energy transfer - as adenosine triphosphate (ATP) and adenosine diphosphate (ADP) - as well as in signal transduction as cyclic adenosine monophosphate, cAMP.
Adenosine diphosphate	Adenosine diphosphate refers to a molecule composed of the sugar ribose, the base adenine, and two phosphate groups; a component of ATP.
Creatine phosphate	Compound unique to muscles that contains a high-energy phosphate bond is creatine phosphate or phosphocreatine.
Glucose	Glucose, a simple monosaccharide sugar, is one of the most important carbohydrates and is used as a source of energy in animals and plants. Glucose is one of the main products of photosynthesis and starts respiration.
Sugar	A sugar is the simplest molecule that can be identified as a carbohydrate. These include monosaccharides and disaccharides, trisaccharides and the oligosaccharides. The term "glyco-" indicates the presence of a sugar in an otherwise non-carbohydrate substance.
Glycogen	Glycogen refers to a complex, extensively branched polysaccharide of many glucose monomers; serves as an energy-storage molecule in liver and muscle cells.
Blood	Blood is a circulating tissue composed of fluid plasma and cells. The main function of blood is to supply nutrients (oxygen, glucose) and constitutional elements to tissues and to remove waste products.
Acid	An acid is a water-soluble, sour-tasting chemical compound that when dissolved in water, gives a solution with a pH of less than 7.
Pyruvic acid	Pyruvic acid is created by the body when sugars are metabolized (through glycolysis). A molecule of glucose breaks down into two pyruvic acid molecules, which are then used to provide further energy.
Glycolysis	Glycolysis refers to the multistep chemical breakdown of a molecule of glucose into two molecules of pyruvic acid; the first stage of cellular respiration in all organisms; occurs in the cytoplasmic fluid.

Go to **Cram101.com** for the Practice Tests for this Chapter.

Lactic acid	Lactic acid accumulates in skeletal muscles during extensive anaerobic exercise, causing temporary muscle pain. Lactic acid is quickly removed from muscles when they resume aerobic metabolism.
Aerobic	An aerobic organism is an organism that has an oxygen based metabolism. Aerobes, in a process known as cellular respiration, use oxygen to oxidize substrates (for example sugars and fats) in order to obtain energy.
Plasma	Fluid portion of circulating blood is called plasma.
Fatty acid	A fatty acid is a carboxylic acid (or organic acid), often with a long aliphatic tail (long chains), either saturated or unsaturated.
Acetyl	The acetyl radical contains a methyl group single-bonded to a carbonyl. The carbon of the carbonyl has an lone electron available, with which it forms a chemical bond to the remainder of the molecule.
Mitochondria	Cytoplasmic organelles responsible for ATP generation for cellular activities are referred to as mitochondria.
Krebs cycle	The Krebs cycle is a series of chemical reactions of central importance in all living cells that utilize oxygen as part of cellular respiration. In these aerobic organisms, the Krebs cycle is a metabolic pathway that forms part of the break down of carbohydrates, fats and proteins into carbon dioxide and water in order to generate energy.
Phosphorylation	Phosphorylation refers to reaction in which a phosphate group becomes covalently coupled to another molecule.
Oxidative phosphorylation	Oxidative phosphorylation is a biochemical process in cells. It is the final metabolic pathway of cellular respiration, after glycolysis and the citric acid cycle.
Tissue	A collection of interconnected cells that perform a similar function within an organism is called tissue.
Striated muscle	Striated muscle refers to contractile tissue characterized by multinucleated cells containing highly ordered arrangements of actin and myosin microfilaments. Also known as skeletal muscle.
Myofibril	Myofibril is a cylindrical organelle, found within muscle cells. They are bundles of filaments that run from one end of the cell to the other and are attached to the cell surface membrane at each end.
Striation	Striation refers to the tiny grooves of muscle across major muscle groups characteristic of a well-developed body.
Actin	A protein in a muscle fiber that, together with myosin, is responsible for contraction and relaxation is actin.
Sarcomere	A sarcomere is the basic unit of a cross striated muscle's myofibril. They are multi-protein complexes composed of three different filament systems. A sarcomere is defined as the segment between two neighboring Z-lines (or Z-discs).
A band	A band is a dark band corresponding to an area where actin and myosin filaments overlap in cardiac or skeletal muscle.
I band	I band refers to the area near the edge of the sarcomere where there are only thin filaments.
Actin filament	An actin filament is a helical protein filament formed by the polymerization of globular actin molecules. They provide mechanical support for the cell, determine the cell shape, enable cell movements; and participate in certain cell junctions.
ATPase	ATPase is a class of enzymes that catalyze the decomposition of adenosine triphosphate into

Go to **Cram101.com** for the Practice Tests for this Chapter.

adenosine diphosphate and a free phosphate ion. This dephosphorylation reaction releases energy, which the enzyme harnesses to drive other chemical reactions that would not otherwise occur. This process is widely used in all known forms of life.

Enzyme	An enzyme is a protein that catalyzes, or speeds up, a chemical reaction. They are essential to sustain life because most chemical reactions in biological cells would occur too slowly, or would lead to different products, without them.
Potential energy	Stored energy as a result of location or spatial arrangement is referred to as potential energy.
Extension	Movement increasing the angle between parts at a joint is referred to as extension.
Troponin	A molecule found in thin filaments of muscle that helps regulate when muscle cells contract is referred to as troponin.
Calcium	Calcium is the chemical element in the periodic table that has the symbol Ca and atomic number 20. Calcium is a soft grey alkaline earth metal that is used as a reducing agent in the extraction of thorium, zirconium and uranium. Calcium is also the fifth most abundant element in the Earth's crust.
Tropomyosin	Protein that blocks muscle contraction until calcium ions are present is referred to as tropomyosin.
Adenosine triphosphate	Organic molecule that stores energy and releases energy for use in cellular processes is adenosine triphosphate.
Channel	Channel, in communications (sometimes called communications channel), refers to the medium used to convey information from a sender (or transmitter) to a receiver.
Depolarization	Depolarization is a decrease in the absolute value of a cell's membrane potential. Thus, changes in membrane voltage in which the membrane potential becomes less positive or less negative are both depolarizations.
Transverse	A transverse (also known as axial or horizontal) plane is an X-Y plane, parallel to the ground, which (in humans) separates the superior from the inferior, or put another way, the head from the feet.
Membrane potential	Membrane potential is the electrical potential difference (voltage) across a cell's plasma membrane.
Blocking	A sudden break or interuption in the flow of thinking or speech that is seen as an absence in thought is refered to as blocking.
Capillary	A capillary is the smallest of a body's blood vessels, measuring 5-10 micro meters. They connect arteries and veins, and most closely interact with tissues. Their walls are composed of a single layer of cells, the endothelium. This layer is so thin that molecules such as oxygen, water and lipids can pass through them by diffusion and enter the tissues.
Capillaries	Capillaries refer to the smallest of the blood vessels and the sites of exchange between the blood and tissue cells.
Distribution	Distribution in pharmacology is a branch of pharmacokinetics describing reversible transfer of drug from one location to another within the body.
Stimulus	Stimulus in a nervous system, a factor that triggers sensory transduction.
Activation	As reflected by facial expressions, the degree of arousal a person is experiencing is referred to as activation.
Motor unit	A motor neuron and all the muscle fibers it controls is called the motor unit.

Go to **Cram101.com** for the Practice Tests for this Chapter.

Respiratory system	The respiratory system is the biological system of any organism that engages in gas exchange.In humans and other mammals, the respiratory system consists of the airways, the lungs, and the respiratory muscles that mediate the movement of air into and out of the body.
Alveoli	Alveoli are anatomical structures that have the form of a hollow cavity. In the lung, the pulmonary alveoli are spherical outcroppings of the respiratory bronchioles and are the primary sites of gas exchange with the blood.
Lungs	Lungs are the essential organs of respiration in air-breathing vertebrates. Their principal function is to transport oxygen from the atmosphere into the bloodstream, and to excrete carbon dioxide from the bloodstream into the atmosphere.
Red blood cells	Red blood cells are the most common type of blood cell and are the vertebrate body's principal means of delivering oxygen from the lungs or gills to body tissues via the blood.
Red blood cell	The red blood cell is the most common type of blood cell and is the vertebrate body's principal means of delivering oxygen from the lungs or gills to body tissues via the blood.
Hemoglobin	Hemoglobin is the iron-containing oxygen-transport metalloprotein in the red cells of the blood in mammals and other animals. Hemoglobin transports oxygen from the lungs to the rest of the body, such as to the muscles, where it releases the oxygen load.
Carbon dioxide	Carbon dioxide is an atmospheric gas comprized of one carbon and two oxygen atoms. A very widely known chemical compound, it is frequently called by its formula CO_2. In its solid state, it is commonly known as dry ice.
Steady state	Steady state is a system in which a particular variable is not changing but energy must be continuously added to maintain this variable constant.
Buffer	A chemical substance that resists changes in pH by accepting H^+ ions from or donating H^+ ions to solutions is called a buffer.
Value	Value is worth in general, and it is thought to be connected to reasons for certain practices, policies, actions, beliefs or emotions. Value is "that which one acts to gain and/or keep."
Bicarbonate	A Bicarbonate or, more properly, a hydrogen carbonate is a polyatomic ion. It is the intermediate form in the deprotonation of carbonic acid: removing the first proton from carbonic acid forms bicarbonate; removing the second proton leads to the carbonate ion.
Adipose tissue	Adipose tissue is an anatomical term for loose connective tissue composed of adipocytes. Its main role is to store energy in the form of fat, although it also cushions and insulates the body. It has an important endocrine function in producing recently-discovered hormones such as leptin, resistin and TNFalpha.
Tolerance	Drug tolerance occurs when a subject's reaction to a drug decreases so that larger doses are required to achieve the same effect.
Variable	A characteristic or aspect in which people, objects, events, or conditions vary is called variable.
Ventilation	Ventilation refers to a mechanism that provides contact between an animal's respiratory surface and the air or water to which it is exposed. It is also called breathing.
Constant	A behavior or characteristic that does not vary from one observation to another is referred to as a constant.
Cardiovascular system	The circulatory system or cardiovascular system is the organ system which circulates blood around the body of most animals.
Criterion	Criterion refers to a standard of comparison. For performance appraisal, it is the definition

Go to **Cram101.com** for the Practice Tests for this Chapter.

of good performance.

Protocol	Protocol is a document with the aim of guiding decisions and criteria in specific areas of healthcare, as defined by an authoritative examination of current evidence. It details the activities to be executed in specific situations.
Predisposition	Predisposition refers to an inclination or diathesis to respond in a certain way, either inborn or acquired. In abnormal psychology, it is a factor that lowers the ability to withstand stress and inclines the individual toward pathology.
Critical concentration	Concentration of a protein monomer, such as actin or tubulin, that is in equilibrium with the assembled form of the protein is called critical concentration.
Cardiovascular disease	Cardiovascular disease refers to afflictions in the mechanisms, including the heart, blood vessels, and their controllers, that are responsible for transporting blood to the body's tissues and organs. Psychological factors may play important roles in such diseases and their treatments.
Affect	Affect is the scientific term used to describe a subject's externally displayed mood. This can be assesed by the nurse by observing facial expression, tone of voice, and body language.
Tidal volume	Tidal volume (TV) is the amount of air breathed in or out during normal human respiration. It is normally from 450 to 500 mL.
Heart rate	Heart rate is a term used to describe the frequency of the cardiac cycle. It is considered one of the four vital signs. Usually it is calculated as the number of contractions of the heart in one minute and expressed as "beats per minute".
Ventricle	In the heart, a ventricle is a heart chamber which collects blood from an atrium (another heart chamber) and pumps it out of the heart.
Venous blood	In the circulatory system, venous blood or peripheral blood is blood returning to the heart. With one exception (the pulmonary vein) this blood is deoxygenated and high in carbon dioxide, having released oxygen and absorbed CO_2 in the tissues.
Medicine	Medicine is the branch of health science and the sector of public life concerned with maintaining or restoring human health through the study, diagnosis and treatment of disease and injury.
Acute	In medicine, an acute disease is a disease with either or both of: a rapid onset; and a short course (as opposed to a chronic course).
Arteriole	An arteriole is a blood vessel that extends and branches out from an artery and leads to capillaries. They have thick muscular walls and are the primary site of vascular resistance.
Artery	Vessel that takes blood away from the heart to the tissues and organs of the body is called an artery.
Blood pressure	Blood pressure is the pressure exerted by the blood on the walls of the blood vessels.
Peripheral resistance	Peripheral resistance refers to the impedance of blood flow by the arterioles. An increase in peripheral resistance causes a rise in blood pressure.
Blood vessel	A blood vessel is a part of the circulatory system and function to transport blood throughout the body. The most important types, arteries and veins, are so termed because they carry blood away from or towards the heart, respectively.
Aorta	The largest artery in the human body, the aorta originates from the left ventricle of the heart and brings oxygenated blood to all parts of the body in the systemic circulation.
Arch of the aorta	The arch of the aorta begins at the level of the upper border of the second sternocostal articulation of the right side, and runs at first upward, backward, and to the left in front

of the trachea; it is then directed backward on the left side of the trachea and finally passes downward on the left side of the body of the fourth thoracic vertebra, at the lower border of which it becomes continuous with the descending aorta. It thus forms two curvatures: one with its convexity upward, the other with its convexity forward and to the left. Its upper border is usually about 2.5 cm. below the superior border to the manubrium sterni.

Carotid artery	In human anatomy, the carotid artery refers to a number of major arteries in the head and neck.
Baroreceptors	Baroreceptors refer to pressure sensors located in the heart, aortic arch, and carotid sinuses that trigger autonomic reflexes in response to fluctuations in blood pressure.
Baroreceptor	A baroreceptor in the human body detects the pressure of blood flowing though it, and can send messages to the central nervous system to increase or decrease total peripheral resistance and cardiac output.
Control center	Control center refers to one of three interdependent components of homeostatic control mechanisms; determines the set point.
Diastolic blood pressure	The pressure present in a large artery when the heart is at the resting phase of the cardiac cycle is called diastolic blood pressure.
Coronary	Referring to the heart or the blood vessels of the heart is referred to as coronary.
Aerobic exercise	Exercise in which oxygen is used to produce ATP is aerobic exercise.
Ischemia	Narrowing of arteries caused by plaque buildup within the arteries is called ischemia.
Myocardium	Myocardium is the muscular tissue of the heart. The myocardium is composed of specialized cardiac muscle cells with an ability not possessed by muscle tissue elsewhere in the body.
Coronary arteries	Arteries that directly supply the heart with blood are referred to as coronary arteries.
Coronary artery	An artery that supplies blood to the wall of the heart is called a coronary artery.
Puberty	A time in the life of a developing individual characterized by the increasing production of sex hormones, which cause it to reach sexual maturity is called puberty.
Elevation	Elevation refers to upward movement of a part of the body.
Valsalva maneuver	A Valsalva maneuver is any attempted exhalation against a closed glottis or against a closed mouth and nose. A Valsalva maneuver performed against a closed glottis results in a drastic increase in pressure in the thoracic cavity, the airtight section of the torso that houses the lungs and heart.
Adaptation	A biological adaptation is an anatomical structure, physiological process or behavioral trait of an organism that has evolved over a period of time by the process of natural selection such that it increases the expected long-term reproductive success of the organism.
Core temperature	Core temperature is the operating temperature of an organism, specifically in deep structures of the body such as the liver, in comparison to temperatures of peripheral tissues.
Basal metabolic rate	Basal metabolic rate, is the rate of metabolism that occurs when an individual is at rest in a warm environment and is in the post absorptive state, and has not eaten for at least 12 hours.
Metabolic rate	Energy expended by the body per unit time is called metabolic rate.
Radiation	The emission of electromagnetic waves by all objects warmer than absolute zero is referred to as radiation.

Solution	Solution refers to homogenous mixture formed when a solute is dissolved in a solvent.
Skin	Skin is an organ of the integumentary system composed of a layer of tissues that protect underlying muscles and organs.
Insight	Insight refers to a sudden awareness of the relationships among various elements that had previously appeared to be independent of one another.
Dehydration	Dehydration is the removal of water from an object. Medically, dehydration is a serious and potentially life-threatening condition in which the body contains an insufficient volume of water for normal functioning.
Acclimatization	The word acclimatization is used to describe the process of an organism adjusting to changes in its environment, often involving temperature or climate. Acclimatization usually occurs in a short time, and within one organism's lifetime.
Risk factor	A risk factor is a variable associated with an increased risk of disease or infection but risk factors are not necessarily causal.
Dizygotic	Dizygotic twins each have their own amnion and chorion and may or may not share a placenta.
Monozygotic	Monozygotic is the division of one egg and one sperm cell into two zygotes shortly after fertilization.
Concept	A mental category used to class together objects, relations, events, abstractions, or qualities that have common properties is called concept.
Course	Pattern of development and change of a disorder over time is a course.
Adjustment	Adjustment is an attempt to cope with a given situation.
Assessment	In clinical practice, the process by which a mental health professional gathers and compiles information about a client for the purpose of describing the person's problems or disorder and developing a plan of treatment is an assessment.
Longitudinal study	Longitudinal study refers to a type of developmental study in which the same group of participants is followed and measured at different ages.
Rehabilitation	Rehabilitation is the restoration of lost capabilities, or the treatment aimed at producing it. Also refers to treatment for dependency on psychoactive substances such as alcohol, prescription drugs, and illicit drugs such as cocaine, heroin or amphetamines.
Compatibility	The capability of living together in harmony is referred to as compatibility.
Nitrate	Nitrate refers to a salt of nitric acid; a compound containing the radical NO_3; biologically, the final form of nitrogen from the oxidation of organic nitrogen compounds.
Stress	Stress refers to a condition that is a response to factors that change the human systems normal state.

Go to **Cram101.com** for the Practice Tests for this Chapter.